MznLnx

Missing Links Exam Preps

Exam Prep for

Calculus

Stewart, 5th Edition

The MznLnx Exam Prep is your link from the texbook and lecture to your exams.
The MznLnx Exam Preps are unauthorized and comprehensive reviews of your textbooks.

All material provided by MznLnx and Rico Publications (c) 2010
Textbook publishers and textbook authors do not particpate in or contribute to these reviews.

MznLnx

Rico Publications

Exam Prep for Calculus
5th Edition
Stewart

Publisher: Raymond Houge
Assistant Editor: Michael Rouger
Text and Cover Designer: Lisa Buckner
Marketing Manager: Sara Swagger
Project Manager, Editorial Production: Jerry Emerson
Art Director: Vernon Lowerui

Product Manager: Dave Mason
Editorial Assitant: Rachel Guzmanji
Pedagogy: Debra Long
Cover Image: Jim Reed/Getty Images
Text and Cover Printer: City Printing, Inc.
Compositor: Media Mix, Inc.

(c) 2010 Rico Publications

ALL RIGHTS RESERVED. No part of this work covered by the copyright may be reproduced or used in any form or by an means--graphic, electronic, or mechanical, including photocopying, recording, taping, Web distribution, information storage, and retrieval systems, or in any other manner--without the written permission of the publisher.

Printed in the United States
ISBN:

For more information about our products, contact us at:
Dave.Mason@RicoPublications.com

For permission to use material from this text or product, submit a request online to:
Dave.Mason@RicoPublications.com

Contents

CHAPTER 1
Functions and Models — 1

CHAPTER 2
Limits and Rates of Change — 13

CHAPTER 3
Derivatives — 20

CHAPTER 4
Applications of Differentiation — 41

CHAPTER 5
Integrals — 51

CHAPTER 6
Applications of Integration — 57

CHAPTER 7
Inverse Functions — 64

CHAPTER 8
Techniques of Integration — 76

CHAPTER 9
Further Applications of Integration — 86

CHAPTER 10
Differential Equations — 93

CHAPTER 11
Parametric Equations and Polar Coordinates — 103

CHAPTER 12
Infinite Sequences and Series — 116

CHAPTER 13
Vectors and the Geometrq of Space — 135

CHAPTER 14
Vector Functions — 145

CHAPTER 15
Partial Derivatives — 154

CHAPTER 16
Multiple Integrals — 166

CHAPTER 17
Vector Calculus — 176

CHAPTER 18
Second-Order Differential Equations — 186

ANSWER KEY — 190

TO THE STUDENT

COMPREHENSIVE

The *MznLnx* Exam Prep series is designed to help you pass your exams. Editors at MznLnx review your textbooks and then prepare these practice exams to help you master the textbook material. Unlike study guides, workbooks, and practice tests provided by the texbook publisher and textbook authors, *MznLnx* gives you **all** of the material in each chapter in exam form, not just samples, so you can be sure to nail your exam.

MECHANICAL

The MznLnx Exam Prep series creates exams that will help you learn the subject matter as well as test you on your understanding. Each question is designed to help you master the concept. Just working through the exams, you gain an understanding of the subject--its a simple mechanical process that produces success.

INTEGRATED STUDY GUIDE AND REVIEW

MznLnx is not just a set of exams designed to test you, its also a comprehensive review of the subject content. Each exam question is also a review of the concept, making sure that you will get the answer correct without having to go to other sources of material. You learn as you go! Its the easiest way to pass an exam.

HUMOR

Studying can be tedious and dry. MznLnx's instructional design includes moderate humor within the exam questions on occassion, to break the tedium and revitalize the brain

Chapter 1. Functions and Models

1. In mathematics, the concept of a '_____' is used to describe the behavior of a function as its argument or input either 'gets close' to some point, or as the argument becomes arbitrarily large; or the behavior of a sequence's elements as their index increases indefinitely. Limits are used in calculus and other branches of mathematical analysis to define derivatives and continuity.

   In formulas, _____ is usually abbreviated as lim

   a. 15 theorem
   c. BIBO stability
   b. BDDC
   d. Limit

2. The _____ is a method of finding the area of a shape by inscribing inside it a sequence of polygons whose areas converge to the area of the containing shape. If the sequence is correctly constructed, the difference in area between the nth polygon and the containing shape will become arbitrarily small as n becomes large. As this difference becomes arbitrarily small, the possible values for the area of the shape are systematically 'exhausted' by the lower bound areas successively established by the sequence members.

   a. Method of exhaustion
   c. BDDC
   b. BIBO stability
   d. 15 theorem

3. A _____ of a curve is a line that (locally) intersects two points on the curve. The word secant comes from the Latin secare, for to cut.

   It can be used to approximate the tangent to a curve, at some point P. If the secant to a curve is defined by two points, P and Q, with P fixed and Q variable, as Q approaches P along the curve, the direction of the secant approaches that of the tangent at P, assuming there is just one.

   a. Kappa curve
   c. Witch of Agnesi
   b. Curve
   d. Secant line

4. In geometry, the _____ (or simply the tangent) to a curve at a given point is the straight line that 'just touches' the curve at that point (in the sense explained more precisely below.) As it passes through the point of tangency, the _____ is 'going in the same direction' as the curve, and in this sense it is the best straight-line approximation to the curve at that point. The same definition applies to space curves and curves in n-dimensional Euclidean space.

   a. Sphere
   c. Lie derivative
   b. Minimal surface
   d. Tangent line

5. In physics, _____ is defined as the rate of change of position. it is vector physical quantity; both speed and direction are required to define it. In the SI (metric) system, it is measured in meters per second: (m/s) or ms^{-1}.

   a. BIBO stability
   c. Velocity
   b. 15 theorem
   d. BDDC

6. In mathematics, a (topological) _____ is defined as follows: let I be an interval of real numbers (i.e. a non-empty connected subset of $\mathbb{R}$); then a _____ γ is a continuous mapping $\gamma : I \to X$, where X is a topological space. The _____ γ is said to be simple if it is injective, i.e. if for all x, y in I, we have $\gamma(x) = \gamma(y) \implies x = y$. If I is a closed bounded interval $[a, b]$, we also allow the possibility $\gamma(a) = \gamma(b)$ (this convention makes it possible to talk about closed simple _____.)

Chapter 1. Functions and Models

a. Prolate cycloid
b. Closed curve
c. Tractrix
d. Curve

7. _____ is a means of calculating the volume of a solid of revolution, when integrating along the axis of revolution. This method models the generated 3 dimensional shape as a 'stack' of an infinite number of disks of infinitesimal thickness. It is possible to use 'washers' instead of 'disks' (the washer method) to obtain 'hollow' solids of revolutions, and uses the same principles that underlie _____.

a. Shell integration
b. Surface of revolution
c. Multiple integral
d. Disk integration

8. The _____ is one of the oldest concepts in mathematical analysis. It provides a rigorous definition of the idea of a sequence converging towards a point called the limit.

Intuitively, suppose we have a sequence of points (i.e. an infinite set of points labelled using the natural numbers) in some sort of mathematical object (for example the real numbers or a vector space) which has a concept of nearness (such as 'all points within a given distance of a fixed point'.)

a. Table of limits
b. 15 theorem
c. Squeeze Theorem
d. Limit of a sequence

9. _____ are a set of problems generally thought to have been devised by Zeno of Elea to support Parmenides's doctrine that 'all is one' and that, contrary to the evidence of our senses, the belief in plurality and change is mistaken, and in particular that motion is nothing but an illusion. It is usually assumed, based on Plato's Parmenides 128c-d, that Zeno took on the project of creating these paradoxes because other philosophers had created paradoxes against Parmenides's view. Thus Zeno can be interpreted as saying that to assume there is plurality is even more absurd than assuming there is only 'the One' (Parmenides 128d.)

a. 15 theorem
b. BDDC
c. Zeno's paradoxes
d. BIBO stability

10. In mathematics, a _____ is an ordered list of objects (or events). Like a set, it contains members (also called elements or terms), and the number of terms (possibly infinite) is called the length of the _____. Unlike a set, order matters, and the exact same elements can appear multiple times at different positions in the _____.

a. Y-intercept
b. BDDC
c. 15 theorem
d. Sequence

11. A _____ is perfectly round geometrical object in three-dimensional space, such as the shape of a round ball. Like a circle in two dimensions, a perfect _____ is completely symmetrical around its center, with all points on the surface lying the same distance r from the center point. This distance r is known as the radius of the _____.

a. Minimal surface
b. Sphere
c. Differentiable manifold
d. Tortuosity

12. The mechanisms of _____; a point mass m_1 attracts another point mass m_2 by a force F_2 which is proportional to the product of the two masses and inversely proportional to the square of the distance (r) between them. Regardless of masses or distance, the magnitudes of $|F_1|$ and $|F_2|$ will always be equal. G is the gravitational constant.

_____ is an empirical physical law describing the gravitational attraction between bodies with mass.

Chapter 1. Functions and Models

a. Newton's law of universal gravitation
b. BIBO stability
c. 15 theorem
d. BDDC

13. In economics, the _____ functional form of production functions is widely used to represent the relationship of an output to inputs. It was proposed by Knut Wicksell (1851-1926), and tested against statistical evidence by Charles Cobb and Paul Douglas in 1900-1928.

For production, the function is

$$Y = AL^\alpha K^\beta,$$

where:

- Y = total production (the monetary value of all goods produced in a year)
- L = labor input
- K = capital input
- A = total factor productivity
- α and β are the output elasticities of labor and capital, respectively. These values are constants determined by available technology.

Output elasticity measures the responsiveness of output to a change in levels of either labor or capital used in production, ceteris paribus. For example if α = 0.15, a 1% increase in labor would lead to approximately a 0.15% increase in output.

a. 15 theorem
b. BIBO stability
c. BDDC
d. Cobb-Douglas

14. The terms '_____' and 'independent variable' are used in similar but subtly different ways in mathematics and statistics as part of the standard terminology in those subjects. They are used to distinguish between two types of quantities being considered, separating them into those available at the start of a process and those being created by it, where the latter (dependent variables) are dependent on the former (independent variables.)

In traditional calculus, a function is defined as a relation between two terms called variables because their values vary.

a. BDDC
b. BIBO stability
c. Dependent variable
d. 15 theorem

15. In mathematics, the _____ (or replacement set) of a given function is the set of 'input' values for which the function is defined. For instance, the _____ of cosine would be all real numbers, while the _____ of the square root would be only numbers greater than or equal to 0 (ignoring complex numbers in both cases.) In a representation of a function in a xy Cartesian coordinate system, the _____ is represented on the x axis (or abscissa.)

a. BIBO stability
b. 15 theorem
c. BDDC
d. Domain

Chapter 1. Functions and Models

16. In vector calculus, the _____ of a scalar field is a vector field which points in the direction of the greatest rate of increase of the scalar field, and whose magnitude is the greatest rate of change.

A generalization of the _____ for functions on a Euclidean space which have values in another Euclidean space is the Jacobian. A further generalization for a function from one Banach space to another is the Fréchet derivative.

   a. Parametric derivative
   b. Gradient
   c. Smooth function
   d. Leibniz's notation

17. The terms 'dependent variable' and '_____' are used in similar but subtly different ways in mathematics and statistics as part of the standard terminology in those subjects. They are used to distinguish between two types of quantities being considered, separating them into those available at the start of a process and those being created by it, where the latter (dependent variables) are dependent on the former (independent variables.)

In traditional calculus, a function is defined as a relation between two terms called variables because their values vary.

   a. ACTRAN
   b. ALGOR
   c. AUSM
   d. Independent variable

18. In mathematics, the _____ of a function is the set of all 'output' values produced by that function. Sometimes it is called the image, or more precisely, the image of the domain of the function. If a function is a surjection then its _____ is equal to its codomain.
   a. Surjective
   b. Range
   c. Piecewise-defined function
   d. Constant function

19. The _____ is a test to determine if a relation or its graph is a function or not. For a relation or graph to be a function, it can have at most a single y-value for each x-value. Thus, a vertical line drawn at any x-position on the graph of a function will intersect the graph at most once.
   a. BDDC
   b. Vertical Line Test
   c. BIBO stability
   d. 15 theorem

20. In mathematics, a _____ is a function whose definition is dependent on the value of the independent variable. Mathematically, a real-valued function f of a real variable x is a relationship whose definition is given differently on disjoint subsets of its domain

The word piecewise is also used to describe any property of a _____ that holds for each piece but may not hold for the whole domain of the function.

   a. Piecewise-defined function
   b. Constant function
   c. Surjective
   d. Range

21. In mathematics, the _____ (or modulus) of a real number is its numerical value without regard to its sign. So, for example, 3 is the _____ of both 3 and −3.

The _____ of a number a is denoted by $|a|$.

- a. ACTRAN
- b. Exponential function
- c. Area hyperbolic functions
- d. Absolute value

22. A _____ is an algebraic equation in which each term is either a constant or the product of a constant and (the first power of) a single variable. Linear equations can have one, two, three or more variables. Linear equations occur with great regularity in applied mathematics.
    - a. 15 theorem
    - b. Linear equation
    - c. Cubic function
    - d. BDDC

23. In mathematics, a _____ is a method for approximating the total area underneath a curve on a graph, otherwise known as an integral. It may also be used to define the integration operation.

Consider a function $f: D \to \mathbf{R}$, where D is a subset of the real numbers $\mathbf{R}$, and let $I = [a, b]$ be a closed interval contained in D. A finite set of points $\{x_0, x_1, x_2, \ldots x_n\}$ such that $a = x_0 < x_1 < x_2 \ldots < x_n = b$ creates a partition

$$P = \{[x_0, x_1), [x_1, x_2), \ldots [x_{n-1}, x_n]\}$$

of I.

- a. Disk integration
- b. Riemann sum
- c. Signed measure
- d. Surface of revolution

24. In mathematics, an _____, is the apparent shape of a circle viewed obliquely from outside it, as distinct from a hyperbola which is the shape seen from inside. It is the finite or bounded case of a conic section as a shape cut in a cone by a plane, the unbounded cases being the parabola, which like the _____ remains connected, and the hyperbola, which separates into two connected components or branches.

Equivalently an _____ can be defined as the locus of points, or path traced out, in a plane such that the sum of the distances from the moving point to two fixed points remains constant.

- a. Ellipse
- b. ACTRAN
- c. ALGOR
- d. AUSM

25. In mathematics, a _____ (in one variable) is an infinite series of the form

$$f(x) = \sum_{n=0}^{\infty} a_n (x-c)^n = a_0 + a_1(x-c)^1 + a_2(x-c)^2 + a_3(x-c)^3 + \cdots$$

where a_n represents the coefficient of the nth term, c is a constant, and x varies around c (for this reason one sometimes speaks of the series as being centered at c

In many situations c is equal to zero, for instance when considering a Maclaurin series.

a. Mountain pass theorem
b. Caccioppoli set
c. Differential calculus
d. Power series

26. In mathematics, even functions and odd functions are functions which satisfy particular symmetry relations, with respect to taking additive inverses. They are important in many areas of mathematical analysis, especially the theory of power series and Fourier series. They are named for the parity of the powers of the power functions which satisfy each condition: the function $f(x) = x^n$ is an _____ if n is an even integer, and it is an odd function if n is an odd integer.

a. Even function
b. Operational calculus
c. Integral of secant cubed
d. Infinite series

27. In mathematics, even functions and odd functions are functions which satisfy particular symmetry relations, with respect to taking additive inverses. They are important in many areas of mathematical analysis, especially the theory of power series and Fourier series. They are named for the parity of the powers of the power functions which satisfy each condition: the function $f(x) = x^n$ is an even function if n is an even integer, and it is an _____ if n is an odd integer.

a. Integral of secant cubed
b. Even function
c. Integration by substitution
d. Odd function

28. In mathematics, a function on the real numbers is called a _____ (or staircase function) if it can be written as a finite linear combination of indicator functions of intervals. Informally speaking, a _____ is a piecewise constant function having only finitely many pieces.

a. Hyperbolic tangent
b. Multiplicative inverse
c. Hyperbolic sine
d. Step function

29. _____ generally conveys two primary meanings. The first is an imprecise sense of harmonious or aesthetically-pleasing proportionality and balance; such that it reflects beauty or perfection. The second meaning is a precise and well-defined concept of balance or 'patterned self-similarity' that can be demonstrated or proved according to the rules of a formal system: by geometry, through physics or otherwise.

a. 15 theorem
b. BIBO stability
c. BDDC
d. Symmetry

30. In mathematics, a _____ is a function which preserves the given order. This concept first arose in calculus, and was later generalized to the more abstract setting of order theory.

In calculus, a function f defined on a subset of the real numbers with real values is called monotonic (also monotonically increasing or non-decreasing), if for all x and y such that $x \geq y$ one has $f(x) \geq f(y)$, so f preserves the order.

a. 15 theorem
b. Pettis integral
c. Pseudo-differential operator
d. Monotonic function

31. In physics, and more specifically kinematics, _____ is the change in velocity over time. Because velocity is a vector, it can change in two ways: a change in magnitude and/or a change in direction. In one dimension, _____ is the rate at which something speeds up or slows down.

a. AUSM
b. ALGOR
c. ACTRAN
d. Acceleration

32. In statistics, given a (random) sample $(Y_i, X_{i1}, \ldots, X_{ip})$, $i = 1, \ldots, n$ the most general form of _____ is formulated as

$$Y_i = \beta_0 + \beta_1 \phi_1(X_{i1}) + \ldots + \beta_p \phi_p(X_{ip}) + \varepsilon_i \quad i = 1, \ldots, n$$

where $\phi_1, \ldots, \phi_p$ may be nonlinear functions.

In matrix notation this model can be written as

$$Y = X\beta + \varepsilon$$

where Y is an n × 1 column vector, X is an n × (p + 1) matrix, β is a (p + 1) × 1 vector of (unobservable) parameters, and ε is an n × 1 vector of errors, which are uncorrelated random variables each with expected value 0 and variance σ². Note that depending on the context the sample can be seen as fixed (observable), or random.

a. BIBO stability
b. BDDC
c. 15 theorem
d. Linear model

33. In mathematics, a _____ is a set (or locus) of points in the plane such that each point p on the oval bears a special relation to two other, fixed points q_1 and q_2: the product of the distance from p to q_1 and the distance from p to q_2 is constant. That is, if we define the function dist(x,y) to be the distance from a point x to a point y, then all points p on a _____ satisfy the equation

$$\text{dist}(q_1, p) \times \text{dist}(q_2, p) = b^2$$

where b is a constant.

The points q_1 and q_2 are called the foci of the oval.

a. Folium of Descartes
b. Cassini oval
c. Tractrix
d. Secant line

34. _____ is finding a curve which has the best fit to a series of data points and possibly other constraints. This section is an introduction to both interpolation (where an exact fit to constraints is expected) and regression analysis. Both are sometimes used for extrapolation.

a. Curve fitting
b. Well-posed problem
c. Series acceleration
d. Propagation of uncertainty

Chapter 1. Functions and Models

35. In mathematics, _____ is the process of constructing new data points outside a discrete set of known data points. It is similar to the process of interpolation, which constructs new points between known points, but the results of extrapolations are often less meaningful, and are subject to greater uncertainty. Example illustration of the _____ problem, consisting of assigning a meaningful value at the blue box, at x = 7, given the red data points.

A sound choice of which _____ method to apply relies on a prior knowledge of the process that created the existing data points.

    a. ALGOR
    b. ACTRAN
    c. AUSM
    d. Extrapolation

36. In the mathematical subfield of numerical analysis, _____ is a method of constructing new data points within the range of a discrete set of known data points.

In engineering and science one often has a number of data points, as obtained by sampling or experimentation, and tries to construct a function which closely fits those data points. This is called curve fitting or regression analysis.

    a. ACTRAN
    b. Interpolation
    c. ALGOR
    d. AUSM

37. The method of _____ or ordinary _____ is used to solve overdetermined systems. _____ is often applied in statistical contexts, particularly regression analysis.

_____ can be interpreted as a method of fitting data. The best fit in the _____ sense is that instance of the model for which the sum of squared residuals has its least value, a residual being the difference between an observed value and the value given by the model.

    a. Least squares
    b. 15 theorem
    c. BIBO stability
    d. BDDC

38. In statistics, _____ is a form of regression analysis in which the relationship between one or more independent variables and another variable, called dependent variable, is modeled by a least squares function, called _____ equation. This function is a linear combination of one or more model parameters, called regression coefficients. A _____ equation with one independent variable represents a straight line.

    a. Standard deviation
    b. Normal distribution
    c. Poisson distribution
    d. Linear regression

39. In mathematics, a _____ is a constant multiplicative factor of a certain object. For example, in the expression $9x^2$, the _____ of x^2 is 9.

The object can be such things as a variable, a vector, a function, etc.

    a. Difference polynomial
    b. Coefficient
    c. Leading coefficient
    d. Degree of the polynomial

Chapter 1. Functions and Models

40. In mathematics, a _____ is a function of the form

$$f(x) = ax^3 + bx^2 + cx + d,$$

where a is nonzero; or in other words, a polynomial of degree three. The derivative of a _____ is a quadratic function. The integral of a _____ is a quartic function.

   a. BDDC
   b. 15 theorem
   c. Cubic function
   d. Linear equation

41. When a polynomial is expressed as a sum or difference of terms (e.g., in standard or canonical form), the exponent of the term with the highest exponent is the _____. The degree of a term is the sum of the powers of each variable in the term. The words degree and order are used interchangeably.
   a. Sheffer sequence
   b. Coefficient
   c. Quadratic function
   d. Degree of the polynomial

42. A _____, in mathematics, is a polynomial function of the form $f(x) = ax^2 + bx + c$, where $a \neq 0$. The graph of a _____ is a parabola whose major axis is parallel to the y-axis.

The expression $ax^2 + bx + c$ in the definition of a _____ is a polynomial of degree 2 or a 2nd degree polynomial, because the highest exponent of x is 2.

   a. Constant term
   b. Degree of the polynomial
   c. Coefficient
   d. Quadratic function

43. In mathematics, an _____ is informally a function which satisfies a polynomial equation whose coefficients are themselves polynomials. For example, an _____ in one variable x is a solution y for an equation

$$a_n(x)y^n + a_{n-1}(x)y^{n-1} + \cdots + a_0(x) = 0$$

where the coefficients $a_i(x)$ are polynomial functions of x. A function which is not algebraic is called a transcendental function.

   a. AUSM
   b. ACTRAN
   c. ALGOR
   d. Algebraic function

44. In mathematics, a _____ is any function which can be written as the ratio of two polynomial functions.

$$y = \frac{x^2 - 3x - 2}{x^2 - 4}$$

In the case of one variable, x, a _____ is a function of the form

$$f(x) = \frac{P(x)}{Q(x)}$$

where P and Q are polynomial function in x and Q is not the zero polynomial. The domain of f is the set of all points x for which the denominator Q(x) is not zero.

   a. Rational function   b. BIBO stability
   c. 15 theorem   d. BDDC

45. In mathematics, a _____ or reciprocal for a number x, denoted by $1/x$ or x^{-1}, is a number which when multiplied by x yields the multiplicative identity, 1. The _____ of x is also called the reciprocal of x. The _____ of a fraction p/q is q/p.
   a. Heaviside step function   b. Hyperbolic sine
   c. Square root function   d. Multiplicative inverse

46. Trigonometry is a branch of mathematics that deals with triangles, particularly those plane triangles in which one angle has 90 degrees (right triangles.) Trigonometry deals with relationships between the sides and the angles of triangles and with the _____ functions, which describe those relationships.

Trigonometry has applications in both pure mathematics and in applied mathematics, where it is essential in many branches of science and technology.

   a. 15 theorem   b. Trigonometric functions
   c. Trigonometric integrals   d. Trigonometric

47. In mathematics, the _____ are functions of an angle. They are important in the study of triangles and modeling periodic phenomena, among many other applications. _____ are commonly defined as ratios of two sides of a right triangle containing the angle, and can equivalently be defined as the lengths of various line segments from a unit circle.
   a. Trigonometric integrals   b. 15 theorem
   c. Trigonometric   d. Trigonometric functions

48. In infinitesimal calculus, a _____ is traditionally an infinitesimally small change in a variable. For example, if x is a variable, then a change in the value of x is often denoted Δx (or δx when this change is considered to be small.) The _____ dx represents such a change, but is infinitely small.
   a. Differential   b. Related rates
   c. Continuous function   d. Dirichlet integral

49. The _____ is a function in mathematics. The application of this function to a value x is written as exp(x). Equivalently, this can be written in the form e^x, where e is a mathematical constant, the base of the natural logarithm, which equals approximately 2.718281828, and is also known as Euler's number.

a. Area hyperbolic functions
b. ACTRAN
c. Integral part
d. Exponential function

50. Integration is an important concept in mathematics, specifically in the field of calculus and, more broadly, mathematical analysis. Given a function f of a real variable x and an interval [a, b] of the real line, the _____

$$\int_a^b f(x)\,dx,$$

is defined informally to be the net signed area of the region in the xy-plane bounded by the graph of f, the x-axis, and the vertical lines x = a and x = b.

The term '_____' may also refer to the notion of antiderivative, a function F whose derivative is the given function f.

a. Integral test for convergence
b. Integrand
c. Indefinite integral
d. Integral

51. The function $\log_b(x)$ depends on both b and x, but the term _____ in standard usage refers to a function of the form $\log_b(x)$ in which the base b is fixed and so the only argument is x. Thus there is one _____ for each value of the base b (which must be positive and must differ from 1.) Viewed in this way, the base-b _____ is the inverse function of the exponential function b^x.

a. 15 theorem
b. BDDC
c. BIBO stability
d. Logarithm function

52. A _____ is a function that does not satisfy a polynomial equation whose coefficients are themselves polynomials, in contrast to an algebraic function, which does satisfy such an equation. In other words a _____ is a function which 'transcends' algebra in the sense that it cannot be expressed in terms of a finite sequence of the algebraic operations of addition, multiplication, and root extraction.

Examples of transcendental functions include the exponential function, the logarithm, and the trigonometric functions.

a. 15 theorem
b. BDDC
c. BIBO stability
d. Transcendental function

53. The _____, H, also called the unit step function, is a discontinuous function whose value is zero for negative argument and one for positive argument. It seldom matters what value is used for H, since H is mostly used as a distribution. The function is used in the mathematics of control theory and signal processing to represent a signal that switches on at a specified time and stays switched on indefinitely.

a. Heaviside step function
b. Signum function
c. Hyperbolic functions
d. Hyperbolic cosine

54. The _____ is an elementary unary real function, easily computable as the mean of its independent variable and its absolute value.

This function is applied in engineering (e.g., in the theory of DSP.) The name _____ can be derived by the look of its graph.

- a. Ramp function
- b. Bounded function
- c. Monodromy
- d. Differential calculus

55. In mathematics, a _____ is a unicursal quartic curve with three inflection points, given by the equation

$$a^2 y^2 - b^2 x^2 = x^2 y^2$$

The bullet curve has three double points in the real projective plane, at x=0 and y=0, x=0 and z=0, and y=0 and z=0, and is therefore a unicursal (rational) curve of genus zero.

If

$$f(z) = \sum_{n=0}^{\infty} \binom{2n}{n} z^{2n+1} = z + 2z^3 + 6z^5 + 20z^7 + \cdots$$

then

$$y = f\left(\frac{x}{2a}\right) \pm 2b$$

are the two branches of the bullet curve at the origin.

- a. Folium of Descartes
- b. Hypocycloid
- c. Bullet-nose curve
- d. Closed curve

56. _____ is a method of mathematical proof typically used to establish that a given statement is true of all natural numbers. It is done by proving that the first statement in the infinite sequence of statements is true, and then proving that if any one statement in the infinite sequence of statements is true, then so is the next one.

The method can be extended to prove statements about more general well-founded structures, such as trees; this generalization, known as structural induction, is used in mathematical logic and computer science.

- a. BIBO stability
- b. 15 theorem
- c. BDDC
- d. Mathematical induction

Chapter 2. Limits and Rates of Change

1. The _____ is an important second-order linear partial differential equation that describes the propagation of a variety of waves, such as sound waves, light waves and water waves. It arises in fields such as acoustics, electromagnetics, and fluid dynamics. Historically, the problem of a vibrating string such as that of a musical instrument was studied by Jean le Rond d'Alembert, Leonhard Euler, Daniel Bernoulli, and Joseph-Louis Lagrange.
   a. Klein-Gordon equation
   b. Dirac equation
   c. Wave equation
   d. Moment of Inertia

2. In physics, _____ is defined as the rate of change of position. it is vector physical quantity; both speed and direction are required to define it. In the SI (metric) system, it is measured in meters per second: (m/s) or ms^{-1}.
   a. Velocity
   b. BIBO stability
   c. 15 theorem
   d. BDDC

3. In mathematics, the concept of a '_____' is used to describe the behavior of a function as its argument or input either 'gets close' to some point, or as the argument becomes arbitrarily large; or the behavior of a sequence's elements as their index increases indefinitely. Limits are used in calculus and other branches of mathematical analysis to define derivatives and continuity.

   In formulas, _____ is usually abbreviated as lim

   a. Limit
   b. BDDC
   c. 15 theorem
   d. BIBO stability

4. In mathematics, the _____ is a fundamental concept in calculus and analysis concerning the behavior of that function near a particular input. Informally, a function assigns an output f(x) to every input x. The function has a limit L at an input p if f(x) is 'close' to L whenever x is 'close' to p.
   a. 15 theorem
   b. Table of limits
   c. Limit of a sequence
   d. Limit of a function

5. In mathematics, a _____ or rhodonea curve is a sinusoid plotted in polar coordinates. Up to similarity, these curves can all be expressed by a polar equation of the form

   $$r = \cos(k\theta).$$

   If k is an integer, the curve will be _____ shaped with

   - 2k petals if k is even, and
   - k petals if k is odd.

   When k is even, the entire graph of the _____ will be traced out exactly once when the value of θ changes from 0 to 2π. When k is odd, this will happen on the interval between 0 and π. (More generally, this will happen on any interval of length 2π for k even, and π for k odd.)

   a. Cochleoid
   b. Curtate cycloid
   c. Rose
   d. Space curve

Chapter 2. Limits and Rates of Change

6. The _____, H, also called the unit step function, is a discontinuous function whose value is zero for negative argument and one for positive argument. It seldom matters what value is used for H, since H is mostly used as a distribution. The function is used in the mathematics of control theory and signal processing to represent a signal that switches on at a specified time and stays switched on indefinitely.

    a. Hyperbolic functions
    b. Hyperbolic cosine
    c. Signum function
    d. Heaviside step function

7. In calculus, a _____ is either of the two limits of a function f(x) of a real variable x as x approaches a specified point either from below or from above. One should write either:

$$\lim_{x \to a^+} f(x) \text{ or } \lim_{x \downarrow a} f(x)$$

for the limit as x decreases in value approaching a (x approaches a 'from above' or 'from the right'), and similarly

$$\lim_{x \to a^-} f(x) \text{ or } \lim_{x \uparrow a} f(x)$$

for the limit as x increases in value approaching a (x approaches a 'from below' or 'from the left'.)

The two one-sided limits exist and are equal if and only if the limit of f(x) as x approaches a exists.

    a. ALGOR
    b. One-sided limit
    c. AUSM
    d. ACTRAN

8. Cantor defined two kinds of _____ numbers, the ordinal numbers and the cardinal numbers. Ordinal numbers may be identified with well-ordered sets, or counting carried on to any stopping point, including points after an _____ number have already been counted. Generalizing finite and the ordinary _____ sequences which are maps from the positive integers leads to mappings from ordinal numbers, and transfinite sequences.

    a. ACTRAN
    b. ALGOR
    c. Infinite
    d. AUSM

9. An _____ of a real-valued function y = f(x) is a curve which describes the behavior of f as either x or y tends to infinity.

In other words, as one moves along the graph of f(x) in some direction, the distance between it and the _____ eventually becomes smaller than any distance that one may specify.

    a. AUSM
    b. ACTRAN
    c. ALGOR
    d. Asymptote

Chapter 2. Limits and Rates of Change

10. The line x = a is a _____ of a curve y=f(x) if at least one of the following statements is true:

1. $\lim_{x \to a} f(x) = \pm\infty$
2. $\lim_{x \to a^-} f(x) = \pm\infty$
3. $\lim_{x \to a^+} f(x) = \pm\infty$

Intuitively, if x = a is an asymptote of f, then, if we imagine x approaching a from one side, the value of f(x) grows without bound; i.e., f(x) becomes large (positively or negatively), and, in fact, becomes larger than any finite value.

Note that f(x) may or may not be defined at a: what the function is doing precisely at x = a does not affect the asymptote. For example, consider the function

$$f(x) = \begin{cases} \frac{1}{x} & \text{if } x > 0, \\ 5 & \text{if } x \leq 0 \end{cases}$$

As $\lim_{x \to 0^+} f(x) = \infty$, f(x) has a _____ at 0, even though f(0) = 5.

Another example is $f(x) = 1/(x-1)$ which has a _____ of x=1 as shown by the limit

$$\lim_{x \to 1^+} \frac{1}{x-1} = \infty$$

In the graph of $f(x) = x + \frac{1}{x}$, the y-axis (x = 0) and the line y = x are both asymptotes.

When a linear asymptote is not parallel to the x- or y-axis, it is called either an oblique asymptote or equivalently a slant asymptote.

a. Geometric function theory
b. Vertical asymptote
c. Fractional calculus
d. Semi-differentiability

11. The _____ is a method of finding the area of a shape by inscribing inside it a sequence of polygons whose areas converge to the area of the containing shape. If the sequence is correctly constructed, the difference in area between the nth polygon and the containing shape will become arbitrarily small as n becomes large. As this difference becomes arbitrarily small, the possible values for the area of the shape are systematically 'exhausted' by the lower bound areas successively established by the sequence members.

a. BIBO stability
b. BDDC
c. 15 theorem
d. Method of exhaustion

Chapter 2. Limits and Rates of Change

12. In mathematics and computer science, the floor and ceiling functions map a real number to the next smallest or next largest integer. More precisely, floor(x) is the largest integer not greater than x and ceiling(x) is the smallest integer not less than x.

The _____ is also called the greatest integer or entier function, and the floor of a nonnegative x may be called the integral part or integral value of x. Computer languages (other than APL) commonly use ENTIER(x) (Algol), floor(x), or int(x) (C and C++).

a. Hyperbolic tangent
b. Floor function
c. Hyperbolic functions
d. Signum function

13. In calculus, the _____ is a theorem regarding the limit of a function.

The _____ is a technical result which is very important in proofs in calculus and mathematical analysis. It is typically used to confirm the limit of a function via comparison with two other functions whose limits are known or easily computed.

a. 15 theorem
b. Table of limits
c. Limit of a sequence
d. Squeeze Theorem

14. In economics, the _____ functional form of production functions is widely used to represent the relationship of an output to inputs. It was proposed by Knut Wicksell (1851-1926), and tested against statistical evidence by Charles Cobb and Paul Douglas in 1900-1928.

For production, the function is

$Y = AL^{\alpha}K^{\beta}$,

where:

- Y = total production (the monetary value of all goods produced in a year)
- L = labor input
- K = capital input
- A = total factor productivity
- α and β are the output elasticities of labor and capital, respectively. These values are constants determined by available technology.

Output elasticity measures the responsiveness of output to a change in levels of either labor or capital used in production, ceteris paribus. For example if α = 0.15, a 1% increase in labor would lead to approximately a 0.15% increase in output.

a. 15 theorem
b. BDDC
c. BIBO stability
d. Cobb-Douglas

Chapter 2. Limits and Rates of Change

15. Continuous functions are of utmost importance in mathematics and applications. However, not all functions are continuous. If a function is not continuous at a point in its domain, one says that it has a _____ there. The set of all points of _____ of a function may be a discrete set, a dense set, or even the entire domain of the function.
    a. BDDC
    b. BIBO stability
    c. Discontinuity
    d. 15 theorem

16. In mathematics, a _____ is a function for which, intuitively, small changes in the input result in small changes in the output. Otherwise, a function is said to be discontinuous. A _____ with a continuous inverse function is called bicontinuous. An intuitive though imprecise (and inexact) idea of continuity is given by the common statement that a _____ is a function whose graph can be drawn without lifting the chalk from the blackboard.
    a. Continuous function
    b. Leibniz function
    c. Maxima
    d. Dirichlet integral

17. In mathematical analysis, the _____ states that for each value between the least upper bound and greatest lower bound of the image of a continuous function there is a corresponding value in its domain mapping to the original. _____

    - Version I. The _____ states the following: If the function y = f(x) is continuous on the interval [a, b], and u is a number between f(a) and f(b), then there is a c ∈ [a, b] such that f(c) = u.

    - Version II. Suppose that I is an interval [a, b] in the real numbers R and that f : I → R is a continuous function. Then the image set f(I) is also an interval, and either it contains [f(a), f(b)], or it contains [f(b), f(a)]; that is,

        f(I) ⊇ [f(a), f(b)], or f(I) ⊇ [f(b), f(a)].

It is frequently stated in the following equivalent form: Suppose that f : [a, b] → R is continuous and that u is a real number satisfying f(a) < u < f(b) or f(a) > u > f(b).) Then for some c ∈ [a, b], f(c) = u.

This captures an intuitive property of continuous functions: given f continuous on [1, 2], if f(1) = 3 and f(2) = 5 then f must take the value 4 somewhere between 1 and 2.

    a. AUSM
    b. ACTRAN
    c. ALGOR
    d. Intermediate Value Theorem

18. A curve γ is said to be closed or a loop if $I = [a, b]$ and if $\gamma(a) = \gamma(b)$. A _____ is thus a continuous mapping of the circle S^1; a simple _____ is also called a Jordan curve or a Jordan arc. The Jordan curve theorem states that such curves divide the plane into an 'interior' and an 'exterior'.
    a. Closed curve
    b. Kappa curve
    c. Bullet-nose curve
    d. Curve

Chapter 2. Limits and Rates of Change

19. In mathematics, a (topological) _____ is defined as follows: let I be an interval of real numbers (i.e. a non-empty connected subset of $\mathbb{R}$); then a _____ γ is a continuous mapping $\gamma : I \to X$, where X is a topological space. The _____ γ is said to be simple if it is injective, i.e. if for all x, y in I, we have $\gamma(x) = \gamma(y) \implies x = y$. If I is a closed bounded interval $[a, b]$, we also allow the possibility $\gamma(a) = \gamma(b)$ (this convention makes it possible to talk about closed simple _____.)

   a. Prolate cycloid
   b. Tractrix
   c. Curve
   d. Closed curve

20. In geometry, the _____ (or simply the tangent) to a curve at a given point is the straight line that 'just touches' the curve at that point (in the sense explained more precisely below.) As it passes through the point of tangency, the _____ is 'going in the same direction' as the curve, and in this sense it is the best straight-line approximation to the curve at that point. The same definition applies to space curves and curves in n-dimensional Euclidean space.

   a. Minimal surface
   b. Sphere
   c. Tangent line
   d. Lie derivative

21. When a linear asymptote is not parallel to the x- or y-axis, it is called either an oblique asymptote or equivalently a _____. The function f(x) is asymptotic to y = mx + b if

$$\lim_{x \to \infty} f(x) - (mx + b) = 0 \text{ or } \lim_{x \to -\infty} f(x) - (mx + b) = 0$$

Note that y = mx + b is never a vertical asymptote, but can be a horizontal asymptote if m=0 (in which case it is not an oblique asymptote.)

An example is $f(x)=(x^2-1)/x$ which has an oblique asymptote of y=x (m=1, b=0) as seen in the limit

$$\lim_{x \to \infty} f(x) - x$$
$$= \lim_{x \to \infty} \frac{x^2 - 1}{x} - x$$
$$= \lim_{x \to \infty} (x - 1/x) - x$$
$$= \lim_{x \to \infty} -1/x = 0$$

Computationally identifying an oblique asymptote can be more difficult than a horizontal or vertical asymptote, in particular because the m and b might not be known.

   a. Geometric function theory
   b. Horizontal asymptote
   c. Slant asymptote
   d. Second derivative

22. _____ is a means of calculating the volume of a solid of revolution, when integrating along the axis of revolution. This method models the generated 3 dimensional shape as a 'stack' of an infinite number of disks of infinitesimal thickness. It is possible to use 'washers' instead of 'disks' (the washer method) to obtain 'hollow' solids of revolutions, and uses the same principles that underlie _____.

a. Multiple integral	b. Shell integration
c. Surface of revolution	d. Disk integration

23. In mathematics, the simplest case of _____ refers to the study of problems in which one seeks to minimize or maximize a real function by systematically choosing the values of real or integer variables from within an allowed set. This (a scalar real valued objective function) is actually a small subset of this field which comprises a large area of applied mathematics and generalizes to study of means to obtain 'best available' values of some objective function given a defined domain where the elaboration is on the types of functions and the conditions and nature of the objects in the problem domain.

The first _____ technique, which is known as steepest descent, goes back to Gauss.

a. AUSM	b. ACTRAN
c. ALGOR	d. Optimization

Chapter 3. Derivatives

1. In calculus, a branch of mathematics, the _____ is a measurement of how a function changes when its input changes. Loosely speaking, a _____ can be thought of as how much a quantity is changing at some given point. For example, the _____ of the position (or distance) of a vehicle with respect to time is the instantaneous velocity (respectively, instantaneous speed) at which the vehicle is traveling.

The process of finding a _____ is called differentiation. The fundamental theorem of calculus states that differentiation is the reverse process to integration.

    a. Concave upwards   b. Ramp function
    c. Mountain pass theorem   d. Derivative

2. In mathematics and computer science, the floor and ceiling functions map a real number to the next smallest or next largest integer. More precisely, floor(x) is the largest integer not greater than x and ceiling(x) is the smallest integer not less than x.

The _____ is also called the greatest integer or entier function, and the floor of a nonnegative x may be called the integral part or integral value of x. Computer languages (other than APL) commonly use ENTIER(x) (Algol), floor(x), or int(x) (C and C++).

    a. Hyperbolic tangent   b. Hyperbolic functions
    c. Signum function   d. Floor function

3. In geometry, the _____ (or simply the tangent) to a curve at a given point is the straight line that 'just touches' the curve at that point (in the sense explained more precisely below.) As it passes through the point of tangency, the _____ is 'going in the same direction' as the curve, and in this sense it is the best straight-line approximation to the curve at that point. The same definition applies to space curves and curves in n-dimensional Euclidean space.

    a. Minimal surface   b. Tangent line
    c. Lie derivative   d. Sphere

4. In mathematics, the simplest case of _____ refers to the study of problems in which one seeks to minimize or maximize a real function by systematically choosing the values of real or integer variables from within an allowed set. This (a scalar real valued objective function) is actually a small subset of this field which comprises a large area of applied mathematics and generalizes to study of means to obtain 'best available' values of some objective function given a defined domain where the elaboration is on the types of functions and the conditions and nature of the objects in the problem domain.

The first _____ technique, which is known as steepest descent, goes back to Gauss.

    a. ACTRAN   b. AUSM
    c. ALGOR   d. Optimization

5. In mathematics, the _____ (or replacement set) of a given function is the set of 'input' values for which the function is defined. For instance, the _____ of cosine would be all real numbers, while the _____ of the square root would be only numbers greater than or equal to 0 (ignoring complex numbers in both cases.) In a representation of a function in a xy Cartesian coordinate system, the _____ is represented on the x axis (or abscissa.)

Chapter 3. Derivatives

    a. BDDC   b. BIBO stability
    c. 15 theorem   d. Domain

6. In mathematics, a differential operator is an operator defined as a function of the _____. It is helpful, as a matter of notation first, to consider differentiation as an abstract operation, accepting a function and returning another (in the style of a higher-order function in computer science.)

There are certainly reasons not to restrict to linear operators; for instance the Schwarzian derivative is a well-known non-linear operator.

    a. Second partial derivatives test   b. Surface integral
    c. Vector Laplacian   d. Differentiation operator

7. In calculus, _____, was originally the use of expressions such as dx and dy and to represent 'infinitely small' (or infinitesimal) increments of quantities x and y, just as >Δx and >Δy represent finite increments of x and y respectively. So for y being a function of x, or

the derivative of y with respect to x, which later came to be viewed as

was, according to Leibniz, the quotient of an infinitesimal increment of y by an infinitesimal increment of x, or

where the right hand side is Lagrange's notation for the derivative of f at x.

Similarly, although mathematicians usually now view an integral

as a limit

where >Δx is an interval containing x_i, Leibniz viewed it as the sum (the integral sign denoting summation) of infinitely many infinitesimal quantities f(x) dx.

a. Fermat differentiation
b. Notation for differentiation
c. Leibniz's notation
d. Gradient

8. In economics, the _____ functional form of production functions is widely used to represent the relationship of an output to inputs. It was proposed by Knut Wicksell (1851-1926), and tested against statistical evidence by Charles Cobb and Paul Douglas in 1900-1928.

For production, the function is

$$Y = AL^\alpha K^\beta,$$

where:

- Y = total production (the monetary value of all goods produced in a year)
- L = labor input
- K = capital input
- A = total factor productivity
- α and β are the output elasticities of labor and capital, respectively. These values are constants determined by available technology.

Output elasticity measures the responsiveness of output to a change in levels of either labor or capital used in production, ceteris paribus. For example if $\alpha = 0.15$, a 1% increase in labor would lead to approximately a 0.15% increase in output.

a. Cobb-Douglas
b. BDDC
c. BIBO stability
d. 15 theorem

9. In mathematics, a _____ is a function whose values do not vary and thus are constant. For example, if we have the function f(x) = 4, then f is constant since f maps any value to 4. More formally, a function f : A → B is a _____ if f(x) = f(y) for all x and y in A.
a. Range
b. Surjective
c. Piecewise-defined function
d. Constant function

10. In calculus, the _____ function is zero (A constant function is one that does not depend on the independent variable, such as f(x) = 7.)

The rule can be justified in various ways. The derivative is the slope of the tangent to the given function's graph, and the graph of a constant function is a horizontal line, whose slope is zero.

a. Symmetric derivative
b. Linearity of differentiation
c. Derivative of a constant
d. Functional derivative

11. This article will state and prove the _____ for differentiation, and then use it to prove these two formulas.

The _____ for differentiation states that for every natural number n, the derivative of $f(x) = x^n$ is $f'(x) = nx^{n-1}$, that is,

$$(x^n)' = nx^{n-1}.$$

The _____ for integration

$$\int x^n \, dx = \frac{x^{n+1}}{n+1} + C$$

for natural n is then an easy consequence. One just needs to take the derivative of this equality and use the _____ and linearity of differentiation on the right-hand side.

a. Hyperbolic angle
c. Dirichlet integral

b. Limits of integration
d. Power Rule

12. In calculus, the _____ allows you to take constants outside a derivative and concentrate on differentiating the function of x itself. This is a part of the linearity of differentiation.

Suppose you have a function

$$g(x) = k \cdot f(x).$$

where k is a constant.

Use the formula for differentiation from first principles to obtain:

$$g'(x) = \lim_{h \to 0} \frac{g(x+h) - g(x)}{h}$$
$$g'(x) = \lim_{h \to 0} \frac{k \cdot f(x+h) - k \cdot f(x)}{h}$$
$$g'(x) = \lim_{h \to 0} \frac{k(f(x+h) - f(x))}{h}$$
$$g'(x) = k \lim_{h \to 0} \frac{f(x+h) - f(x)}{h} \quad (*)$$
$$g'(x) = k \cdot f'(x).$$

This is the statement of the _____, in Lagrange's notation for differentiation.

a. Product rule
b. Reciprocal Rule
c. Constant factor rule in differentiation
d. Differentiation rules

13. In calculus, the _____ is a formula used to find the derivatives of products of functions. It may be stated thus:

$$(f \cdot g)' = f' \cdot g + f \cdot g'$$

or in the Leibniz notation thus:

$$\frac{d}{dx}(u \cdot v) = u \cdot \frac{dv}{dx} + v \cdot \frac{du}{dx}.$$

Discovery of this rule is credited to Gottfried Leibniz, who demonstrated it using differentials. Here is Leibniz's argument: Let u and v be two differentiable functions of x.

a. Reciprocal Rule
b. Constant factor rule in differentiation
c. Product Rule
d. Quotient Rule

14. In calculus, the _____ is a method of finding the derivative of a function that is the quotient of two other functions for which derivatives exist.

If the function one wishes to differentiate, f(x), can be written as

$$f(x) = \frac{g(x)}{h(x)}$$

and h(x) ≠ 0, then the rule states that the derivative of g(x) / h(x) is equal to:

$$\frac{d}{dx}f(x) = f'(x) = \frac{g'(x)h(x) - g(x)h'(x)}{[h(x)]^2}.$$

Or, more precisely, if all x in some open set containing the number a satisfy h(x) ≠ 0; and g'(a) and h'(a) both exist; then, f'(a) exists as well and:

$$f'(a) = \frac{g'(a)h(a) - g(a)h'(a)}{[h(a)]^2}.$$

The derivative of (4x − 2) / (x² + 1) is:

$$\frac{d}{dx}\left[\frac{(4x-2)}{x^2+1}\right] = \frac{(x^2+1)(4) - (4x-2)(2x)}{(x^2+1)^2}$$
$$= \frac{(4x^2+4) - (8x^2-4x)}{(x^2+1)^2} = \frac{-4x^2+4x+4}{(x^2+1)^2}$$

In the example above, the choices

g(x) = 4x − 2
h(x) = x² + 1

were made. Analogously, the derivative of sin(x) / x² (when x ≠ 0) is:

$$\frac{\cos(x)x^2 - \sin(x)2x}{x^4}$$

Another example is:

$$f(x) = \frac{2x^2}{x^3}$$

whereas g(x) = 2x² and h(x) = x³, and g'(x) = 4x and h'(x) = 3x².

a. Reciprocal Rule
c. Product rule
b. Differentiation rules
d. Quotient Rule

15. In the various subfields of physics, there exist two common usages of the term _____, both with rigorous mathematical frameworks.

- In the study of transport phenomena (heat transfer, mass transfer and fluid dynamics), _____ is defined as the amount that flows through a unit area per unit time. _____ in this definition is a vector.
- In the field of electromagnetism and mathematics, _____ is usually the integral of a vector quantity over a finite surface. The result of this integration is a scalar quantity. The magnetic _____ is thus the integral of the magnetic vector field B over a surface, and the electric _____ is defined similarly. Using this definition, the _____ of the Poynting vector over a specified surface is the rate at which electromagnetic energy flows through that surface. Confusingly, the Poynting vector is sometimes called the power _____, which is an example of the first usage of _____, above. It has units of watts per square metre (WÂ·m⁻²)

One could argue, based on the work of James Clerk Maxwell, that the transport definition precedes the more recent way the term is used in electromagnetism. The specific quote from Maxwell is 'In the case of fluxes, we have to take the integral, over a surface, of the _____ through every element of the surface. The result of this operation is called the surface integral of the _____.

- a. 15 theorem
- b. BDDC
- c. BIBO stability
- d. Flux

16. In mathematics, the _____, is the curve defined as follows.

Starting with a fixed circle, a point O on the circle is chosen. For any other point A on the circle, the secant line OA is drawn. The point M is diametrically opposite O. The line OA intersects the tangent at M at the point N. The line parallel to OM through N, and the line perpendicular to OM through A intersect at P. As the point A is varied, the path of P is the witch.

- a. Closed curve
- b. Cochleoid
- c. Folium of Descartes
- d. Witch of Agnesi

17. In the two-dimensional case, a _____ perpendicularly intersects the tangent line to a curve at a given point.

The _____ is often used in computer graphics to determine a surface's orientation toward a light source for flat shading, or the orientation of each of the corners (vertices) to mimic a curved surface with Phong shading.

For a polygon (such as a triangle), a surface normal can be calculated as the vector cross product of two (non-parallel) edges of the polygon.

- a. PDE surfaces
- b. Prolate
- c. Parametric surface
- d. Normal line

18. _____ is a means of calculating the volume of a solid of revolution, when integrating along the axis of revolution. This method models the generated 3 dimensional shape as a 'stack' of an infinite number of disks of infinitesimal thickness. It is possible to use 'washers' instead of 'disks' (the washer method) to obtain 'hollow' solids of revolutions, and uses the same principles that underlie _____.

- a. Shell integration
- b. Multiple integral
- c. Surface of revolution
- d. Disk integration

19. The _____ is an important second-order linear partial differential equation that describes the propagation of a variety of waves, such as sound waves, light waves and water waves. It arises in fields such as acoustics, electromagnetics, and fluid dynamics. Historically, the problem of a vibrating string such as that of a musical instrument was studied by Jean le Rond d'Alembert, Leonhard Euler, Daniel Bernoulli, and Joseph-Louis Lagrange.

- a. Klein-Gordon equation
- b. Moment of Inertia
- c. Wave equation
- d. Dirac equation

Chapter 3. Derivatives

20. In physics, _____ is defined as the rate of change of position. it is vector physical quantity; both speed and direction are required to define it. In the SI (metric) system, it is measured in meters per second: (m/s) or ms^{-1}.
    a. BIBO stability
    b. 15 theorem
    c. Velocity
    d. BDDC

21. The _____ of a material is defined as its mass per unit volume. The symbol of _____ is ρ '>rho.)

Mathematically:

$$d = \frac{m}{V}$$

where:

    d is the _____,
    m is the mass,
    V is the volume.

  a. BIBO stability
  b. Density
  c. 15 theorem
  d. BDDC

22. _____, linear mass density or linear mass is a measure of mass per unit of length, and it is a characteristic of strings or other one-dimensional objects. The SI unit of _____ is the kilogram per metre (kg/m.) The _____, μ (sometimes denoted by λ), of an object is defined as:

$$\mu = \frac{\partial m}{\partial x}$$

where m is the mass, and x is a coordinate along the (one dimensional) object.

  a. Linear density
  b. BDDC
  c. BIBO stability
  d. 15 theorem

23. An _____ process is a change in which the temperature of the system stays constant: ΔT = 0. This typically occurs when a system is in contact with an outside thermal reservoir (heat bath), and the change occurs slowly enough to allow the system to continually adjust to the temperature of the reservoir through heat exchange. An alternative special case in which a system exchanges no heat with its surroundings (Q = 0) is called an adiabatic process.
    a. AUSM
    b. ACTRAN
    c. ALGOR
    d. Isothermal

24. In vector calculus, the _____ of a scalar field is a vector field which points in the direction of the greatest rate of increase of the scalar field, and whose magnitude is the greatest rate of change.

A generalization of the _____ for functions on a Euclidean space which have values in another Euclidean space is the Jacobian. A further generalization for a function from one Banach space to another is the Fréchet derivative.

   a. Gradient
   b. Smooth function
   c. Leibniz's notation
   d. Parametric derivative

25. Jean Baptiste _____ (March 21, 1768 - May 16, 1830) was a French mathematician and physicist best known for initiating the investigation of Fourier series and their application to problems of heat flow. The Fourier transform is also named in his honour. Fourier is also generally credited with the discovery of the greenhouse effect.

   a. BDDC
   b. 15 theorem
   c. Joseph Fourier
   d. BIBO stability

26. The mechanisms of _____; a point mass m_1 attracts another point mass m_2 by a force F_2 which is proportional to the product of the two masses and inversely proportional to the square of the distance (r) between them. Regardless of masses or distance, the magnitudes of $|F_1|$ and $|F_2|$ will always be equal. G is the gravitational constant.

_____ is an empirical physical law describing the gravitational attraction between bodies with mass.

   a. BDDC
   b. BIBO stability
   c. 15 theorem
   d. Newton's law of universal gravitation

27. The _____ are a pair of first order, non-linear, differential equations frequently used to describe the dynamics of biological systems in which two species interact, one a predator and one its prey. They were proposed independently by Alfred J. Lotka in 1925 and Vito Volterra in 1926.

where

- y is the number of some predator;
- x is the number of its prey;
- dy/dt and dx/dt represents the growth of the two populations against time;
- t represents the time; and
- >α, >β, >γ and >δ are parameters representing the interaction of the two species.

When multiplied out, the equations take a form useful for physical interpretation. Their origin should be considered from a more general framework,

where both functions represent per capita growth rates of the prey and predator, respectively.

a. BDDC
b. BIBO stability
c. 15 theorem
d. Lotka-Volterra equations

28. Trigonometry is a branch of mathematics that deals with triangles, particularly those plane triangles in which one angle has 90 degrees (right triangles.) Trigonometry deals with relationships between the sides and the angles of triangles and with the _____ functions, which describe those relationships.

Trigonometry has applications in both pure mathematics and in applied mathematics, where it is essential in many branches of science and technology.

a. 15 theorem
b. Trigonometric functions
c. Trigonometric integrals
d. Trigonometric

29. In mathematics, the _____ are functions of an angle. They are important in the study of triangles and modeling periodic phenomena, among many other applications. _____ are commonly defined as ratios of two sides of a right triangle containing the angle, and can equivalently be defined as the lengths of various line segments from a unit circle.

a. Trigonometric
b. 15 theorem
c. Trigonometric integrals
d. Trigonometric functions

30. In mathematics, the concept of a '_____' is used to describe the behavior of a function as its argument or input either 'gets close' to some point, or as the argument becomes arbitrarily large; or the behavior of a sequence's elements as their index increases indefinitely. Limits are used in calculus and other branches of mathematical analysis to define derivatives and continuity.

In formulas, _____ is usually abbreviated as lim

a. 15 theorem
b. Limit
c. BIBO stability
d. BDDC

31. In mathematics, a _____ differential equation may refer to one of two related things, both of which are differential equations that can be attacked by a method of separation of variables.

- For ordinary differential equations, it describes a class of equations that can be separated into a pair of integrals. See: Examples of differential equations

- For partial differential equations, it describes a class of equations that can be broken down into differential equations in fewer independent variables. See _____ partial differential equation.

a. Weak solution
b. Lax pair
c. Separable
d. Conserved quantity

32. In infinitesimal calculus, a _____ is traditionally an infinitesimally small change in a variable. For example, if x is a variable, then a change in the value of x is often denoted Δx (or δx when this change is considered to be small.) The _____ dx represents such a change, but is infinitely small.

a. Differential
b. Dirichlet integral
c. Related rates
d. Continuous function

33. A _____ is a mathematical equation for an unknown function of one or several variables that relates the values of the function itself and of its derivatives of various orders. they play a prominent role in engineering, physics, economics and other disciplines.

A simplified real world example of a _____ is modeling the acceleration of a ball falling through the air (considering only gravity and air resistance.)

a. Petrovsky lacuna
b. Lax pair
c. Structural stability
d. Differential equation

34. Integration is an important concept in mathematics, specifically in the field of calculus and, more broadly, mathematical analysis. Given a function f of a real variable x and an interval [a, b] of the real line, the _____

$$\int_a^b f(x)\,dx,$$

is defined informally to be the net signed area of the region in the xy-plane bounded by the graph of f, the x-axis, and the vertical lines x = a and x = b.

The term '_____' may also refer to the notion of antiderivative, a function F whose derivative is the given function f.

a. Integrand
b. Integral test for convergence
c. Indefinite integral
d. Integral

Chapter 3. Derivatives

35. In a totally ordered set all elements are mutually comparable, so such a set can have at most one minimal element and at most one maximal element. Then, due to mutual comparability, the minimal element will also be the least element and the maximal element will also be the greatest element. Thus in a totally ordered set we can simply use the terms minimum and _____.

   a. Dirichlet integral
   b. Hyperbolic angle
   c. Maximum
   d. Complex analysis

36. In calculus, the _____ is a formula for the derivative of the composite of two functions.

In intuitive terms, if a variable, y, depends on a second variable, u, which in turn depends on a third variable, x, then the rate of change of y with respect to x can be computed as the rate of change of y with respect to u multiplied by the rate of change of u with respect to x. Schematically,

$$\frac{dy}{dx} = \frac{dy}{du} \cdot \frac{du}{dx}.$$

   a. Chain Rule
   b. Reciprocal Rule
   c. Quotient Rule
   d. Differentiation rules

37. In mathematics, a _____ is a constant multiplicative factor of a certain object. For example, in the expression $9x^2$, the _____ of x^2 is 9.

The object can be such things as a variable, a vector, a function, etc.

   a. Leading coefficient
   b. Coefficient
   c. Degree of the polynomial
   d. Difference polynomial

38. A _____ has several distinct meanings.

One meaning is that a first-order ordinary differential equation is homogeneous if it has the form

$$\frac{dy}{dx} = F(y/x).$$

To solve such equations, one makes the change of variables u = y/x, which will transform such an equation into separable one.

Another meaning is a linear _____, which is a differential equation of the form

$$Ly = 0$$

where the differential operator L is a linear operator, and y is the unknown function.

Chapter 3. Derivatives

a. Homogeneous differential equation
c. Nullcline
b. Weak solution
d. Nahm equations

39. In mathematics, a _____ represents the application of one function to the results of another. For instance, the functions f: X → Y and g: Y → Z can be composed by first computing f(x) and then applying a function g to the output of f(x).)

Thus one obtains a function g â˜ f: X → Z defined by (g â˜ f)(x) = g(f(x)) for all x in X. The notation g â˜ f is read as 'g circle f', or 'g composed with f', 'g after f', 'g following f', or just 'g of f'.

a. Surjective
c. Constant function
b. Composite function
d. Range

40. In mathematics, a _____ is a unicursal quartic curve with three inflection points, given by the equation

$$a^2 y^2 - b^2 x^2 = x^2 y^2$$

The bullet curve has three double points in the real projective plane, at x=0 and y=0, x=0 and z=0, and y=0 and z=0, and is therefore a unicursal (rational) curve of genus zero.

If

$$f(z) = \sum_{n=0}^{\infty} \binom{2n}{n} z^{2n+1} = z + 2z^3 + 6z^5 + 20z^7 + \cdots$$

then

$$y = f\left(\frac{x}{2a}\right) \pm 2b$$

are the two branches of the bullet curve at the origin.

a. Bullet-nose curve
c. Closed curve
b. Hypocycloid
d. Folium of Descartes

41. In mathematics, a (topological) _____ is defined as follows: let I be an interval of real numbers (i.e. a non-empty connected subset of $\mathbb{R}$); then a _____ γ is a continuous mapping $\gamma : I \to X$, where X is a topological space. The _____ γ is said to be simple if it is injective, i.e. if for all x, y in I, we have $\gamma(x) = \gamma(y) \implies x = y$. If I is a closed bounded interval $[a, b]$, we also allow the possibility $\gamma(a) = \gamma(b)$ (this convention makes it possible to talk about closed simple _____.)

a. Curve
c. Tractrix
b. Closed curve
d. Prolate cycloid

Chapter 3. Derivatives

42. _____ is the motion of a simple harmonic oscillator, a motion that is neither driven nor damped. The motion is periodic - as it repeats itself at standard intervals in a specific manner - and sinusoidal, with constant amplitude; the acceleration of a body executing _____ is directly proportional to the displacement of the body from the equilibrium position and is always directed towards the equilibrium position.

The motion is characterized by its amplitude (which is always positive), its period, the time for a single oscillation, its frequency, the reciprocal of the period (i.e. the number of cycles per unit time), and its phase, which determines the starting point on the sine wave.

    a. BDDC
    c. Simple harmonic motion
    b. 15 theorem
    d. Holonomic

43. In acoustics and telecommunication, a _____ of a wave is a component frequency of the signal that is an integer multiple of the fundamental frequency. For example, if the fundamental frequency is f, the harmonics have frequencies f, 2f, 3f, 4f, etc. The harmonics have the property that they are all periodic at the fundamental frequency, therefore the sum of harmonics is also periodic at that frequency.

    a. Harmonic
    c. 15 theorem
    b. BDDC
    d. BIBO stability

44. In Geometry, the _____ is an algebraic curve defined by the equation

$$x^3 + y^3 - 3axy = 0$$

It forms a loop in the first quadrant with a double point at the origin and asymptote

$$x + y + a = 0$$

It is symmetrical about y = x.

    a. Folium of Descartes
    c. Curve
    b. Cochleoid
    d. Prolate cycloid

45. In calculus, a method called _____ can be applied to implicitly defined functions. This method is an application of the chain rule allowing one to calculate the derivative of a function given implicitly.

As explained in the introduction, y can be given as a function of x implicitly rather than explicitly. When we have an equation R (x,y) = 0, we may be able to solve it for y and then differentiate. However, sometimes it is simpler to differentiate R(x,y) with respect to x and then solve for dy / dx.

    a. Implicit function
    c. Ordinary differential equation
    b. Implicit differentiation
    d. Automatic differentiation

46. In mathematics, an _____ is a generalization for the concept of a function in which the dependent variable has not been given 'explicitly' in terms of the independent variable. To give a function f explicitly is to provide a prescription for determining the output value of the function y in terms of the input value x:

Chapter 3. Derivatives

$$y = f(x.)$$

By contrast, the function is implicit if the value of y is obtained from x by solving an equation of the form:

$$R(x,y) = 0.$$

a. Implicit function
c. Implicit differentiation
b. Automatic differentiation
d. Ordinary differential equation

47. In mathematics, the _____ of a non-negative integer n, denoted by n!, is the product of all positive integers less than or equal to n. For example,

$$5! = 1 \times 2 \times 3 \times 4 \times 5 = 120$$

and

$$6! = 1 \times 2 \times 3 \times 4 \times 5 \times 6 = 720.$$

The notation n! was introduced by Christian Kramp in 1808.

The _____ function is formally defined by

$$n! = \prod_{k=1}^{n} k \qquad \forall n \in \mathbb{N}$$

or recursively defined by

$$n! = \begin{cases} n \leq 1 & 1 \\ n > 1 & n(n-1)! \end{cases} \qquad \forall n \in \mathbb{N}.$$

Both of the above definitions incorporate the instance

$$0! = 1$$

as an instance of the fact that the product of no numbers at all is 1.

a. 15 theorem
c. BDDC
b. Constraint counting
d. Factorial

Chapter 3. Derivatives

48. _____ are a set of problems generally thought to have been devised by Zeno of Elea to support Parmenides's doctrine that 'all is one' and that, contrary to the evidence of our senses, the belief in plurality and change is mistaken, and in particular that motion is nothing but an illusion. It is usually assumed, based on Plato's Parmenides 128c-d, that Zeno took on the project of creating these paradoxes because other philosophers had created paradoxes against Parmenides's view. Thus Zeno can be interpreted as saying that to assume there is plurality is even more absurd than assuming there is only 'the One' (Parmenides 128d.)
   a. 15 theorem
   b. BDDC
   c. BIBO stability
   d. Zeno's paradoxes

49. A plane curve is a curve for which X is the Euclidean plane -- these are the examples first encountered -- or in some cases the projective plane. A _____ is a curve for which X is of three dimensions, usually Euclidean space; a skew curve is a _____ which lies in no plane. These definitions also apply to algebraic curves
   a. Space curve
   b. Folium of Descartes
   c. Hypocycloid
   d. Curtate cycloid

50. In mathematics, two vectors are _____ if they are perpendicular, i.e., they form a right angle. For example, a subway and the street above, although they do not physically intersect, are _____ if they cross at a right angle.
   a. AUSM
   b. ALGOR
   c. ACTRAN
   d. Orthogonal

51. In mathematics, _____ are a family of curves in the plane that intersect a given family of curves at right angles. The problem is classical, but is now understood by means of complex analysis; see for example harmonic conjugate.

For a family of level curves described by g(x,y) = C, where C is a constant, the _____ may be found as the level curves of a new function f(x,y) by solving the partial differential equation

$$\nabla f \cdot \nabla g = 0$$

for f(x,y).

   a. ACTRAN
   b. AUSM
   c. Orthogonal trajectories
   d. ALGOR

52. A _____ is the path a moving object follows through space. The object might be a projectile or a satellite, for example. It thus includes the meaning of orbit - the path of a planet, an asteroid or a comet as it travels around a central mass.
   a. BIBO stability
   b. 15 theorem
   c. BDDC
   d. Trajectory

53. In mathematics, an _____ is a particular type of curve: a hypocycloid with four cusps. Astroids are also superellipses: all astroids are scaled versions of the curve specified by the equation

$$x^{2/3} + y^{2/3} = 1$$

Its modern name comes from the Greek word for 'star'.

a. ALGOR
c. ACTRAN
b. Astroid
d. Epicycloid

54. A _____ is closed curve with one cusp.

In geometry, the _____ is an epicycloid with one cusp.

Rolling circle around another fixed circle produces _____ (red curve) Conformal mapping from circle to _____

- epicycloid produced as the path (or locus) of a point on the circumference of a circle as that circle rolls around another fixed circle with the same radius.

- limaçon with one cusp. The cusp is formed when the ratio of a to b in the equation is equal to one.

a. BIBO stability
c. Cardioid
b. BDDC
d. 15 theorem

55. The _____ is a curve, with a Cartesian equation of

$$x^4 = x^2 + y^2,$$

or, in polar coordinates,

$$r = \sec^2 \theta.$$

This quartic curve was studied by the Greek astronomer and mathematician Eudoxus of Cnidus (c. 408 BC - c.347 BC) in relation to the classical problem of doubling the cube.

- List of curves

a. Dolbeault operator
c. Kampyle of Eudoxus
b. Tschirnhausen cubic
d. Macbeath surface

56. The _____, named after the mathematician Ehrenfried Walther von Tschirnhaus, is a plane curve which is defined by either of these formulae:

$y^2 = x^3 + 3x^2$

$a = r\cos^3(\theta / 3.)$

Chapter 3. Derivatives

a. Dolbeault operator
b. Strophoid
c. Kampyle of Eudoxus
d. Tschirnhausen cubic

57. In mathematics, an _____, is the apparent shape of a circle viewed obliquely from outside it, as distinct from a hyperbola which is the shape seen from inside. It is the finite or bounded case of a conic section as a shape cut in a cone by a plane, the unbounded cases being the parabola, which like the _____ remains connected, and the hyperbola, which separates into two connected components or branches.

Equivalently an _____ can be defined as the locus of points, or path traced out, in a plane such that the sum of the distances from the moving point to two fixed points remains constant.

a. ALGOR
b. ACTRAN
c. AUSM
d. Ellipse

58. Let f be a differentiable function, and let f'(x) be its derivative. The derivative of f'(x) (if it has one) is written f''(x) and is called the _____ of f. Similarly, the derivative of a _____, if it exists, is written f'''(x) and is called the third derivative of f.
a. Stationary phase approximation
b. Horizontal asymptote
c. Ramp function
d. Second derivative

59. In physics, and more specifically kinematics, _____ is the change in velocity over time. Because velocity is a vector, it can change in two ways: a change in magnitude and/or a change in direction. In one dimension, _____ is the rate at which something speeds up or slows down.
a. Acceleration
b. AUSM
c. ALGOR
d. ACTRAN

60. Let f be a differentiable function, and let f'(x) be its derivative. The derivative of f'(x) (if it has one) is written f''(x) and is called the second derivative of f. Similarly, the derivative of a second derivative, if it exists, is written f'''(x) and is called the _____ of f.
a. Third derivative
b. Second derivative
c. Geometric function theory
d. Semi-differentiability

61.

In differential calculus, _____ problems involve finding a rate that a quantity changes by relating the population of the earth. The rate of change is usually with respect to people who have died.

a. Binomial series
b. Reflection formula
c. Complex analysis
d. Related rates

62. In mathematics, a _____ is an approximation of a general function using a linear function (more precisely, an affine function.)

Given a differentiable function f of one real variable, Taylor's theorem for n=1 states that

$$f(x) = f(a) + f'(a)(x-a) + R_2$$

where R_2 is the remainder term. The _____ is obtained by dropping the remainder:

$$f(x) \approx f(a) + f'(a)(x-a)$$

which is true for x close to a.

   a. Linearity of differentiation
   b. Differentiation of trigonometric functions
   c. Smooth function
   d. Linear approximation

63. In mathematics and its applications, _____ refers to finding the linear approximation to a function at a given point. In the study of dynamical systems, _____ is a method for assessing the local stability of an equilibrium point of a system of nonlinear differential equations or discrete dynamical systems. This method is used in fields such as engineering, physics, economics, and ecology.
   a. Stationary point
   b. Symmetrically continuous
   c. Point of inflection
   d. Linearization

64. In mathematics, an _____ on a real vector space is a choice of which ordered bases are 'positively' oriented and which are 'negatively' oriented. In the three-dimensional Euclidean space, the two possible basis orientations are called right-handed and left-handed (or right-chiral and left-chiral), respectively. However, the choice of _____ is independent of the handedness or chirality of the bases (although right-handed bases are typically declared to be positively oriented, they may also be assigned a negative _____.)
   a. Unit vector
   b. ACTRAN
   c. Orientation
   d. ALGOR

65. In mathematics, an _____ is a function built from a finite number of exponentials, logarithms, constants, one variable, and nth roots through composition and combinations using the four elementary operations (+ - × ÷.) The trigonometric functions and their inverses are assumed to be included in the elementary functions by using complex variables and the relations between the trigonometric functions and the exponential and logarithm functions.

Elementary functions are considered a subset of special functions.

   a. ACTRAN
   b. AUSM
   c. ALGOR
   d. Elementary function

66. The _____ in some data is the discrepancy between an exact value and some approximation to it. An _____ can occur because

1. the measurement of the data is not precise (due to the instruments), or
2. approximations are used instead of the real data (e.g., 3.14 instead of π.)

Chapter 3. Derivatives

In the mathematical field of numerical analysis, the numerical stability of an algorithm in numerical analysis indicates how the error is propagated by the algorithm.

One commonly distinguishes between the relative error and the absolute error. The absolute error is the magnitude of the difference between the exact value and the approximation.

a. Approximation error
b. ALGOR
c. AUSM
d. ACTRAN

67. One commonly distinguishes between the _____ and the absolute error. The absolute error is the magnitude of the difference between the exact value and the approximation. The _____ is the absolute error divided by the magnitude of the exact value.
    a. Relative error
    b. Series acceleration
    c. Numerical integration
    d. Meshfree methods

68. A _____, sometimes known as an energy shield, force shield typically made of energy or charged particles, that protects a person, area or object from attacks or intrusions.

A University of Washington in Seattle group has been experimenting with using a bubble of charged plasma to surround a spacecraft, contained by a fine mesh of superconducting wire. This would protect the spacecraft from interstellar radiation and some particles without needing physical shielding.

   a. BDDC
   b. BIBO stability
   c. 15 theorem
   d. Force field

69. In calculus, _____ gives a sequence of approximations of a differentiable function around a given point by polynomials (the Taylor polynomials of that function) whose coefficients depend only on the derivatives of the function at that point. The theorem also gives precise estimates on the size of the error in the approximation. The theorem is named after the mathematician Brook Taylor, who stated it in 1712, though the result was first discovered 41 years earlier in 1671 by James Gregory.
    a. Leibniz differential
    b. Continuous function
    c. Complex analysis
    d. Taylor's theorem

70. In geometry, a _____ is a three-dimensional figure formed by six parallelograms. It is to a parallelogram as a cube is to a square: Euclidean geometry supports all four notions but affine geometry admits only parallelograms and parallelepipeds. Three equivalent definitions of _____ are

   - a polyhedron with six faces (hexahedron), each of which is a parallelogram,
   - a hexahedron with three pairs of parallel faces, and
   - a prism of which the base is a parallelogram.

The cuboid (six rectangular faces), cube (six square faces), and the rhombohedron (six rhombus faces) are all specific cases of _____.

Parallelepipeds are a subclass of the prismatoids.

a. Parallelepiped   b. BIBO stability
c. 15 theorem   d. BDDC

71. In mathematics, an _____ is an infinite series of the form

$$\sum_{n=0}^{\infty}(-1)^n a_n,$$

with $a_n \geq 0$ (or $a_n \leq 0$) for all n. A finite sum of this kind is an alternating sum. An _____ converges if the terms a_n converge to 0 monotonically.

a. Uniform convergence   b. Alternating Series
c. Extreme value   d. Infinite series

72. In mathematics, the _____ is a conic section, the intersection of a right circular conical surface and a plane parallel to a generating straight line of that surface. Given a point (the focus) and a line (the directrix) that lie in a plane, the locus of points in that plane that are equidistant to them is a _____.

A particular case arises when the plane is tangent to the conical surface of a circle.

a. BIBO stability   b. 15 theorem
c. BDDC   d. Parabola

Chapter 4. Applications of Differentiation

1. The largest and the smallest element of a set are called extreme values, absolute extrema, or extreme records.

For a differentiable function f, if $f(x_0)$ is an _____ for the set of all values f(x), and if x_0 is in the interior of the domain of f, then x_0 is a critical point, by Fermat's theorem.

In the case of a general partial order one should not confuse a least element (smaller than all other) and a minimal element (nothing is smaller.)

- a. Integration by substitution
- b. Infinitesimal
- c. Extreme Value Theorem
- d. Extreme value

2. In mathematics, the simplest case of _____ refers to the study of problems in which one seeks to minimize or maximize a real function by systematically choosing the values of real or integer variables from within an allowed set. This (a scalar real valued objective function) is actually a small subset of this field which comprises a large area of applied mathematics and generalizes to study of means to obtain 'best available' values of some objective function given a defined domain where the elaboration is on the types of functions and the conditions and nature of the objects in the problem domain.

The first _____ technique, which is known as steepest descent, goes back to Gauss.

- a. Optimization
- b. ALGOR
- c. AUSM
- d. ACTRAN

3. In mathematics, a (topological) _____ is defined as follows: let I be an interval of real numbers (i.e. a non-empty connected subset of $\mathbb{R}$); then a _____ γ is a continuous mapping $\gamma : I \to X$, where X is a topological space. The _____ γ is said to be simple if it is injective, i.e. if for all x, y in I, we have $\gamma(x) = \gamma(y) \implies x = y$. If I is a closed bounded interval $[a, b]$, we also allow the possibility $\gamma(a) = \gamma(b)$ (this convention makes it possible to talk about closed simple _____.)

- a. Prolate cycloid
- b. Tractrix
- c. Closed curve
- d. Curve

4. In a totally ordered set all elements are mutually comparable, so such a set can have at most one minimal element and at most one maximal element. Then, due to mutual comparability, the minimal element will also be the least element and the maximal element will also be the greatest element. Thus in a totally ordered set we can simply use the terms minimum and _____.

- a. Hyperbolic angle
- b. Maximum
- c. Dirichlet integral
- d. Complex analysis

5. In a totally ordered set all elements are mutually comparable, so such a set can have at most one minimal element and at most one maximal element. Then, due to mutual comparability, the minimal element will also be the least element and the maximal element will also be the greatest element. Thus in a totally ordered set we can simply use the terms _____ and maximum.

- a. Periodic function
- b. Taylor's theorem
- c. Calculus controversy
- d. Minimum

Chapter 4. Applications of Differentiation

6. In calculus, the _____ states that if a real-valued function f is continuous in the closed and bounded interval [a,b], then f must attain its maximum and minimum value, each at least once. That is, there exist numbers c and d in [a,b] such that:

$$f(c) \geq f(x) \geq f(d) \quad \text{for all } x \in [a, b].$$

A related theorem is the boundedness theorem which states that a continuous function f in the closed interval [a,b] is bounded on that interval. That is, there exist real numbers m and M such that:

$$m \leq f(x) \leq M \quad \text{for all } x \in [a, b].$$

The _____ enriches the boundedness theorem by saying that not only is the function bounded, but it also attains its least upper bound as its maximum and its greatest lower bound as its minimum.

a. Extreme Value Theorem
c. Uniform convergence
b. Integral of secant cubed
d. Infinitesimal

7. In mathematics, a _____ (or critical number) is a point on the domain of a function where:

- one dimension: the derivative (or slope of the line when visualized) is equal to zero or a point where the function ceases to be differentiable.
- in general: there are two distinct concepts: either the derivative (Jacobian) vanishes, or it is not of full rank (or, in either case, the function is not differentiable); these agree in one dimension.

Note that in one dimension, a critical value or critical number x of function f is the domain element at which the derivative is zero or undefined, whereas the associated ordered pair (x, y) is the _____. In higher dimensions a critical value is in the range whereas a _____ is in the domain.

There are two situations in which a point becomes a _____ of a function of one variable. The first of which is that the value of the first derivative is equal to zero.

a. Critical point
c. Differentiation operator
b. Differential operator
d. Shift theorem

8. In mathematics, a _____ is a constant multiplicative factor of a certain object. For example, in the expression $9x^2$, the _____ of x^2 is 9.

The object can be such things as a variable, a vector, a function, etc.

a. Coefficient
c. Degree of the polynomial
b. Leading coefficient
d. Difference polynomial

9. In mathematics, an _____ is an infinite series of the form

$$\sum_{n=0}^{\infty}(-1)^n a_n,$$

with $a_n \geq 0$ (or $a_n \leq 0$) for all n. A finite sum of this kind is an alternating sum. An _____ converges if the terms a_n converge to 0 monotonically.

- a. Infinite series
- b. Alternating Series
- c. Uniform convergence
- d. Extreme value

10. In probability theory and statistics, the _____ (or expectation value or mean and for continuous random variables with a density function it is the probability density -weighted integral of the possible values.

The term '_____' can be misleading.

- a. ALGOR
- b. ACTRAN
- c. AUSM
- d. Expected value

11. In calculus, the _____ states, roughly, that given a section of a smooth curve, there is at least one point on that section at which the derivative (slope) of the curve is equal (parallel) to the 'average' derivative of the section. It is used to prove theorems that make global conclusions about a function on an interval starting from local hypotheses about derivatives at points of the interval.

This theorem can be understood concretely by applying it to motion: If a car travels one hundred miles in one hour, so its average speed during that time was 100 miles per hour.

- a. Mean Value Theorem
- b. First derivative test
- c. Leibniz differential
- d. Fresnel integrals

12. In calculus, a branch of mathematics, the _____ is a measurement of how a function changes when its input changes. Loosely speaking, a _____ can be thought of as how much a quantity is changing at some given point. For example, the _____ of the position (or distance) of a vehicle with respect to time is the instantaneous velocity (respectively, instantaneous speed) at which the vehicle is traveling.

The process of finding a _____ is called differentiation. The fundamental theorem of calculus states that differentiation is the reverse process to integration.

- a. Ramp function
- b. Mountain pass theorem
- c. Concave upwards
- d. Derivative

13. In calculus, the _____ determines whether a given critical point of a function is a maximum, a minimum, or neither.

Suppose that f is a function and we want to determine if f has a maximum or minimum at x. If f is increasing to the left of x and decreasing to the right of x, then x is a local maximum of f.

- a. Functional integration
- b. Hyperbolic angle
- c. Test for Divergence
- d. First Derivative Test

14. In differential calculus, an inflection point, or _____ (or inflexion) is a point on a curve at which the curvature changes sign. The curve changes from being concave upwards (positive curvature) to concave downwards (negative curvature), or vice versa. If one imagines driving a vehicle along the curve, it is a point at which the steering-wheel is momentarily 'straight', being turned from left to right or vice versa.

- a. Linearity of differentiation
- b. Second derivative test
- c. Reduced derivative
- d. Point of inflection

15. Let f be a differentiable function, and let f'(x) be its derivative. The derivative of f'(x) (if it has one) is written f''(x) and is called the _____ of f. Similarly, the derivative of a _____, if it exists, is written f'''(x) and is called the third derivative of f.

- a. Ramp function
- b. Stationary phase approximation
- c. Horizontal asymptote
- d. Second Derivative

16. In calculus, a branch of mathematics, the _____ is a criterion often useful for determining whether a given stationary point of a function is a local maximum or a local minimum.

The test states: If the function f is twice differentiable at a stationary point x, meaning that $f'(x) = 0$, then:

- If $f''(x) < 0$ then f has a local maximum at x.
- If $f''(x) > 0$ then f has a local minimum at x.
- If $f''(x) = 0$, the _____ says nothing about the point x, has a possible inflection point.

In the last case, the function may have a local maximum or minimum there, but the function is sufficiently 'flat' that this is undetected by the second derivative. In this case one has to examine the third derivative. Such an example is f(x) = x^4.

- a. Parametric derivative
- b. Stationary point
- c. Metric derivative
- d. Second Derivative Test

17. In mathematics, the concept of a '_____' is used to describe the behavior of a function as its argument or input either 'gets close' to some point, or as the argument becomes arbitrarily large; or the behavior of a sequence's elements as their index increases indefinitely. Limits are used in calculus and other branches of mathematical analysis to define derivatives and continuity.

In formulas, _____ is usually abbreviated as lim

Chapter 4. Applications of Differentiation

a. 15 theorem
b. BDDC
c. BIBO stability
d. Limit

18. An _____ of a real-valued function y = f(x) is a curve which describes the behavior of f as either x or y tends to infinity.

In other words, as one moves along the graph of f(x) in some direction, the distance between it and the _____ eventually becomes smaller than any distance that one may specify.

a. AUSM
b. Asymptote
c. ALGOR
d. ACTRAN

19. Suppose f is a function. Then the line y = a is a _____ for f if

$$\lim_{x \to \infty} f(x) = a \text{ or } \lim_{x \to -\infty} f(x) = a.$$

Intuitively, this means that f(x) can be made as close as desired to a by making x big enough. How big is big enough depends on how close one wishes to make f(x) to a.

a. Mountain pass theorem
b. Bounded function
c. Horizontal asymptote
d. Vertical asymptote

20. Cantor defined two kinds of _____ numbers, the ordinal numbers and the cardinal numbers. Ordinal numbers may be identified with well-ordered sets, or counting carried on to any stopping point, including points after an _____ number have already been counted. Generalizing finite and the ordinary _____ sequences which are maps from the positive integers leads to mappings from ordinal numbers, and transfinite sequences.

a. AUSM
b. ACTRAN
c. Infinite
d. ALGOR

21. In mathematics, even functions and odd functions are functions which satisfy particular symmetry relations, with respect to taking additive inverses. They are important in many areas of mathematical analysis, especially the theory of power series and Fourier series. They are named for the parity of the powers of the power functions which satisfy each condition: the function f(x) = x^n is an _____ if n is an even integer, and it is an odd function if n is an odd integer.

a. Operational calculus
b. Integral of secant cubed
c. Infinite series
d. Even function

22. In vector calculus, the _____ of a scalar field is a vector field which points in the direction of the greatest rate of increase of the scalar field, and whose magnitude is the greatest rate of change.

A generalization of the _____ for functions on a Euclidean space which have values in another Euclidean space is the Jacobian. A further generalization for a function from one Banach space to another is the Fréchet derivative.

Chapter 4. Applications of Differentiation

a. Gradient
b. Smooth function
c. Parametric derivative
d. Leibniz's notation

23. In mathematics, a _____ is an ordered list of objects (or events). Like a set, it contains members (also called elements or terms), and the number of terms (possibly infinite) is called the length of the _____. Unlike a set, order matters, and the exact same elements can appear multiple times at different positions in the _____.

a. Y-intercept
b. 15 theorem
c. BDDC
d. Sequence

24. In mathematics, even functions and odd functions are functions which satisfy particular symmetry relations, with respect to taking additive inverses. They are important in many areas of mathematical analysis, especially the theory of power series and Fourier series. They are named for the parity of the powers of the power functions which satisfy each condition: the function f(x) = x^n is an even function if n is an even integer, and it is an _____ if n is an odd integer.

a. Integral of secant cubed
b. Even function
c. Integration by substitution
d. Odd function

25. _____ generally conveys two primary meanings. The first is an imprecise sense of harmonious or aesthetically-pleasing proportionality and balance; such that it reflects beauty or perfection. The second meaning is a precise and well-defined concept of balance or 'patterned self-similarity' that can be demonstrated or proved according to the rules of a formal system: by geometry, through physics or otherwise.

a. Symmetry
b. BDDC
c. 15 theorem
d. BIBO stability

26. In mathematics, a _____ is a function that repeats its values in regular intervals or periods. The most important examples are the trigonometric functions, which repeat over intervals of length 2π. Periodic functions are used throughout science to describe oscillations, waves, and other phenomena that exhibit periodicity.

a. Test for Divergence
b. Term test
c. Nth term
d. Periodic function

27. The line x = a is a _____ of a curve y=f(x) if at least one of the following statements is true:

1. $\lim_{x \to a} f(x) = \pm\infty$
2. $\lim_{x \to a^-} f(x) = \pm\infty$
3. $\lim_{x \to a^+} f(x) = \pm\infty$

Intuitively, if x = a is an asymptote of f, then, if we imagine x approaching a from one side, the value of f(x) grows without bound; i.e., f(x) becomes large (positively or negatively), and, in fact, becomes larger than any finite value.

Note that f(x) may or may not be defined at a: what the function is doing precisely at x = a does not affect the asymptote. For example, consider the function

$$f(x) = \begin{cases} \frac{1}{x} & \text{if } x > 0, \\ 5 & \text{if } x \leq 0 \end{cases}$$

As $x \to 0^+$, $\lim f(x) = \infty$, f(x) has a _____ at 0, even though f(0) = 5.

Another example is $f(x) = 1/(x-1)$ which has a _____ of x=1 as shown by the limit

$$\lim_{x \to 1^+} \frac{1}{x-1} = \infty$$

In the graph of $f(x) = x + \frac{1}{x}$, the y-axis (x = 0) and the line y = x are both asymptotes.

When a linear asymptote is not parallel to the x- or y-axis, it is called either an oblique asymptote or equivalently a slant asymptote.

- a. Fractional calculus
- c. Vertical asymptote
- b. Geometric function theory
- d. Semi-differentiability

28. In mathematics a _____ is a construction in vector calculus which associates a vector to every point in a (locally) Euclidean space.

Vector fields are often used in physics to model, for example, the speed and direction of a moving fluid throughout space, or the strength and direction of some force, such as the magnetic or gravitational force, as it changes from point to point.

In the rigorous mathematical treatment, (tangent) vector fields are defined on manifolds as sections of a manifold's tangent bundle.

- a. 15 theorem
- c. BIBO stability
- b. BDDC
- d. Vector field

29. When a linear asymptote is not parallel to the x- or y-axis, it is called either an oblique asymptote or equivalently a _____. The function f(x) is asymptotic to y = mx + b if

$$\lim_{x \to \infty} f(x) - (mx+b) = 0 \text{ or } \lim_{x \to -\infty} f(x) - (mx+b) = 0$$

Chapter 4. Applications of Differentiation

Note that y = mx + b is never a vertical asymptote, but can be a horizontal asymptote if m=0 (in which case it is not an oblique asymptote.)

An example is $f(x)=(x^2-1)/x$ which has an oblique asymptote of y=x (m=1, b=0) as seen in the limit

$$\lim_{x \to \infty} f(x) - x$$
$$= \lim_{x \to \infty} \frac{x^2 - 1}{x} - x$$
$$= \lim_{x \to \infty} (x - 1/x) - x$$
$$= \lim_{x \to \infty} -1/x = 0$$

Computationally identifying an oblique asymptote can be more difficult than a horizontal or vertical asymptote, in particular because the m and b might not be known.

a. Geometric function theory
b. Horizontal asymptote
c. Second derivative
d. Slant asymptote

30. In the differential geometry of surfaces, an _____ is a curve always tangent to an asymptotic direction of the surface (where they exist.) It is sometimes called an asymptotic line, although it need not be a line.

An asymptotic direction is one in which the normal curvature is zero.

a. ALGOR
b. ACTRAN
c. Epicycloid
d. Asymptotic curve

31. In mathematics, an _____ is a function built from a finite number of exponentials, logarithms, constants, one variable, and nth roots through composition and combinations using the four elementary operations (+ - × ÷.) The trigonometric functions and their inverses are assumed to be included in the elementary functions by using complex variables and the relations between the trigonometric functions and the exponential and logarithm functions.

Elementary functions are considered a subset of special functions.

a. AUSM
b. ALGOR
c. ACTRAN
d. Elementary function

32. In economics, the _____ functional form of production functions is widely used to represent the relationship of an output to inputs. It was proposed by Knut Wicksell (1851-1926), and tested against statistical evidence by Charles Cobb and Paul Douglas in 1900-1928.

Chapter 4. Applications of Differentiation

For production, the function is

$$Y = AL^\alpha K^\beta,$$

where:

- Y = total production (the monetary value of all goods produced in a year)
- L = labor input
- K = capital input
- A = total factor productivity
- α and β are the output elasticities of labor and capital, respectively. These values are constants determined by available technology.

Output elasticity measures the responsiveness of output to a change in levels of either labor or capital used in production, ceteris paribus. For example if α = 0.15, a 1% increase in labor would lead to approximately a 0.15% increase in output.

a. Cobb-Douglas
b. 15 theorem
c. BIBO stability
d. BDDC

33. A _____ is the portion of a solid--normally a cone or pyramid--which lies between two parallel planes cutting the solid. The term is commonly used in computer graphics to describe the 3d area which is visible on the screen (which is formed by a clipped pyramid.)

Each plane section is a base of the _____.

a. BDDC
b. Frustum
c. BIBO stability
d. 15 theorem

34. A _____ is a model used within physics to explain how gravity exists in the universe. In its original concept, gravity was a force between point masses. Following Newton, Laplace attempted to model gravity as some kind of radiation field or fluid, and since the 19th century explanations for gravity have usually been sought in terms of a field model, rather than a point attraction.

a. Gravitational field
b. BIBO stability
c. BDDC
d. 15 theorem

35. In mathematics and computer science, the floor and ceiling functions map a real number to the next smallest or next largest integer. More precisely, floor(x) is the largest integer not greater than x and ceiling(x) is the smallest integer not less than x.

The _____ is also called the greatest integer or entier function, and the floor of a nonnegative x may be called the integral part or integral value of x. Computer languages (other than APL) commonly use ENTIER(x) (Algol), floor(x), or int(x) (C and C++).

a. Signum function
b. Hyperbolic tangent
c. Hyperbolic functions
d. Floor function

36. In infinitesimal calculus, a _____ is traditionally an infinitesimally small change in a variable. For example, if x is a variable, then a change in the value of x is often denoted Δx (or δx when this change is considered to be small.) The _____ dx represents such a change, but is infinitely small.
   a. Related rates
   b. Dirichlet integral
   c. Continuous function
   d. Differential

37. In calculus, an _____, primitive or indefinite integral of a function f is a function F whose derivative is equal to f, i.e., F >' = f. The process of solving for antiderivatives is antidifferentiation (or indefinite integration.) Antiderivatives are related to definite integrals through the fundamental theorem of calculus: the definite integral of a function over an interval is equal to the difference between the values of an _____ evaluated at the endpoints of the interval.
   a. Integrand
   b. Antiderivative
   c. Indefinite integral
   d. Order of integration

38. The _____, are the five positions in an orbital configuration where a small object affected only by gravity can theoretically be stationary relative to two larger objects (such as a satellite with respect to the Earth and Moon.) The _____ mark positions where the combined gravitational pull of the two large masses provides precisely the centripetal force required to rotate with them. They are analogous to geostationary orbits in that they allow an object to be in a 'fixed' position in space rather than an orbit in which its relative position changes continuously.
   a. BDDC
   b. BIBO stability
   c. 15 theorem
   d. Lagrangian points

39. A _____ is a mathematical equation for an unknown function of one or several variables that relates the values of the function itself and of its derivatives of various orders. they play a prominent role in engineering, physics, economics and other disciplines.

A simplified real world example of a _____ is modeling the acceleration of a ball falling through the air (considering only gravity and air resistance.)

   a. Petrovsky lacuna
   b. Lax pair
   c. Differential equation
   d. Structural stability

40. In mathematics, a _____ (or direction field) is a graphical representation of the solutions of a first-order differential equation. It is achieved without solving the differential equation analytically, and thence it is useful. The representation may be used to qualitatively visualise solutions, or to numerically approximate them.
   a. Standard part function
   b. The Method of Mechanical Theorems
   c. Fresnel integrals
   d. Slope field

Chapter 5. Integrals

1. The _____ is one of the oldest concepts in mathematical analysis. It provides a rigorous definition of the idea of a sequence converging towards a point called the limit.

Intuitively, suppose we have a sequence of points (i.e. an infinite set of points labelled using the natural numbers) in some sort of mathematical object (for example the real numbers or a vector space) which has a concept of nearness (such as 'all points within a given distance of a fixed point'.)

    a. 15 theorem
    b. Squeeze Theorem
    c. Limit of a sequence
    d. Table of limits

2. In mathematics, the concept of a '_____' is used to describe the behavior of a function as its argument or input either 'gets close' to some point, or as the argument becomes arbitrarily large; or the behavior of a sequence's elements as their index increases indefinitely. Limits are used in calculus and other branches of mathematical analysis to define derivatives and continuity.

In formulas, _____ is usually abbreviated as lim

    a. BIBO stability
    b. BDDC
    c. 15 theorem
    d. Limit

3. In mathematics, a _____ is an ordered list of objects (or events). Like a set, it contains members (also called elements or terms), and the number of terms (possibly infinite) is called the length of the _____. Unlike a set, order matters, and the exact same elements can appear multiple times at different positions in the _____.

    a. 15 theorem
    b. Sequence
    c. BDDC
    d. Y-intercept

4. _____ is the addition of a set of numbers; the result is their sum or total. An interim or present total of a _____ process is termed the running total. The 'numbers' to be summed may be natural numbers, complex numbers, matrices, or still more complicated objects.

    a. BDDC
    b. 15 theorem
    c. BIBO stability
    d. Summation

5. In mathematics, a (topological) _____ is defined as follows: let I be an interval of real numbers (i.e. a non-empty connected subset of $\mathbb{R}$); then a _____ γ is a continuous mapping $\gamma : I \to X$, where X is a topological space. The _____ γ is said to be simple if it is injective, i.e. if for all x, y in I, we have $\gamma(x) = \gamma(y) \implies x = y$. If I is a closed bounded interval $[a, b]$, we also allow the possibility $\gamma(a) = \gamma(b)$ (this convention makes it possible to talk about closed simple _____.)

    a. Curve
    b. Tractrix
    c. Prolate cycloid
    d. Closed curve

6. Integration is an important concept in mathematics, specifically in the field of calculus and, more broadly, mathematical analysis. Given a function f of a real variable x and an interval [a, b] of the real line, the _____

$$\int_a^b f(x)\, dx,$$

is defined informally to be the net signed area of the region in the xy-plane bounded by the graph of f, the x-axis, and the vertical lines x = a and x = b.

The term '_____' may also refer to the notion of antiderivative, a function F whose derivative is the given function f.

    a. Integral test for convergence   b. Integrand
    c. Indefinite integral   d. Integral

7. In mathematics, the _____ of a function y = f(x) is a function that, in some fashion, 'undoes' the effect of f The _____ of f is denoted f^{-1}. The statements y=f(x) and x=f^{-1}(y) are equivalent.
    a. ACTRAN   b. Inverse
    c. AUSM   d. ALGOR

8. If a function has an integral, it is said to be integrable. The function for which the integral is calculated is called the _____. The region over which a function is being integrated is called the domain of integration.
    a. Integration by parts   b. Order of integration
    c. Integral test for convergence   d. Integrand

9. In mathematics, a _____ is a method for approximating the total area underneath a curve on a graph, otherwise known as an integral. It may also be used to define the integration operation.

Consider a function $f: D \rightarrow \mathbf{R}$, where D is a subset of the real numbers $\mathbf{R}$, and let $I = [a, b]$ be a closed interval contained in D. A finite set of points $\{x_0, x_1, x_2, ... x_n\}$ such that $a = x_0 < x_1 < x_2 ... < x_n = b$ creates a partition

$$P = \{[x_0, x_1), [x_1, x_2), ... [x_{n-1}, x_n]\}$$

of I.

    a. Disk integration   b. Riemann sum
    c. Signed measure   d. Surface of revolution

10. In infinitesimal calculus, a _____ is traditionally an infinitesimally small change in a variable. For example, if x is a variable, then a change in the value of x is often denoted Δx (or δx when this change is considered to be small.) The _____ dx represents such a change, but is infinitely small.
    a. Related rates   b. Continuous function
    c. Dirichlet integral   d. Differential

11. The _____ is a doubly ruled surface shaped like a saddle. In a suitable coordinate system, it can be represented by the equation

$$z = \frac{x^2}{a^2} - \frac{y^2}{b^2}.$$

This is a _____ that opens up along the x-axis and down along the y-axis.

Paraboloid of revolution

With a = b an elliptic paraboloid is a paraboloid of revolution: a surface obtained by revolving a parabola around its axis.

   a. PDE surfaces   b. Prolate
   c. Hyperbolic paraboloid   d. Parametric surface

12. In mathematics, a _____ is a quadric surface of special kind. There are two kinds of paraboloids: elliptic and hyperbolic. The elliptic _____ is shaped like an oval cup and can have a maximum or minimum point.
   a. Parametric surface   b. Normal line
   c. Normal vector   d. Paraboloid

13. An _____ process is a change in which the temperature of the system stays constant: ΔT = 0. This typically occurs when a system is in contact with an outside thermal reservoir (heat bath), and the change occurs slowly enough to allow the system to continually adjust to the temperature of the reservoir through heat exchange. An alternative special case in which a system exchanges no heat with its surroundings (Q = 0) is called an adiabatic process.
   a. ACTRAN   b. ALGOR
   c. AUSM   d. Isothermal

14. In mathematics, an _____ (or purely _____) is a complex number whose squared value is a real number not greater than zero. The imaginary unit, denoted by i or j, is an example of an _____. If y is a real number, then i · y is an _____, because:

$$(i \cdot y)^2 = i^2 \cdot y^2 = -y^2 \leq 0.$$

Imaginary numbers were defined in 1572 by Rafael Bombelli.

   a. Univalent function   b. Imaginary number
   c. Entire function   d. Edge-of-the-wedge theorem

15. In mathematics, the _____ are analogs of the ordinary trigonometric or circular functions. The basic _____ are the hyperbolic sine 'sinh', and the hyperbolic cosine 'cosh', from which are derived the hyperbolic tangent 'tanh', etc., in analogy to the derived trigonometric functions. The inverse _____ are the area hyperbolic sine 'arsinh' (also called 'asinh', or sometimes by the misnomer of 'arcsinh') and so on.
   a. Step function   b. Hyperbolic tangent
   c. Hyperbolic functions   d. Hyperbolic sine

16. The _____ specifies the relationship between the two central operations of calculus, differentiation and integration.

The first part of the theorem, sometimes called the first _____, shows that an indefinite integration can be reversed by a differentiation.

The second part, sometimes called the second _____, allows one to compute the definite integral of a function by using any one of its infinitely many antiderivatives.

    a. Minimum
    c. Calculus controversy
    b. Partial sum
    d. Fundamental Theorem of Calculus

17. In calculus, a branch of mathematics, the _____ is a measurement of how a function changes when its input changes. Loosely speaking, a _____ can be thought of as how much a quantity is changing at some given point. For example, the _____ of the position (or distance) of a vehicle with respect to time is the instantaneous velocity (respectively, instantaneous speed) at which the vehicle is traveling.

The process of finding a _____ is called differentiation. The fundamental theorem of calculus states that differentiation is the reverse process to integration.

    a. Ramp function
    c. Mountain pass theorem
    b. Derivative
    d. Concave upwards

18. In mathematics, the trigonometric integrals are a family of integrals which involve trigonometric functions. A number of the basic trigonometric integrals are discussed at the list of integrals of trigonometric functions. Plot of Si(x) for 0 ≤ x ≤ 8π.

The different _____ definitions are:

$$\mathrm{Si}(x) = \int_0^x \frac{\sin t}{t}\, dt$$

$$\mathrm{si}(x) = -\int_x^\infty \frac{\sin t}{t}\, dt$$

Si(x) is the primitive of sinx / x which is zero for x = 0; si(x) is the primitive of sinx / x which is zero for $x = \infty$.

    a. 15 theorem
    c. Sine integral
    b. Trigonometric integrals
    d. Trigonometric

19. In calculus, an antiderivative, primitive or _____ of a function f is a function F whose derivative is equal to f, i.e., F ' = f. The process of solving for antiderivatives is antidifferentiation (or indefinite integration.) Antiderivatives are related to definite integrals through the fundamental theorem of calculus: the definite integral of a function over an interval is equal to the difference between the values of an antiderivative evaluated at the endpoints of the interval.

a. Indefinite integral
b. Arc length
c. Integration by parts operator
d. Integral test for convergence

20. In calculus, a method called _____ can be applied to implicitly defined functions. This method is an application of the chain rule allowing one to calculate the derivative of a function given implicitly.

As explained in the introduction, y can be given as a function of x implicitly rather than explicitly. When we have an equation R (x,y) = 0, we may be able to solve it for y and then differentiate. However, sometimes it is simpler to differentiate R(x,y) with respect to x and then solve for dy / dx.

a. Automatic differentiation
b. Ordinary differential equation
c. Implicit function
d. Implicit differentiation

21. In mathematics, a _____ is a constant multiplicative factor of a certain object. For example, in the expression $9x^2$, the _____ of x^2 is 9.

The object can be such things as a variable, a vector, a function, etc.

a. Coefficient
b. Difference polynomial
c. Leading coefficient
d. Degree of the polynomial

22. In mathematics, a _____ is a basic technique used to simplify problems in which the original variables are replaced with new ones; the new and old variables being related in some specified way. The intent is that the problem expressed in new variables may be simpler, or else equivalent to a better understood problem.

A very simple example of a useful variable change can be seen in the problem of finding the roots of the eighth order polynomial:

$$x^8 + 3x^4 + 2 = 0$$

Eighth order polynomial equations are generally impossible to solve in terms of elementary functions.

a. 15 theorem
b. BDDC
c. Cubic function
d. Change of variables

23. Just as the definite integral of a positive function of one variable represents the area of the region between the graph of the function and the x-axis, the _____ of a positive function of two variables represents the volume of the region between the surface defined by the function (on the three dimensional Cartesian plane where z = f(x,y)) and the plane which contains its domain. (Note that the same volume can be obtained via the triple integral -- the integral of a function in three variables -- of the constant function f(x, y, z) = 1 over the above-mentioned region between the surface and the plane.) If there are more variables, a multiple integral will yield hypervolumes of multi-dimensional functions.

a. Double integral
b. Nonelementary integral
c. Linearity of integration
d. Sum rule in integration

24. In calculus, and more generally in mathematical analysis, _____ is a rule that transforms the integral of products of functions into other, hopefully simpler, integrals. The rule arises from the product rule of differentiation.

If u = f(x), v = g(x), and the differentials du = f '(x) dx and dv = g'(x) dx; then in its simplest form the product rule is:

$$\int u\,dv = uv - \int v\,du.$$

Suppose f(x) and g(x) are two continuously differentiable functions.

a. Integration by parametric derivatives
b. Integration by parts
c. Arc length
d. Integrand

25. However, in algebra and in particular in algebraic combinatorics, the term '_____' is often used instead to refer to elements of the ring of symmetric functions, where that ring is a specific limit of the rings of symmetric polynomials in n indeterminates, as n goes to infinity. This ring serves as universal structure in which relations between symmetric polynomials can be expressed in a way independent of the number n of indeterminates (but its elements are neither polynomials nor functions.) Among other things, this ring plays an important role in the representation theory of the symmetric groups.

a. Symmetric function
b. Leading coefficient
c. Binomial type
d. Difference polynomial

Chapter 6. Applications of Integration

1. In mathematics, the hyperbolic functions are analogs of the ordinary trigonometric functions. The basic hyperbolic functions are the hyperbolic sine 'sinh', and the _____ 'cosh', from which are derived the hyperbolic tangent 'tanh', etc., in analogy to the derived trigonometric functions. The inverse hyperbolic functions are the area hyperbolic sine 'arsinh' (also called 'asinh', or sometimes by the misnomer of 'arcsinh') and so on.
    a. Hyperbolic cosine
    b. Heaviside step function
    c. Multiplicative inverse
    d. Signum function

2. In common usage, a cylinder is taken to mean a finite section of a right _____ with its ends closed to form two circular surfaces, as in the figure (right.) If the cylinder has a radius r and length (height) h, then its volume is given by

$$V = \pi r^2 h$$

and its surface area is:

- the area of the top (πr^2) +
- the area of the bottom (πr^2) +
- the area of the side $(2\pi r h)$.

Therefore without the top or bottom (lateral area), the surface area is

$$A = 2\pi r h.$$

With the top and bottom, the surface area is

$$A = 2\pi r^2 + 2\pi r h = 2\pi r(r + h).$$

For a given volume, the cylinder with the smallest surface area has h = 2r. For a given surface area, the cylinder with the largest volume has h = 2r, i.e. the cylinder fits in a cube (height = diameter.)

Cylindric sections are the intersections of cylinders with planes.

    a. 15 theorem
    b. Cylinder
    c. BDDC
    d. Circular cylinder

3. A _____ is one of the most curvilinear basic geometric shapes:It has two faces, zero vertices, and zero edges. The surface formed by the points at a fixed distance from a given straight line, the axis of the _____. The solid enclosed by this surface and by two planes perpendicular to the axis is also called a _____.
    a. Right circular cylinder
    b. 15 theorem
    c. BDDC
    d. Cylinder

Chapter 6. Applications of Integration

4. In geometry, a _____ is a three-dimensional figure formed by six parallelograms. It is to a parallelogram as a cube is to a square: Euclidean geometry supports all four notions but affine geometry admits only parallelograms and parallelepipeds. Three equivalent definitions of _____ are

- a polyhedron with six faces (hexahedron), each of which is a parallelogram,
- a hexahedron with three pairs of parallel faces, and
- a prism of which the base is a parallelogram.

The cuboid (six rectangular faces), cube (six square faces), and the rhombohedron (six rhombus faces) are all specific cases of _____.

Parallelepipeds are a subclass of the prismatoids.

a. Parallelepiped
b. BIBO stability
c. 15 theorem
d. BDDC

5. In common usage, a cylinder is taken to mean a finite section of a _____ with its ends closed to form two circular surfaces, as in the figure (right.) If the cylinder has a radius r and length (height) h, then its volume is given by

$$V = \pi r^2 h$$

and its surface area is:

- the area of the top (πr^2) +
- the area of the bottom (πr^2) +
- the area of the side $(2\pi r h)$.

Therefore without the top or bottom (lateral area), the surface area is

$$A = 2\pi r h.$$

With the top and bottom, the surface area is

$$A = 2\pi r^2 + 2\pi r h = 2\pi r(r + h).$$

For a given volume, the cylinder with the smallest surface area has h = 2r. For a given surface area, the cylinder with the largest volume has h = 2r, i.e. the cylinder fits in a cube (height = diameter.)

Cylindric sections are the intersections of cylinders with planes.

a. 15 theorem
b. Cylinder
c. BDDC
d. Right circular cylinder

Chapter 6. Applications of Integration

6. The _____, named after the mathematician Ehrenfried Walther von Tschirnhaus, is a plane curve which is defined by either of these formulae:

$y^2 = x^3 + 3x^2$

$a = r\cos^3(\theta / 3.)$

   a. Kampyle of Eudoxus
   b. Tschirnhausen cubic
   c. Strophoid
   d. Dolbeault operator

7. _____ is a means of calculating the volume of a solid of revolution, when integrating along the axis of revolution. This method models the generated 3 dimensional shape as a 'stack' of an infinite number of disks of infinitesimal thickness. It is possible to use 'washers' instead of 'disks' (the washer method) to obtain 'hollow' solids of revolutions, and uses the same principles that underlie _____.
   a. Multiple integral
   b. Surface of revolution
   c. Disk integration
   d. Shell integration

8. In vector calculus, there are two ways of multiplying three vectors together, to make a _____ of vectors. Three vectors defining a parallelepiped

The scalar _____ is defined as the dot product of one of the vectors with the cross product of the other two.

Geometrically, the scalar _____

$$\mathbf{a} \cdot (\mathbf{b} \times \mathbf{c})$$

is the (signed) volume of the parallelepiped defined by the three vectors given.

   a. Divergence Theorem
   b. Gradient theorem
   c. Divergence
   d. Triple product

9. In mathematics, engineering, and manufacturing, a _____ is a solid figure obtained by rotating a plane curve around some straight line (the axis) that lies on the same plane.

Assuming that the curve does not cross the axis, the solid's volume is equal to the length of the circle described by the figure's centroid, times the figure's area (Pappus's second centroid Theorem.)

Rotating a curve

A representative disk is a three-dimensional volume element of a _____.

Chapter 6. Applications of Integration

    a. Sum rule in integration
    b. Risch algorithm
    c. Riemann sum
    d. Solid of revolution

10. In geometry, a _____ (pl. tori) is a surface of revolution generated by revolving a circle in three dimensional space about an axis coplanar with the circle, which does not touch the circle. Examples of tori include the surfaces of doughnuts and inner tubes.
    a. PDE surfaces
    b. Prolate
    c. Normal vector
    d. Torus

11. In linear algebra, the null vector or _____ is the vector (0, 0, …, 0) in Euclidean space, all of whose components are zero. It is usually written $\vec{0}$ or 0 or simply 0. A _____ has no direction.
    a. Zero vector
    b. Direction vector
    c. Scalar multiplication
    d. Dot product

12. The _____ is the derived unit of energy in the International System of Units. It is defined as:

$$1\,\text{J} = 1\,\text{kg} \cdot \text{m}^2 \cdot \text{s}^{-2}$$

One _____ is the amount of energy required to perform the following physical actions:

- The work done by a force of one newton travelling through a distance of one metre;
- The work required to move an electric charge of one coulomb through an electrical potential difference of one volt; or one coulomb volt, with the symbol C·V;
- The work done to produce the power of one watt continuously for one second; or one watt second (compare kilowatt hour), with the symbol W·s. Thus a kilowatt hour is 3,600,000 joules or 3.6 megajoules;

1 _____ is equal to:

- 1×10^7 ergs (exactly)
- 1.6022×10^{19} eV (electronvolts)
- 0.2390 cal (gram calories or small calories)
- 2.3901×10^{-4} kcal (kilocalories, kilogram calories, large calories or food calories)
- 9.4782×10^{-4} BTU (British thermal unit)
- 0.7376 ft·lbf (foot-pound force)
- 23.7 ft·pdl (foot-poundals)
- 2.7778×10^{-7} kilowatt-hour
- 2.7778×10^{-4} watt-hour
- 9.8692×10^{-3} litre-atmosphere
- 1×10^{-44} Foe (exactly)

Chapter 6. Applications of Integration

Units defined in terms of the _____ include:

- 1 thermochemical calorie = 4.184 J
- 1 International Table calorie = 4.1868 J
- 1 watt hour = 3600 J
- 1 kilowatt hour = 3.6 × 10⁶ J (or 3.6 MJ)
- 1 ton TNT exploding = 4.184 GJ

Useful to remember:

- 1 _____ = 1 newton × 1 meter = 1 watt × 1 second

One _____ in everyday life is approximately:

- the energy required to lift a small apple one metre straight up.
- the energy released when that same apple falls one meter to the ground.
- the energy released as heat by a quiet person, every hundredth of a second.
- the energy required to heat one gram of dry, cool air by 1 degree Celsius.
- one hundredth of the energy a person can receive by drinking a drop of beer.
- the kinetic energy of an adult human moving a distance of about a handspan every second.

- Conversion of units
- Orders of magnitude (energy)
- Fluence

a. BIBO stability
c. Joule
b. BDDC
d. 15 theorem

13. In physics, and more specifically kinematics, _____ is the change in velocity over time. Because velocity is a vector, it can change in two ways: a change in magnitude and/or a change in direction. In one dimension, _____ is the rate at which something speeds up or slows down.
    a. AUSM
    b. ALGOR
    c. Acceleration
    d. ACTRAN

14. The most commonly encountered form of Hooke's law is probably the spring equation, which relates the force exerted by a spring to the distance it is stretched by a _____, k, measured in force per length.

$$F = -kx$$

The negative sign indicates that the force exerted by the spring is in direct opposition to the direction of displacement. It is called a 'restoring force', as it tends to restore the system to equilibrium.

Chapter 6. Applications of Integration

a. 15 theorem
b. Spring constant
c. Navier-Stokes equations
d. Polar moment of inertia

15. In infinitesimal calculus, a _____ is traditionally an infinitesimally small change in a variable. For example, if x is a variable, then a change in the value of x is often denoted Δx (or δx when this change is considered to be small.) The _____ dx represents such a change, but is infinitely small.

a. Continuous function
b. Dirichlet integral
c. Differential
d. Related rates

16. The mechanisms of _____; a point mass m_1 attracts another point mass m_2 by a force F_2 which is proportional to the product of the two masses and inversely proportional to the square of the distance (r) between them. Regardless of masses or distance, the magnitudes of $|F_1|$ and $|F_2|$ will always be equal. G is the gravitational constant.

_____ is an empirical physical law describing the gravitational attraction between bodies with mass.

a. BDDC
b. 15 theorem
c. BIBO stability
d. Newton's law of universal gravitation

17. In probability theory and statistics, the _____ (or expectation value or mean and for continuous random variables with a density function it is the probability density -weighted integral of the possible values.

The term '_____' can be misleading.

a. ALGOR
b. AUSM
c. ACTRAN
d. Expected value

18. In calculus, the _____ states, roughly, that given a section of a smooth curve, there is at least one point on that section at which the derivative (slope) of the curve is equal (parallel) to the 'average' derivative of the section. It is used to prove theorems that make global conclusions about a function on an interval starting from local hypotheses about derivatives at points of the interval.

This theorem can be understood concretely by applying it to motion: If a car travels one hundred miles in one hour, so its average speed during that time was 100 miles per hour.

a. Fresnel integrals
b. Leibniz differential
c. First derivative test
d. Mean Value Theorem

19. Integration is an important concept in mathematics, specifically in the field of calculus and, more broadly, mathematical analysis. Given a function f of a real variable x and an interval [a, b] of the real line, the _____

$$\int_a^b f(x)\,dx,$$

is defined informally to be the net signed area of the region in the xy-plane bounded by the graph of f, the x-axis, and the vertical lines x = a and x = b.

The term '_____' may also refer to the notion of antiderivative, a function F whose derivative is the given function f.

a. Integral
b. Indefinite integral
c. Integral test for convergence
d. Integrand

Chapter 7. Inverse Functions

1. In mathematics, the _____ of a function y = f(x) is a function that, in some fashion, 'undoes' the effect of f The _____ of f is denoted f^{-1}. The statements y=f(x) and x=f^{-1}(y) are equivalent.
   a. ACTRAN
   b. Inverse
   c. AUSM
   d. ALGOR

2. In mathematics, if f is a function from A to B then an _____ for f is a function in the opposite direction, from B to A, with the property that a round trip (a composition) from A to B to A (or from B to A to B) returns each element of the initial set to itself. Thus, if an input x into the function f produces an output y, then inputting y into the _____ f^{-1} (read f inverse, not to be confused with exponentiation) produces the output x. Not every function has an inverse; those that do are called invertible.
   a. Inverse function
   b. Augustin-Jean Fresnel
   c. Aristotle
   d. Augustin Louis Cauchy

3. In vector calculus, the _____ of a scalar field is a vector field which points in the direction of the greatest rate of increase of the scalar field, and whose magnitude is the greatest rate of change.

   A generalization of the _____ for functions on a Euclidean space which have values in another Euclidean space is the Jacobian. A further generalization for a function from one Banach space to another is the Fréchet derivative.

   a. Smooth function
   b. Gradient
   c. Parametric derivative
   d. Leibniz's notation

4. In mathematics, the _____ is a test used to determine if a function is injective, surjective or bijective.

   Suppose there is a function f : X → Y with a graph., and you have a horizontal line of X x Y :
   $$y_0 \in Y, \{(x, y_0) : x \in X\} = (X \times y_0)$$

   - If the function is injective, then it can be visualized as one whose graph is never intersected by any horizontal line more than once.
   - If and only if f is surjective, any horizontal line will intersect the graph at least at one point (when the horizontal line is in the codomain.)
   - If f is bijective, any horizontal line will intersect the graph at exactly one point.

   This test is also used to find whether or not the inverse of the function is indeed a function as well. This is due to the reflective properties of the function over y=x.

   a. BDDC
   b. Horizontal Line Test
   c. BIBO stability
   d. 15 theorem

5. An injective function is called an injection, and is also said to be a _____ function (not to be confused with _____ correspondence, i.e. a bijective function.)

   A function f that is not injective is sometimes called many-to-one. (However, this terminology is also sometimes used to mean 'single-valued', i.e. each argument is mapped to at most one value.)

Chapter 7. Inverse Functions

a. Onto
b. Injective function
c. One-to-one
d. One-to-one function

6. An injective function is called an injection, and is also said to be a _____ (not to be confused with one-to-one correspondence, i.e. a bijective function.)

A function f that is not injective is sometimes called many-to-one. (However, this terminology is also sometimes used to mean 'single-valued', i.e. each argument is mapped to at most one value.)

a. Injective function
b. One-to-one
c. Onto
d. One-to-one function

7. Integration is an important concept in mathematics, specifically in the field of calculus and, more broadly, mathematical analysis. Given a function f of a real variable x and an interval [a, b] of the real line, the _____

$$\int_a^b f(x)\,dx,$$

is defined informally to be the net signed area of the region in the xy-plane bounded by the graph of f, the x-axis, and the vertical lines x = a and x = b.

The term '_____' may also refer to the notion of antiderivative, a function F whose derivative is the given function f.

a. Integral test for convergence
b. Integrand
c. Indefinite integral
d. Integral

8. In physics, _____ is defined as the rate of change of position. it is vector physical quantity; both speed and direction are required to define it. In the SI (metric) system, it is measured in meters per second: (m/s) or ms^{-1}.

a. 15 theorem
b. BDDC
c. BIBO stability
d. Velocity

9. In calculus, a branch of mathematics, the _____ is a measurement of how a function changes when its input changes. Loosely speaking, a _____ can be thought of as how much a quantity is changing at some given point. For example, the _____ of the position (or distance) of a vehicle with respect to time is the instantaneous velocity (respectively, instantaneous speed) at which the vehicle is traveling.

The process of finding a _____ is called differentiation. The fundamental theorem of calculus states that differentiation is the reverse process to integration.

a. Concave upwards
b. Derivative
c. Mountain pass theorem
d. Ramp function

Chapter 7. Inverse Functions

10. The _____ is a function in mathematics. The application of this function to a value x is written as exp(x). Equivalently, this can be written in the form e^x, where e is a mathematical constant, the base of the natural logarithm, which equals approximately 2.718281828, and is also known as Euler's number.

    a. Integral part   b. Exponential function
    c. ACTRAN   d. Area hyperbolic functions

11. In infinitesimal calculus, a _____ is traditionally an infinitesimally small change in a variable. For example, if x is a variable, then a change in the value of x is often denoted Δx (or δx when this change is considered to be small.) The _____ dx represents such a change, but is infinitely small.

    a. Differential   b. Dirichlet integral
    c. Related rates   d. Continuous function

12. In geometry, an _____ is a plane curve produced by tracing the path of a chosen point of a circle -- called epicycle -- which rolls without slipping around a fixed circle. It is a particular kind of roulette.

If the smaller circle has radius r, and the larger circle has radius R = kr, then the parametric equations for the curve can be given by either:

$$x(\theta) = (R+r)\cos\theta - r\cos\left(\frac{R+r}{r}\theta\right)$$
$$y(\theta) = (R+r)\sin\theta - r\sin\left(\frac{R+r}{r}\theta\right),$$

or:

$$x(\theta) = r(k+1)\cos\theta - r\cos((k+1)\theta)$$
$$y(\theta) = r(k+1)\sin\theta - r\sin((k+1)\theta).$$

If k is an integer, then the curve is closed, and has k cusps (i.e., sharp corners, where the curve is not differentiable.)

    a. Asymptotic curve   b. Epicycloid
    c. ACTRAN   d. ALGOR

13. In mathematics, the concept of a '_____' is used to describe the behavior of a function as its argument or input either 'gets close' to some point, or as the argument becomes arbitrarily large; or the behavior of a sequence's elements as their index increases indefinitely. Limits are used in calculus and other branches of mathematical analysis to define derivatives and continuity.

In formulas, _____ is usually abbreviated as lim

Chapter 7. Inverse Functions

a. BIBO stability
b. BDDC
c. 15 theorem
d. Limit

14. In mathematics, a _____ is an ordered list of objects (or events). Like a set, it contains members (also called elements or terms), and the number of terms (possibly infinite) is called the length of the _____. Unlike a set, order matters, and the exact same elements can appear multiple times at different positions in the _____.

a. BDDC
b. 15 theorem
c. Y-intercept
d. Sequence

15. A _____, sometimes known as an energy shield, force shield typically made of energy or charged particles, that protects a person, area or object from attacks or intrusions.

A University of Washington in Seattle group has been experimenting with using a bubble of charged plasma to surround a spacecraft, contained by a fine mesh of superconducting wire. This would protect the spacecraft from interstellar radiation and some particles without needing physical shielding.

a. 15 theorem
b. BIBO stability
c. BDDC
d. Force field

16. The _____ of a quantity whose value decreases with time is the interval required for the quantity to decay to half of its initial value. The concept originated in describing how long it takes atoms to undergo radioactive decay but also applies in a wide variety of other situations.

The term '_____' dates to 1907.

a. BDDC
b. Half-life
c. 15 theorem
d. BIBO stability

17. A _____ is a mathematical equation for an unknown function of one or several variables that relates the values of the function itself and of its derivatives of various orders. they play a prominent role in engineering, physics, economics and other disciplines.

A simplified real world example of a _____ is modeling the acceleration of a ball falling through the air (considering only gravity and air resistance.)

a. Structural stability
b. Differential equation
c. Lax pair
d. Petrovsky lacuna

18. In mathematics, a _____ is an infinite series that is not convergent, meaning that the infinite sequence of the partial sums of the series does not have a limit.

If a series converges, the individual terms of the series must approach zero. Thus any series in which the individual terms do not approach zero diverges.

a. 15 theorem
b. BIBO stability
c. BDDC
d. Divergent series

19. In integral calculus we would want to write a fractional algebraic expression as the sum of its _____ in order to take the integral of each simple fraction separately. Once the original denominator, D_0, has been factored we set up a fraction for each factor in the denominator. We may use a subscripted D to represent the denominator of the respective _____ which are the factors in D_0.

a. Hurwitz quaternion order
b. Completing the square
c. Partial fractions
d. Multinomial theorem

20. _____ (including exponential decay) occurs when the growth rate of a mathematical function is proportional to the function's current value. In the case of a discrete domain of definition with equal intervals it is also called geometric growth or geometric decay (the function values form a geometric progression.)

_____ is said to follow an exponential law; the simple-_____ model is known as the Malthusian growth model.

a. Inseparable differential equation
b. Oscillating
c. Exponential growth
d. Isomonodromic deformation

21. In probability theory and statistics, the _____ (or expectation value or mean and for continuous random variables with a density function it is the probability density -weighted integral of the possible values.

The term '_____' can be misleading.

a. ACTRAN
b. ALGOR
c. AUSM
d. Expected value

22. In statistics, _____ is a simple measure of the variability or dispersion of a data set. A low _____ indicates that all of the data points are very close to the same value (the mean), while high _____ indicates that the data is 'spread out' over a large range of values.

For example, the average height for adult men in the United States is about 70 inches, with a _____ of around 3 inches.

a. Moment
b. Poisson distribution
c. Normal distribution
d. Standard deviation

23. The _____ of a material is defined as its mass per unit volume. The symbol of _____ is ρ '>rho.)

Mathematically:

$$d = \frac{m}{V}$$

Chapter 7. Inverse Functions

where:

    d is the _____,
    m is the mass,
    V is the volume.

a. BIBO stability
b. BDDC
c. 15 theorem
d. Density

24. The function $\log_b(x)$ depends on both b and x, but the term _____ in standard usage refers to a function of the form $\log_b(x)$ in which the base b is fixed and so the only argument is x. Thus there is one _____ for each value of the base b (which must be positive and must differ from 1.) Viewed in this way, the base-b _____ is the inverse function of the exponential function b^x.

a. 15 theorem
b. Logarithm function
c. BIBO stability
d. BDDC

25. In economics, the _____ functional form of production functions is widely used to represent the relationship of an output to inputs. It was proposed by Knut Wicksell (1851-1926), and tested against statistical evidence by Charles Cobb and Paul Douglas in 1900-1928.

For production, the function is

$$Y = AL^{\alpha}K^{\beta},$$

where:

- Y = total production (the monetary value of all goods produced in a year)
- L = labor input
- K = capital input
- A = total factor productivity
- α and β are the output elasticities of labor and capital, respectively. These values are constants determined by available technology.

Output elasticity measures the responsiveness of output to a change in levels of either labor or capital used in production, ceteris paribus. For example if α = 0.15, a 1% increase in labor would lead to approximately a 0.15% increase in output.

a. BDDC
b. Cobb-Douglas
c. 15 theorem
d. BIBO stability

Chapter 7. Inverse Functions

26. The _____ in some data is the discrepancy between an exact value and some approximation to it. An _____ can occur because

    1. the measurement of the data is not precise (due to the instruments), or
    2. approximations are used instead of the real data (e.g., 3.14 instead of π.)

In the mathematical field of numerical analysis, the numerical stability of an algorithm in numerical analysis indicates how the error is propagated by the algorithm.

One commonly distinguishes between the relative error and the absolute error. The absolute error is the magnitude of the difference between the exact value and the approximation.

    a. AUSM
    b. ACTRAN
    c. Approximation error
    d. ALGOR

27. In number theory, the _____ describes the asymptotic distribution of the prime numbers. The _____ gives a rough description of how the primes are distributed.

Roughly speaking, the _____ states that if you randomly select a number nearby some large number N, the chance of it being prime is about 1 / ln(N), where ln(N) denotes the natural logarithm of N. For example, near N = 10,000, about one in nine numbers is prime, whereas near N = 1,000,000,000, only one in every 21 numbers is prime.

    a. Character sum
    b. Prime Number Theorem
    c. Kloosterman sum
    d. Selberg sieve

28. In mathematics, an _____ on a real vector space is a choice of which ordered bases are 'positively' oriented and which are 'negatively' oriented. In the three-dimensional Euclidean space, the two possible basis orientations are called right-handed and left-handed (or right-chiral and left-chiral), respectively. However, the choice of _____ is independent of the handedness or chirality of the bases (although right-handed bases are typically declared to be positively oriented, they may also be assigned a negative _____.)

    a. Unit vector
    b. ALGOR
    c. Orientation
    d. ACTRAN

29. In mathematics, a (topological) _____ is defined as follows: let I be an interval of real numbers (i.e. a non-empty connected subset of $\mathbb{R}$); then a _____ γ is a continuous mapping $\gamma : I \to X$, where X is a topological space. The _____ γ is said to be simple if it is injective, i.e. if for all x, y in I, we have $\gamma(x) = \gamma(y) \implies x = y$. If I is a closed bounded interval $[a, b]$, we also allow the possibility $\gamma(a) = \gamma(b)$ (this convention makes it possible to talk about closed simple _____.)

    a. Prolate cycloid
    b. Tractrix
    c. Closed curve
    d. Curve

30. In mathematics, specifically in calculus and complex analysis, the _____ of a function f is defined by the formula

$$\frac{f'}{f}$$

where f ' is the derivative of f.

When f is a function f(x) of a real variable x, and takes real, strictly positive values, this is indeed the formula for (log f)', that is, the derivative of the natural logarithm of f, as follows directly from the chain rule.

Many properties of the real logarithm also apply to the _____, even when the function does not take values in the positive reals.

- a. Difference quotient
- b. Symmetric derivative
- c. Linearity of differentiation
- d. Logarithmic derivative

31. This article will state and prove the _____ for differentiation, and then use it to prove these two formulas.

The _____ for differentiation states that for every natural number n, the derivative of $f(x) = x^n$ is $f'(x) = nx^{n-1}$, that is,

$$(x^n)' = nx^{n-1}.$$

The _____ for integration

$$\int x^n \, dx = \frac{x^{n+1}}{n+1} + C$$

for natural n is then an easy consequence. One just needs to take the derivative of this equality and use the _____ and linearity of differentiation on the right-hand side.

- a. Dirichlet integral
- b. Hyperbolic angle
- c. Limits of integration
- d. Power Rule

32. Call S_N the _____ to N of the sequence {a_n}, or _____ of the series. A series is the sequence of partial sums, {S_N}.

Chapter 7. Inverse Functions

When talking about series, one can refer either to the sequence $\{S_N\}$ of the partial sums, or to the sum of the series,

$$\sum_{n=0}^{\infty} a_n$$

i.e., the limit of the sequence of partial sums - it is clear which one is meant from context.

a. Periodic function
b. Root test
c. Minimum
d. Partial sum

33. In mathematics, the _____ is a special function defined on the complex plane given the symbol Ei.

For real, nonzero values of x, the _____ Ei(x) can be defined as

$$\mathrm{Ei}(x) = \int_{-\infty}^{x} \frac{e^t}{t}\, dt.$$

The definition above can be used for positive values of x, but the integral has to be understood in terms of the Cauchy principal value, due to the singularity in the integrand at zero. For complex values of the argument, the definition becomes ambiguous due to branch points at 0 and ∞. In general, a branch cut is taken on the negative real axis and Ei can be defined by analytic continuation elsewhere on the complex plane.

a. ACTRAN
b. Exponential integral
c. ALGOR
d. Exponential sum

34. In mathematics, the _____ or cyclometric functions are the inverse functions of the trigonometric functions. The principal inverses are listed in the following table.

If x is allowed to be a complex number, then the range of y applies only to its real part.

a. ACTRAN
b. AUSM
c. ALGOR
d. Inverse trigonometric functions

35. Trigonometry is a branch of mathematics that deals with triangles, particularly those plane triangles in which one angle has 90 degrees (right triangles.) Trigonometry deals with relationships between the sides and the angles of triangles and with the _____ functions, which describe those relationships.

Trigonometry has applications in both pure mathematics and in applied mathematics, where it is essential in many branches of science and technology.

Chapter 7. Inverse Functions

a. Trigonometric integrals
b. Trigonometric
c. 15 theorem
d. Trigonometric functions

36. In mathematics, the _____ are functions of an angle. They are important in the study of triangles and modeling periodic phenomena, among many other applications. _____ are commonly defined as ratios of two sides of a right triangle containing the angle, and can equivalently be defined as the lengths of various line segments from a unit circle.
   a. 15 theorem
   b. Trigonometric
   c. Trigonometric functions
   d. Trigonometric integrals

37. In physics and geometry, the _____ is the theoretical shape of a hanging flexible chain or cable when supported at its ends and acted upon by a uniform gravitational force (its own weight) and in equilibrium. The curve has a U shape that is similar in appearance to the parabola, though it is a different curve.
   a. BDDC
   b. 15 theorem
   c. BIBO stability
   d. Catenary

38. The _____ is a doubly ruled surface shaped like a saddle. In a suitable coordinate system, it can be represented by the equation

$$z = \frac{x^2}{a^2} - \frac{y^2}{b^2}.$$

This is a _____ that opens up along the x-axis and down along the y-axis.

Paraboloid of revolution

With a = b an elliptic paraboloid is a paraboloid of revolution: a surface obtained by revolving a parabola around its axis.

   a. PDE surfaces
   b. Prolate
   c. Parametric surface
   d. Hyperbolic paraboloid

39. In mathematics, a _____ is a quadric surface of special kind. There are two kinds of paraboloids: elliptic and hyperbolic. The elliptic _____ is shaped like an oval cup and can have a maximum or minimum point.
   a. Normal vector
   b. Normal line
   c. Parametric surface
   d. Paraboloid

40. The _____ is an important partial differential equation which describes the distribution of heat (or variation in temperature) in a given region over time. For a function u(x,y,z,t) of three spatial variables (x,y,z) and the time variable t, the _____ is

$$\frac{\partial u}{\partial t} - k\left(\frac{\partial^2 u}{\partial x^2} + \frac{\partial^2 u}{\partial y^2} + \frac{\partial^2 u}{\partial z^2}\right) = 0$$

or equivalently

$$\frac{\partial u}{\partial t} = k\nabla^2 u$$

where k is a constant.

The _____ is of fundamental importance in diverse scientific fields.

    a. 15 theorem
    b. Heat equation
    c. BIBO stability
    d. BDDC

41. In mathematics, the _____ are analogs of the ordinary trigonometric or circular functions. The basic _____ are the hyperbolic sine 'sinh', and the hyperbolic cosine 'cosh', from which are derived the hyperbolic tangent 'tanh', etc., in analogy to the derived trigonometric functions. The inverse _____ are the area hyperbolic sine 'arsinh' (also called 'asinh', or sometimes by the misnomer of 'arcsinh') and so on.

    a. Hyperbolic sine
    b. Step function
    c. Hyperbolic tangent
    d. Hyperbolic functions

42. The _____, H, also called the unit step function, is a discontinuous function whose value is zero for negative argument and one for positive argument. It seldom matters what value is used for H, since H is mostly used as a distribution. The function is used in the mathematics of control theory and signal processing to represent a signal that switches on at a specified time and stays switched on indefinitely.

    a. Hyperbolic cosine
    b. Signum function
    c. Hyperbolic functions
    d. Heaviside step function

43. In calculus and other branches of mathematical analysis, an _____ is an algebraic expression obtained in the context of limits. Limits involving algebraic operations are often performed by replacing subexpressions by their limits; if the expression obtained after this substitution does not give enough information to determine the original limit, it is known as an _____. The indeterminate forms include 0^0, $0/0$, 1^∞, $\infty - \infty$, ∞/∞, $0\times\infty$, and ∞^0.

    a. Indeterminate form
    b. ACTRAN
    c. ALGOR
    d. AUSM

44. In calculus, the _____ states, roughly, that given a section of a smooth curve, there is at least one point on that section at which the derivative (slope) of the curve is equal (parallel) to the 'average' derivative of the section. It is used to prove theorems that make global conclusions about a function on an interval starting from local hypotheses about derivatives at points of the interval.

This theorem can be understood concretely by applying it to motion: If a car travels one hundred miles in one hour, so its average speed during that time was 100 miles per hour.

    a. Mean Value Theorem
    b. Leibniz differential
    c. First derivative test
    d. Fresnel integrals

Chapter 7. Inverse Functions

45. _____ is the concept of adding accumulated interest back to the principal, so that interest is earned on interest from that moment on. The act of declaring interest to be principal is called compounding (i.e., interest is compounded.) A loan, for example, may have its interest compounded every month: in this case, a loan with $100 principal and 1% interest per month would have a balance of $101 at the end of the first month.
   a. BIBO stability
   b. Compound interest
   c. 15 theorem
   d. BDDC

46. Cantor defined two kinds of _____ numbers, the ordinal numbers and the cardinal numbers. Ordinal numbers may be identified with well-ordered sets, or counting carried on to any stopping point, including points after an _____ number have already been counted. Generalizing finite and the ordinary _____ sequences which are maps from the positive integers leads to mappings from ordinal numbers, and transfinite sequences.
   a. AUSM
   b. Infinite
   c. ACTRAN
   d. ALGOR

47. The terms of the series are often produced according to a certain rule, such as by a formula, by an algorithm, by a sequence of measurements, or even by a random number generator. As there are an infinite number of terms, this notion is often called an _____. Unlike finite summations, series need tools from mathematical analysis to be fully understood and manipulated.
   a. Extreme value
   b. Integration by substitution
   c. Extreme Value Theorem
   d. Infinite series

Chapter 8. Techniques of Integration

1. In calculus, and more generally in mathematical analysis, _____ is a rule that transforms the integral of products of functions into other, hopefully simpler, integrals. The rule arises from the product rule of differentiation.

If u = f(x), v = g(x), and the differentials du = f '(x) dx and dv = g'(x) dx; then in its simplest form the product rule is:

$$\int u\,dv = uv - \int v\,du.$$

Suppose f(x) and g(x) are two continuously differentiable functions.

    a. Integration by parametric derivatives   b. Integrand
    c. Arc length   d. Integration by parts

2. In mathematics, _____ refers to the rewriting of an expression into a simpler form. For example, the process of rewriting a fraction into one with the smallest whole-number denominator possible (while keeping the numerator an integer) is called 'reducing a fraction'. Rewriting a radical (or 'root') expression with the smallest possible whole number under the radical symbol is called 'reducing a radical'.

    a. Reduction   b. BDDC
    c. 15 theorem   d. BIBO stability

3. Trigonometry is a branch of mathematics that deals with triangles, particularly those plane triangles in which one angle has 90 degrees (right triangles.) Trigonometry deals with relationships between the sides and the angles of triangles and with the _____ functions, which describe those relationships.

Trigonometry has applications in both pure mathematics and in applied mathematics, where it is essential in many branches of science and technology.

    a. Trigonometric   b. 15 theorem
    c. Trigonometric integrals   d. Trigonometric functions

4. In mathematics, the _____ are functions of an angle. They are important in the study of triangles and modeling periodic phenomena, among many other applications. _____ are commonly defined as ratios of two sides of a right triangle containing the angle, and can equivalently be defined as the lengths of various line segments from a unit circle.

    a. Trigonometric   b. Trigonometric integrals
    c. 15 theorem   d. Trigonometric functions

5. In mathematics, the _____ are a family of integrals which involve trigonometric functions. A number of the basic _____ are discussed at the list of integrals of trigonometric functions.

The different sine integral definitions are:

$$\text{Si}(x) = \int_0^x \frac{\sin t}{t}\, dt$$

$$\text{si}(x) = -\int_x^\infty \frac{\sin t}{t}\, dt$$

Si(x) is the primitive of sinx / x which is zero for x = 0; si(x) is the primitive of sinx / x which is zero for $x = \infty$.

- a. Trigonometric
- b. Trigonometric integrals
- c. Trigonometric functions
- d. 15 theorem

6. Integration is an important concept in mathematics, specifically in the field of calculus and, more broadly, mathematical analysis. Given a function f of a real variable x and an interval [a, b] of the real line, the _____

$$\int_a^b f(x)\, dx ,$$

is defined informally to be the net signed area of the region in the xy-plane bounded by the graph of f, the x-axis, and the vertical lines x = a and x = b.

The term '_____' may also refer to the notion of antiderivative, a function F whose derivative is the given function f.

- a. Indefinite integral
- b. Integral test for convergence
- c. Integrand
- d. Integral

7. A _____ has several distinct meanings.

One meaning is that a first-order ordinary differential equation is homogeneous if it has the form

$$\frac{dy}{dx} = F(y/x).$$

To solve such equations, one makes the change of variables u = y/x, which will transform such an equation into separable one.

Another meaning is a linear _____, which is a differential equation of the form

$$Ly = 0$$

where the differential operator L is a linear operator, and y is the unknown function.

a. Nahm equations
b. Nullcline
c. Weak solution
d. Homogeneous differential equation

8. In mathematics, the _____ of a function y = f(x) is a function that, in some fashion, 'undoes' the effect of f The _____ of f is denoted f⁻¹. The statements y=f(x) and x=f⁻¹(y) are equivalent.

a. ACTRAN
b. AUSM
c. Inverse
d. ALGOR

9. In mathematics, _____ is the substitution of trigonometric functions for other expressions. One may use the trigonometric identities to simplify certain integrals containing radical expressions:

- If the integrand contains

$$\sqrt{a^2 - x^2},$$

let

$$x = a \sin \theta$$

and use the identity

$$1 - \sin^2\theta = \cos^2\theta.$$

- If the integrand contains

$$\sqrt{a^2 + x^2}$$

let $x = a \tan \theta$
and use the identity

$$1 + \tan^2 \theta = \sec^2 \theta.$$

- If the integrand contains

$$\sqrt{x^2 - a^2}$$

let

$$x = a \sec \theta$$

and use the identity

$$\sec^2 \theta - 1 = \tan^2 \theta.$$

In the integral

$$\int \frac{dx}{\sqrt{a^2 - x^2}}$$

we may use

$$x = a\sin(\theta), \ dx = a\cos(\theta)\, d\theta$$
$$\theta = \arcsin\left(\frac{x}{a}\right)$$

so that the integral becomes

$$\int \frac{dx}{\sqrt{a^2 - x^2}} = \int \frac{a\cos(\theta)\, d\theta}{\sqrt{a^2 - a^2\sin^2(\theta)}} = \int \frac{a\cos(\theta)\, d\theta}{\sqrt{a^2(1 - \sin^2(\theta))}}$$
$$= \int \frac{a\cos(\theta)\, d\theta}{\sqrt{a^2\cos^2(\theta)}} = \int d\theta = \theta + C = \arcsin\left(\frac{x}{a}\right) + C$$

Note that the above step requires that a > 0 and cos(θ) > 0; we can choose the a to be the positive square root of a^2; and we impose the restriction on θ to be −π/2 < θ < π/2 by using the arcsin function.

For a definite integral, one must figure out how the bounds of integration change. For example, as x goes from 0 to a/2, then sin (θ) goes from 0 to 1/2, so θ goes from 0 to π/6.

    a. Trigonometric substitution   b. Surface of revolution
    c. Signed measure   d. Linearity of integration

10. In infinitesimal calculus, a _____ is traditionally an infinitesimally small change in a variable. For example, if x is a variable, then a change in the value of x is often denoted Δx (or δx when this change is considered to be small.) The _____ dx represents such a change, but is infinitely small.
    a. Continuous function   b. Dirichlet integral
    c. Related rates   d. Differential

11. A _____ is a mathematical equation for an unknown function of one or several variables that relates the values of the function itself and of its derivatives of various orders. they play a prominent role in engineering, physics, economics and other disciplines.

A simplified real world example of a _____ is modeling the acceleration of a ball falling through the air (considering only gravity and air resistance.)

 a. Lax pair   b. Structural stability
 c. Petrovsky lacuna   d. Differential equation

12. In mathematics, a _____ is an ordered list of objects (or events). Like a set, it contains members (also called elements or terms), and the number of terms (possibly infinite) is called the length of the _____. Unlike a set, order matters, and the exact same elements can appear multiple times at different positions in the _____.

 a. 15 theorem   b. Y-intercept
 c. BDDC   d. Sequence

13. Cantor defined two kinds of _____ numbers, the ordinal numbers and the cardinal numbers. Ordinal numbers may be identified with well-ordered sets, or counting carried on to any stopping point, including points after an _____ number have already been counted. Generalizing finite and the ordinary _____ sequences which are maps from the positive integers leads to mappings from ordinal numbers, and transfinite sequences.

 a. ALGOR   b. AUSM
 c. Infinite   d. ACTRAN

14. In mathematics, an _____, is the apparent shape of a circle viewed obliquely from outside it, as distinct from a hyperbola which is the shape seen from inside. It is the finite or bounded case of a conic section as a shape cut in a cone by a plane, the unbounded cases being the parabola, which like the _____ remains connected, and the hyperbola, which separates into two connected components or branches.

Equivalently an _____ can be defined as the locus of points, or path traced out, in a plane such that the sum of the distances from the moving point to two fixed points remains constant.

 a. AUSM   b. ALGOR
 c. ACTRAN   d. Ellipse

15. In mathematics, a _____ is a differential equation of the form

$$Ly = f$$

where the differential operator L is a linear operator, y is the unknown function, and the right hand side f is a given function (called the source term.) The linearity condition on L rules out operations such as taking the square of the derivative of y; but permits, for example, taking the second derivative of y. Therefore a fairly general form of such an equation would be

$$a_n(x)D^n y(x) + a_{n-1}(x)D^{n-1}y(x) + \cdots + a_1(x)Dy(x) + a_0(x)y(x) = f(x)$$

where D is the differential operator d/dx (i.e. Dy = y' , D^2y = y',...), and the a_i are given functions.

Chapter 8. Techniques of Integration

a. Linear differential equation
b. Nullcline
c. Separable
d. Petrovsky lacuna

16. In geometry, a _____ (pl. tori) is a surface of revolution generated by revolving a circle in three dimensional space about an axis coplanar with the circle, which does not touch the circle. Examples of tori include the surfaces of doughnuts and inner tubes.

a. Normal vector
b. PDE surfaces
c. Prolate
d. Torus

17. In integral calculus we would want to write a fractional algebraic expression as the sum of its _____ in order to take the integral of each simple fraction separately. Once the original denominator, D_0, has been factored we set up a fraction for each factor in the denominator. We may use a subscripted D to represent the denominator of the respective _____ which are the factors in D_0.

a. Partial fractions
b. Multinomial theorem
c. Hurwitz quaternion order
d. Completing the square

18. In mathematics, a _____ is any function which can be written as the ratio of two polynomial functions.

$$y = \frac{x^2 - 3x - 2}{x^2 - 4}$$

In the case of one variable, x, a _____ is a function of the form

$$f(x) = \frac{P(x)}{Q(x)}$$

where P and Q are polynomial function in x and Q is not the zero polynomial. The domain of f is the set of all points x for which the denominator Q(x) is not zero.

a. Rational function
b. BDDC
c. BIBO stability
d. 15 theorem

19. When a linear asymptote is not parallel to the x- or y-axis, it is called either an oblique asymptote or equivalently a _____. The function f(x) is asymptotic to y = mx + b if

$$\lim_{x \to \infty} f(x) - (mx + b) = 0 \quad \text{or} \quad \lim_{x \to -\infty} f(x) - (mx + b) = 0$$

Note that y = mx + b is never a vertical asymptote, but can be a horizontal asymptote if m=0 (in which case it is not an oblique asymptote.)

Chapter 8. Techniques of Integration

An example is $f(x)=(x^2-1)/x$ which has an oblique asymptote of y=x (m=1, b=0) as seen in the limit

$$\lim_{x \to \infty} f(x) - x$$
$$= \lim_{x \to \infty} \frac{x^2 - 1}{x} - x$$
$$= \lim_{x \to \infty} (x - 1/x) - x$$
$$= \lim_{x \to \infty} -1/x = 0$$

Computationally identifying an oblique asymptote can be more difficult than a horizontal or vertical asymptote, in particular because the m and b might not be known.

- a. Geometric function theory
- b. Slant asymptote
- c. Second derivative
- d. Horizontal asymptote

20. An _____ of a real-valued function y = f(x) is a curve which describes the behavior of f as either x or y tends to infinity.

In other words, as one moves along the graph of f(x) in some direction, the distance between it and the _____ eventually becomes smaller than any distance that one may specify.

- a. Asymptote
- b. AUSM
- c. ACTRAN
- d. ALGOR

21. _____ is the motion of a simple harmonic oscillator, a motion that is neither driven nor damped. The motion is periodic - as it repeats itself at standard intervals in a specific manner - and sinusoidal, with constant amplitude; the acceleration of a body executing _____ is directly proportional to the displacement of the body from the equilibrium position and is always directed towards the equilibrium position.

The motion is characterized by its amplitude (which is always positive), its period, the time for a single oscillation, its frequency, the reciprocal of the period (i.e. the number of cycles per unit time), and its phase, which determines the starting point on the sine wave.

- a. Simple harmonic motion
- b. Holonomic
- c. 15 theorem
- d. BDDC

22. In calculus, a branch of mathematics, the _____ is a measurement of how a function changes when its input changes. Loosely speaking, a _____ can be thought of as how much a quantity is changing at some given point. For example, the _____ of the position (or distance) of a vehicle with respect to time is the instantaneous velocity (respectively, instantaneous speed) at which the vehicle is traveling.

The process of finding a _____ is called differentiation. The fundamental theorem of calculus states that differentiation is the reverse process to integration.

Chapter 8. Techniques of Integration

a. Derivative
b. Ramp function
c. Concave upwards
d. Mountain pass theorem

23. In acoustics and telecommunication, a _____ of a wave is a component frequency of the signal that is an integer multiple of the fundamental frequency. For example, if the fundamental frequency is f, the harmonics have frequencies f, 2f, 3f, 4f, etc. The harmonics have the property that they are all periodic at the fundamental frequency, therefore the sum of harmonics is also periodic at that frequency.

a. Harmonic
b. BDDC
c. BIBO stability
d. 15 theorem

24. In mathematics, an _____ is a function built from a finite number of exponentials, logarithms, constants, one variable, and nth roots through composition and combinations using the four elementary operations (+ - × ÷.) The trigonometric functions and their inverses are assumed to be included in the elementary functions by using complex variables and the relations between the trigonometric functions and the exponential and logarithm functions.

Elementary functions are considered a subset of special functions.

a. ALGOR
b. AUSM
c. ACTRAN
d. Elementary function

25. An _____ process is a change in which the temperature of the system stays constant: ΔT = 0. This typically occurs when a system is in contact with an outside thermal reservoir (heat bath), and the change occurs slowly enough to allow the system to continually adjust to the temperature of the reservoir through heat exchange. An alternative special case in which a system exchanges no heat with its surroundings (Q = 0) is called an adiabatic process.

a. Isothermal
b. ACTRAN
c. AUSM
d. ALGOR

26. In numerical analysis, _____ constitutes a broad family of algorithms for calculating the numerical value of a definite integral, and by extension, the term is also sometimes used to describe the numerical solution of differential equations The term numerical quadrature is more or less a synonym for _____, especially as applied to one-dimensional integrals.

a. Multigrid method
b. Meshfree methods
c. Galerkin methods
d. Numerical integration

27. In mathematics, the _____ is a way to approximately calculate the definite integral

$$\int_a^b f(x)\,dx.$$

The _____ works by approximating the region under the graph of the function f by a trapezoid and calculating its area. It follows that

$$\int_a^b f(x)\,dx \approx (b-a)\frac{f(a)+f(b)}{2}.$$

Chapter 8. Techniques of Integration

To calculate this integral more accurately, one first splits the interval of integration [a,b] into n smaller subintervals, and then applies the _____ on each of them. One obtains the composite _____:

$$\int_a^b f(x)\, dx \approx \frac{b-a}{n} \left[\frac{f(a)+f(b)}{2} + \sum_{k=1}^{n-1} f\left(a + k\frac{b-a}{n}\right) \right].$$

This can alternatively be written as:

$$\int_a^b f(x)\, dx \approx \frac{b-a}{2n} \left(f(x_0) + 2f(x_1) + 2f(x_2) + \cdots + 2f(x_{n-1}) + f(x_n) \right)$$

where

$$x_k = a + k\frac{b-a}{n}, \text{ for } k = 0, 1, \ldots, n$$

(one can also use a non-uniform grid.)

a. BDDC
b. Trapezoidal Rule
c. 15 theorem
d. BIBO stability

28. In the various subfields of physics, there exist two common usages of the term _____, both with rigorous mathematical frameworks.

- In the study of transport phenomena (heat transfer, mass transfer and fluid dynamics), _____ is defined as the amount that flows through a unit area per unit time. _____ in this definition is a vector.
- In the field of electromagnetism and mathematics, _____ is usually the integral of a vector quantity over a finite surface. The result of this integration is a scalar quantity. The magnetic _____ is thus the integral of the magnetic vector field B over a surface, and the electric _____ is defined similarly. Using this definition, the _____ of the Poynting vector over a specified surface is the rate at which electromagnetic energy flows through that surface. Confusingly, the Poynting vector is sometimes called the power _____, which is an example of the first usage of _____, above. It has units of watts per square metre (W·m^{-2}).

One could argue, based on the work of James Clerk Maxwell, that the transport definition precedes the more recent way the term is used in electromagnetism. The specific quote from Maxwell is 'In the case of fluxes, we have to take the integral, over a surface, of the _____ through every element of the surface. The result of this operation is called the surface integral of the _____.

a. 15 theorem
b. BDDC
c. BIBO stability
d. Flux

Chapter 8. Techniques of Integration

29. In calculus, an _____ is the limit of a definite integral as an endpoint of the interval of integration approaches either a specified real number or ∞ or −∞ or, in some cases, as both endpoints approach limits.

Specifically, an _____ is a limit of the form

$$\lim_{b\to\infty}\int_a^b f(x)\,dx, \qquad \lim_{a\to-\infty}\int_a^b f(x)\,dx,$$

or of the form

$$\lim_{c\to b^-}\int_a^c f(x)\,dx, \qquad \lim_{c\to a^+}\int_c^b f(x)\,dx,$$

in which one takes a limit in one or the other (or sometimes both) endpoints. Improper integrals may also occur at an interior point of the domain of integration, or at multiple such points.

a. ACTRAN
b. ALGOR
c. AUSM
d. Improper integral

30. In vector calculus, the _____ is an operator that measures the magnitude of a vector field's source or sink at a given point; the _____ of a vector field is a (signed) scalar. For example, consider air as it is heated or cooled. The relevant vector field for this example is the velocity of the moving air at a point.

a. Triple product
b. Divergence
c. Divergence Theorem
d. Gradient theorem

31. If a function has an integral, it is said to be integrable. The function for which the integral is calculated is called the _____. The region over which a function is being integrated is called the domain of integration.

a. Integral test for convergence
b. Integration by parts
c. Order of integration
d. Integrand

32. In probability theory and statistics, the _____ (or expectation value or mean and for continuous random variables with a density function it is the probability density-weighted integral of the possible values.

The term '_____' can be misleading.

a. AUSM
b. ALGOR
c. ACTRAN
d. Expected value

33. In physics, _____ is defined as the rate of change of position. it is vector physical quantity; both speed and direction are required to define it. In the SI (metric) system, it is measured in meters per second: (m/s) or ms^{-1}.

a. Velocity
b. BDDC
c. 15 theorem
d. BIBO stability

86   Chapter 9. Further Applications of Integration

1. For some curves there is a smallest number L that is an upper bound on the length of any polygonal approximation. If such a number exists, then the curve is said to be rectifiable and the curve is defined to have _____ L.

Let C be a curve in Euclidean (or, generally, a metric) space X = R^n, so C is the image of a continuous function f : [a, b] → X of the interval [a, b] into X.

    a. Integrand   b. Integration by parametric derivatives
    c. Order of integration   d. Arc length

2. In mathematics, a (topological) _____ is defined as follows: let I be an interval of real numbers (i.e. a non-empty connected subset of $\mathbb{R}$); then a _____ γ is a continuous mapping $\gamma : I \to X$, where X is a topological space. The _____ γ is said to be simple if it is injective, i.e. if for all x, y in I, we have $\gamma(x) = \gamma(y) \implies x = y$. If I is a closed bounded interval $[a, b]$, we also allow the possibility $\gamma(a) = \gamma(b)$ (this convention makes it possible to talk about closed simple _____.)

    a. Tractrix   b. Prolate cycloid
    c. Curve   d. Closed curve

3. A _____ is a type of manifold that is locally similar enough to Euclidean space to allow one to do calculus Any manifold can be described by a collection of charts, also known as an atlas.

    a. Lie derivative   b. Tortuosity
    c. Differentiable manifold   d. Minimal surface

4. Smooth functions with given closed support are used in the construction of smooth partitions of unity ; these are essential in the study of smooth manifolds, for example to show that Riemannian metrics can be defined globally starting from their local existence. A simple case is that of a bump function on the real line, that is, a _____ f that takes the value 0 outside an interval [a,b] and such that

        f(x) > 0 for a < x < b.

Given a number of overlapping intervals on the line, bump functions can be constructed on each of them, and on semi-infinite intervals (->∞, c] and [d,+>∞) to cover the whole line, such that the sum of the functions is always 1.

    a. Functional derivative   b. Smooth function
    c. Linear approximation   d. Symmetrically continuous

5. In vector calculus, the _____ of a scalar field is a vector field which points in the direction of the greatest rate of increase of the scalar field, and whose magnitude is the greatest rate of change.

A generalization of the _____ for functions on a Euclidean space which have values in another Euclidean space is the Jacobian. A further generalization for a function from one Banach space to another is the Fréchet derivative.

    a. Smooth function   b. Parametric derivative
    c. Gradient   d. Leibniz's notation

Chapter 9. Further Applications of Integration

6. A _____ is a surface created by rotating a curve lying on some plane (the generatrix) around a straight line (the axis of rotation) that lies on the same plane.

Examples of surfaces generated by a straight line are the cylindrical and conical surfaces. A circle that is rotated about a (coplanar) axis through the center generates a sphere.

a. Surface of revolution
b. Solid of revolution
c. Nonelementary integral
d. Disk integration

7. _____ is how much exposed area an object has. It is expressed in square units. If an object has flat faces, its _____ can be calculated by adding together the areas of its faces.

a. Surface area
b. Plane curve
c. Gyroid
d. Lipschitz domain

8. In mathematics, engineering, and manufacturing, a _____ is a solid figure obtained by rotating a plane curve around some straight line (the axis) that lies on the same plane.

Assuming that the curve does not cross the axis, the solid's volume is equal to the length of the circle described by the figure's centroid, times the figure's area (Pappus's second centroid Theorem.)

Rotating a curve

A representative disk is a three-dimensional volume element of a _____.

a. Riemann sum
b. Sum rule in integration
c. Solid of revolution
d. Risch algorithm

9. The _____ of a material is defined as its mass per unit volume. The symbol of _____ is ρ '>rho.)

Mathematically:

$$d = \frac{m}{V}$$

where:

    d is the _____,
    m is the mass,
    V is the volume.

a. 15 theorem
b. BDDC
c. Density
d. BIBO stability

10. A quantity is said to be subject to _____ if it decreases at a rate proportional to its value. Symbolically, this can be expressed as the following differential equation, where N is the quantity and λ is a positive number called the decay constant.

$$\frac{dN}{dt} = -\lambda N.$$

The solution to this equation is:

$$N(t) = N_0 e^{-\lambda t}.$$

Here N(t) is the quantity at time t, and N_0 = N(0) is the initial quantity, i.e. the quantity at time t = 0.

- a. ACTRAN
- b. ALGOR
- c. Exponential decay
- d. Exponential sum

11. _____ are a set of problems generally thought to have been devised by Zeno of Elea to support Parmenides's doctrine that 'all is one' and that, contrary to the evidence of our senses, the belief in plurality and change is mistaken, and in particular that motion is nothing but an illusion. It is usually assumed, based on Plato's Parmenides 128c-d, that Zeno took on the project of creating these paradoxes because other philosophers had created paradoxes against Parmenides's view. Thus Zeno can be interpreted as saying that to assume there is plurality is even more absurd than assuming there is only 'the One' (Parmenides 128d.)

- a. Zeno's paradoxes
- b. BIBO stability
- c. 15 theorem
- d. BDDC

12. The concept of _____ in mathematics evolved from the concept of _____ in physics. The nth _____ of a real-valued function f(x) of a real variable about a value c is

$$\mu'_n = \int_{-\infty}^{\infty} (x - c)^n f(x)\, dx.$$

It is possible to define moments for random variables in a more general fashion than moments for real values. See Moments in metric spaces.

- a. Linear regression
- b. Poisson distribution
- c. Standard deviation
- d. Moment

13. The _____ is an important family of continuous probability distributions, applicable in many fields. Each member of the family may be defined by two parameters, location and scale: the mean and variance respectively. The standard _____ is the _____ with a mean of zero and a variance of one.

- a. Poisson distribution
- b. Linear regression
- c. Continuous random variable
- d. Normal distribution

14. In mathematics, a _____ is a quadric surface of special kind. There are two kinds of paraboloids: elliptic and hyperbolic. The elliptic _____ is shaped like an oval cup and can have a maximum or minimum point.

a. Normal line
c. Normal vector
b. Parametric surface
d. Paraboloid

15. _____ generally conveys two primary meanings. The first is an imprecise sense of harmonious or aesthetically-pleasing proportionality and balance; such that it reflects beauty or perfection. The second meaning is a precise and well-defined concept of balance or 'patterned self-similarity' that can be demonstrated or proved according to the rules of a formal system: by geometry, through physics or otherwise.
   a. BIBO stability
   b. BDDC
   c. 15 theorem
   d. Symmetry

16. A _____ is a model used within physics to explain how gravity exists in the universe. In its original concept, gravity was a force between point masses. Following Newton, Laplace attempted to model gravity as some kind of radiation field or fluid, and since the 19th century explanations for gravity have usually been sought in terms of a field model, rather than a point attraction.
   a. BIBO stability
   b. BDDC
   c. 15 theorem
   d. Gravitational field

17. In the various subfields of physics, there exist two common usages of the term _____, both with rigorous mathematical frameworks.

   - In the study of transport phenomena (heat transfer, mass transfer and fluid dynamics), _____ is defined as the amount that flows through a unit area per unit time. _____ in this definition is a vector.
   - In the field of electromagnetism and mathematics, _____ is usually the integral of a vector quantity over a finite surface. The result of this integration is a scalar quantity. The magnetic _____ is thus the integral of the magnetic vector field B over a surface, and the electric _____ is defined similarly. Using this definition, the _____ of the Poynting vector over a specified surface is the rate at which electromagnetic energy flows through that surface. Confusingly, the Poynting vector is sometimes called the power _____, which is an example of the first usage of _____, above. It has units of watts per square metre (W·m^{-2})

One could argue, based on the work of James Clerk Maxwell, that the transport definition precedes the more recent way the term is used in electromagnetism. The specific quote from Maxwell is 'In the case of fluxes, we have to take the integral, over a surface, of the _____ through every element of the surface. The result of this operation is called the surface integral of the _____.

   a. BDDC
   b. Flux
   c. 15 theorem
   d. BIBO stability

18. In probability theory, a probability distribution is called continuous if its cumulative distribution function is continuous. This is equivalent to saying that for random variables X with the distribution in question, Pr[X = a] = 0 for all real numbers a, i.e.: the probability that X attains the value a is zero, for any number a. If the distribution of X is continuous then X is called a _____.
   a. Moment
   b. Standard deviation
   c. Linear regression
   d. Continuous random variable

19. Determining the _____ segment -- also called rectification of a curve -- was historically difficult. Although many methods were used for specific curves, the advent of calculus led to a general formula that provides closed-form solutions in some cases.

A curve in, say, the plane can be approximated by connecting a finite number of points on the curve using line segments to create a polygonal path. Since it is straightforward to calculate the length of each linear segment (using the theorem of Pythagoras in Euclidean space, for example), the total length of the approximation can be found by summing the lengths of each linear segment.

    a. Surface of revolution
    c. Riemann sum
    b. Nonelementary integral
    d. Length of an irregular arc

20. In mathematics, two vectors are _____ if they are perpendicular, i.e., they form a right angle. For example, a subway and the street above, although they do not physically intersect, are _____ if they cross at a right angle.
    a. Orthogonal
    c. AUSM
    b. ACTRAN
    d. ALGOR

21. In mathematics, _____ are a family of curves in the plane that intersect a given family of curves at right angles. The problem is classical, but is now understood by means of complex analysis; see for example harmonic conjugate.

For a family of level curves described by g(x,y) = C, where C is a constant, the _____ may be found as the level curves of a new function f(x,y) by solving the partial differential equation

$$\nabla f \cdot \nabla g = 0$$

for f(x,y).

    a. ALGOR
    c. AUSM
    b. Orthogonal trajectories
    d. ACTRAN

22. A _____ is the path a moving object follows through space. The object might be a projectile or a satellite, for example. It thus includes the meaning of orbit - the path of a planet, an asteroid or a comet as it travels around a central mass.
    a. Trajectory
    c. BIBO stability
    b. BDDC
    d. 15 theorem

23. In economics, the _____ functional form of production functions is widely used to represent the relationship of an output to inputs. It was proposed by Knut Wicksell (1851-1926), and tested against statistical evidence by Charles Cobb and Paul Douglas in 1900-1928.

For production, the function is

    $Y = AL^\alpha K^\beta$,

where:

- Y = total production (the monetary value of all goods produced in a year)
- L = labor input
- K = capital input
- A = total factor productivity
- α and β are the output elasticities of labor and capital, respectively. These values are constants determined by available technology.

Output elasticity measures the responsiveness of output to a change in levels of either labor or capital used in production, ceteris paribus. For example if α = 0.15, a 1% increase in labor would lead to approximately a 0.15% increase in output.

a. Cobb-Douglas
b. 15 theorem
c. BDDC
d. BIBO stability

24. The mechanisms of _____; a point mass m_1 attracts another point mass m_2 by a force F_2 which is proportional to the product of the two masses and inversely proportional to the square of the distance (r) between them. Regardless of masses or distance, the magnitudes of $|F_1|$ and $|F_2|$ will always be equal. G is the gravitational constant.

_____ is an empirical physical law describing the gravitational attraction between bodies with mass.

a. 15 theorem
b. Newton's law of universal gravitation
c. BIBO stability
d. BDDC

25. In mathematics, a _____ (pdf) is a function that represents a probability distribution in terms of integrals.

Formally, a probability distribution has density f, if f is a non-negative Lebesgue-integrable function $\mathbb{R} \rightarrow \mathbb{R}$ such that the probability of the interval [a, b] is given by

$$\int_a^b f(x)\,dx$$

for any two numbers a and b. This implies that the total integral of f must be 1.

a. BIBO stability
b. BDDC
c. 15 theorem
d. Probability density function

26. In probability theory and statistics, the _____ (or expectation value or mean and for continuous random variables with a density function it is the probability density -weighted integral of the possible values.

The term '_____' can be misleading.

a. ACTRAN
c. AUSM
b. Expected value
d. ALGOR

27. In statistics, _____ is a simple measure of the variability or dispersion of a data set. A low _____ indicates that all of the data points are very close to the same value (the mean), while high _____ indicates that the data is 'spread out' over a large range of values.

For example, the average height for adult men in the United States is about 70 inches, with a _____ of around 3 inches.

a. Standard deviation
c. Normal distribution
b. Poisson distribution
d. Moment

Chapter 10. Differential Equations

1. In infinitesimal calculus, a _____ is traditionally an infinitesimally small change in a variable. For example, if x is a variable, then a change in the value of x is often denoted Δx (or δx when this change is considered to be small.) The _____ dx represents such a change, but is infinitely small.
   - a. Continuous function
   - b. Related rates
   - c. Dirichlet integral
   - d. Differential

2. A _____ is a mathematical equation for an unknown function of one or several variables that relates the values of the function itself and of its derivatives of various orders. they play a prominent role in engineering, physics, economics and other disciplines.

   A simplified real world example of a _____ is modeling the acceleration of a ball falling through the air (considering only gravity and air resistance.)

   - a. Lax pair
   - b. Petrovsky lacuna
   - c. Structural stability
   - d. Differential equation

3. Just as the definite integral of a positive function of one variable represents the area of the region between the graph of the function and the x-axis, the _____ of a positive function of two variables represents the volume of the region between the surface defined by the function (on the three dimensional Cartesian plane where z = f(x,y)) and the plane which contains its domain. (Note that the same volume can be obtained via the triple integral -- the integral of a function in three variables -- of the constant function f(x, y, z) = 1 over the above-mentioned region between the surface and the plane.) If there are more variables, a multiple integral will yield hypervolumes of multi-dimensional functions.
   - a. Linearity of integration
   - b. Nonelementary integral
   - c. Sum rule in integration
   - d. Double integral

4. Integration is an important concept in mathematics, specifically in the field of calculus and, more broadly, mathematical analysis. Given a function f of a real variable x and an interval [a, b] of the real line, the _____

$$\int_a^b f(x)\,dx,$$

is defined informally to be the net signed area of the region in the xy-plane bounded by the graph of f, the x-axis, and the vertical lines x = a and x = b.

The term '_____' may also refer to the notion of antiderivative, a function F whose derivative is the given function f.

   - a. Integral test for convergence
   - b. Integrand
   - c. Integral
   - d. Indefinite integral

5. The most commonly encountered form of Hooke's law is probably the spring equation, which relates the force exerted by a spring to the distance it is stretched by a _____, k, measured in force per length.

$$F = -kx$$

The negative sign indicates that the force exerted by the spring is in direct opposition to the direction of displacement. It is called a 'restoring force', as it tends to restore the system to equilibrium.

a. Navier-Stokes equations
b. Polar moment of inertia
c. 15 theorem
d. Spring constant

6. In mathematics, in the field of differential equations, an initial value problem is an ordinary differential equation together with specified value, called the _____, of the unknown function at a given point in the domain of the solution. In physics or other sciences, modeling a system frequently amounts to solving an initial value problem; in this context, the differential equation is an evolution equation specifying how, given initial conditions, the system will evolve with time.

An initial value problem is a differential equation

$$y'(t) = f(t, y(t)) \quad \text{with} \quad f : \mathbb{R} \times \mathbb{R} \to \mathbb{R}$$

together with a point in the domain of f

$$(t_0, y_0) \in \mathbb{R} \times \mathbb{R},$$

called the _____.

a. Initial condition
b. ALGOR
c. AUSM
d. ACTRAN

7. In mathematics, in the field of differential equations, an _____ is an ordinary differential equation together with specified value, called the initial condition, of the unknown function at a given point in the domain of the solution. In physics or other sciences, modeling a system frequently amounts to solving an _____; in this context, the differential equation is an evolution equation specifying how, given initial conditions, the system will evolve with time.

An _____ is a differential equation

$$y'(t) = f(t, y(t)) \quad \text{with} \quad f : \mathbb{R} \times \mathbb{R} \to \mathbb{R}$$

together with a point in the domain of f

$$(t_0, y_0) \in \mathbb{R} \times \mathbb{R},$$

called the initial condition.

a. ALGOR
b. Initial value problem
c. AUSM
d. ACTRAN

Chapter 10. Differential Equations

8. In mathematics, a _____ to an ordinary or partial differential equation is a function for which the derivatives appearing in the equation may not all exist but which is nonetheless deemed to satisfy the equation in some precisely defined sense. There are many different definitions of _____, appropriate for different classes of equations. One of the most important is based on the notion of distributions.
   a. Nahm equations
   c. Weak solution
   b. Singular perturbation
   d. Riemann-Hilbert correspondence

9. In mathematics, a _____ (or direction field) is a graphical representation of the solutions of a first-order differential equation. It is achieved without solving the differential equation analytically, and thence it is useful. The representation may be used to qualitatively visualise solutions, or to numerically approximate them.
   a. Fresnel integrals
   c. Standard part function
   b. The Method of Mechanical Theorems
   d. Slope field

10. In mathematics, a (topological) _____ is defined as follows: let I be an interval of real numbers (i.e. a non-empty connected subset of $\mathbb{R}$); then a _____ γ is a continuous mapping $\gamma : I \to X$, where X is a topological space. The _____ γ is said to be simple if it is injective, i.e. if for all x, y in I, we have $\gamma(x) = \gamma(y) \implies x = y$. If I is a closed bounded interval $[a, b]$, we also allow the possibility $\gamma(a) = \gamma(b)$ (this convention makes it possible to talk about closed simple _____.)
   a. Curve
   c. Prolate cycloid
   b. Tractrix
   d. Closed curve

11. In mathematics, an autonomous system or _____ is a system of ordinary differential equations which does not depend on the independent variable.

Many laws in physics, where the independent variable is usually assumed to be time, are expressed as autonomous systems because it is assumed the laws of nature which hold now are identical to those for any point in the past or future.

Autonomous systems are closely related to dynamical systems.

   a. Integro-differential equation
   c. Annihilator method
   b. Algebraic differential equation
   d. Autonomous differential equation

12. In mathematics, a _____ differential equation may refer to one of two related things, both of which are differential equations that can be attacked by a method of separation of variables.

   - For ordinary differential equations, it describes a class of equations that can be separated into a pair of integrals. See: Examples of differential equations

   - For partial differential equations, it describes a class of equations that can be broken down into differential equations in fewer independent variables. See _____ partial differential equation.

a. Weak solution
b. Lax pair
c. Conserved quantity
d. Separable

13. In mathematics, two vectors are _____ if they are perpendicular, i.e., they form a right angle. For example, a subway and the street above, although they do not physically intersect, are _____ if they cross at a right angle.
    a. ACTRAN
    b. Orthogonal
    c. AUSM
    d. ALGOR

14. In mathematics, _____ are a family of curves in the plane that intersect a given family of curves at right angles. The problem is classical, but is now understood by means of complex analysis; see for example harmonic conjugate.

For a family of level curves described by g(x,y) = C, where C is a constant, the _____ may be found as the level curves of a new function f(x,y) by solving the partial differential equation

$$\nabla f \cdot \nabla g = 0$$

for f(x,y).

    a. ALGOR
    b. ACTRAN
    c. AUSM
    d. Orthogonal trajectories

15. A _____ is the path a moving object follows through space. The object might be a projectile or a satellite, for example. It thus includes the meaning of orbit - the path of a planet, an asteroid or a comet as it travels around a central mass.
    a. BDDC
    b. 15 theorem
    c. BIBO stability
    d. Trajectory

16. In physics, _____ is defined as the rate of change of position. it is vector physical quantity; both speed and direction are required to define it. In the SI (metric) system, it is measured in meters per second: (m/s) or ms^{-1}.
    a. 15 theorem
    b. Velocity
    c. BIBO stability
    d. BDDC

17. A quantity is said to be subject to _____ if it decreases at a rate proportional to its value. Symbolically, this can be expressed as the following differential equation, where N is the quantity and λ is a positive number called the decay constant.

$$\frac{dN}{dt} = -\lambda N.$$

The solution to this equation is:

$$N(t) = N_0 e^{-\lambda t}.$$

Here N(t) is the quantity at time t, and N_0 = N(0) is the initial quantity, i.e. the quantity at time t = 0.

Chapter 10. Differential Equations

a. ACTRAN
b. ALGOR
c. Exponential sum
d. Exponential decay

18. _____ (including exponential decay) occurs when the growth rate of a mathematical function is proportional to the function's current value. In the case of a discrete domain of definition with equal intervals it is also called geometric growth or geometric decay (the function values form a geometric progression.)

_____ is said to follow an exponential law; the simple-_____ model is known as the Malthusian growth model.

a. Inseparable differential equation
b. Isomonodromic deformation
c. Oscillating
d. Exponential growth

19. The _____ of a quantity whose value decreases with time is the interval required for the quantity to decay to half of its initial value. The concept originated in describing how long it takes atoms to undergo radioactive decay but also applies in a wide variety of other situations.

The term '_____' dates to 1907.

a. 15 theorem
b. BIBO stability
c. Half-life
d. BDDC

20. _____ is the concept of adding accumulated interest back to the principal, so that interest is earned on interest from that moment on. The act of declaring interest to be principal is called compounding (i.e., interest is compounded.) A loan, for example, may have its interest compounded every month: in this case, a loan with $100 principal and 1% interest per month would have a balance of $101 at the end of the first month.

a. 15 theorem
b. BDDC
c. BIBO stability
d. Compound interest

21. Cantor defined two kinds of _____ numbers, the ordinal numbers and the cardinal numbers. Ordinal numbers may be identified with well-ordered sets, or counting carried on to any stopping point, including points after an _____ number have already been counted. Generalizing finite and the ordinary _____ sequences which are maps from the positive integers leads to mappings from ordinal numbers, and transfinite sequences.

a. ACTRAN
b. AUSM
c. ALGOR
d. Infinite

22. The terms of the series are often produced according to a certain rule, such as by a formula, by an algorithm, by a sequence of measurements, or even by a random number generator. As there are an infinite number of terms, this notion is often called an _____. Unlike finite summations, series need tools from mathematical analysis to be fully understood and manipulated.

a. Integration by substitution
b. Extreme value
c. Extreme Value Theorem
d. Infinite series

23. The _____ of an object is the extra energy which it possesses due to its motion. It is defined as the work needed to accelerate a body of a given mass from rest to its current velocity. Having gained this energy during its acceleration, the body maintains this _____ unless its speed changes.

a. Kinetic energy
b. BDDC
c. 15 theorem
d. Potential energy

24. _____ is a PDE solver of Maxwell's equations based on the method of moments. It is a 3-D planar electromagnetic (EM) simulator used for passive circuit analysis. It is presently marketed by Agilent Technologies EEsof division , but the tool was original developed by a Belgian company, Alphabit, a spinoff from IMEC, which was acquired by Hewlett-Packard and later spun out as part of Agilent.

a. Trefftz method
b. Partial Element Equivalent Circuit
c. Stencil
d. Momentum

25. The largest and the smallest element of a set are called extreme values, absolute extrema, or extreme records.

For a differentiable function f, if $f(x_0)$ is an _____ for the set of all values f(x), and if x_0 is in the interior of the domain of f, then x_0 is a critical point, by Fermat's theorem.

In the case of a general partial order one should not confuse a least element (smaller than all other) and a minimal element (nothing is smaller.)

a. Extreme Value
b. Integration by substitution
c. Extreme Value Theorem
d. Infinitesimal

26. In calculus, the _____ states that if a real-valued function f is continuous in the closed and bounded interval [a,b], then f must attain its maximum and minimum value, each at least once. That is, there exist numbers c and d in [a,b] such that:

$$f(c) \geq f(x) \geq f(d) \quad \text{for all } x \in [a, b].$$

A related theorem is the boundedness theorem which states that a continuous function f in the closed interval [a,b] is bounded on that interval. That is, there exist real numbers m and M such that:

$$m \leq f(x) \leq M \quad \text{for all } x \in [a, b].$$

The _____ enriches the boundedness theorem by saying that not only is the function bounded, but it also attains its least upper bound as its maximum and its greatest lower bound as its minimum.

a. Uniform convergence
b. Infinitesimal
c. Integral of secant cubed
d. Extreme Value Theorem

27. The _____ is a polynomial mapping of degree 2, often cited as an archetypal example of how complex, chaotic behaviour can arise from very simple non-linear dynamical equations. The map was popularized in a seminal 1976 paper by the biologist Robert May, in part as a discrete-time demographic model analogous to the logistic equation first created by Pierre François Verhulst. Mathematically, the _____ is written

Chapter 10. Differential Equations

$$(1) \quad x_{n+1} = rx_n(1 - x_n)$$

where:

x_n is a number between zero and one, and represents the population at year n, and hence x_0 represents the initial population (at year 0)

r is a positive number, and represents a combined rate for reproduction and starvation.

a. BDDC
b. BIBO stability
c. 15 theorem
d. Logistic map

28. A _____ or Gompertz function, named after Benjamin Gompertz, is a sigmoid function. It is a type of mathematical model for a time series, where growth is slowest at the start and end of a time period. Graphs of Gompertz curves, showing the effect of varying one of a,b,c while keeping the others constant.

$$y(t) = ae^{be^{ct}}$$

where

- a is the upper asymptote
- c is the growth rate
- b, c are negative numbers
- e is Euler's Number (e = 2.71828...)

The function curve can be derived from Gompertz's law, which states the rate of mortality (decay) falls exponentially with current size. Mathematically

$$k^r \propto \frac{1}{y(t)}$$

where

- $r = \dfrac{y'(t)}{y(t)}$ is the rate of growth.
- k is an arbitrary constant.

Examples of uses for Gompertz curves include:

- Mobile phone uptake, where costs were initially high (so uptake was slow), followed by a period of rapid growth, followed by a slowing of uptake as saturation was reached.
- Population in a confined space, as birth rates first increase and then slow as resource limits are reached.
- Modeling of growth of tumors

Chapter 10. Differential Equations

In the sixties A.K. Laird for the first time successfully used the _____ to fit data of growth of tumors. In fact, tumors are cellular populations growing in a confined space where the availability of nutrients is limited.

a. Spheroidal wave functions
c. Neumann-Dirichlet method

b. Duffing equation
d. Gompertz curve

29. In mathematics, an _____ is a function that is chosen to facilitate the solving of a given ordinary differential equation.

Consider an ordinary differential equation of the form

$$y' + a(x)y = b(x) \quad (1)$$

where y = y(x) is an unknown function of x, and a(x) and b(x) are given functions.

The _____ method works by turning the left hand side into the form of the derivative of a product.

a. Exponential growth
c. Integrating factor

b. Isomonodromic deformation
d. Oscillating

30. In mathematics, a _____ is a differential equation of the form

$$Ly = f$$

where the differential operator L is a linear operator, y is the unknown function, and the right hand side f is a given function (called the source term.) The linearity condition on L rules out operations such as taking the square of the derivative of y; but permits, for example, taking the second derivative of y. Therefore a fairly general form of such an equation would be

$$a_n(x)D^n y(x) + a_{n-1}(x)D^{n-1}y(x) + \cdots + a_1(x)Dy(x) + a_0(x)y(x) = f(x)$$

where D is the differential operator d/dx (i.e. Dy = y' , D²y = y',...), and the a_i are given functions.

a. Nullcline
c. Petrovsky lacuna

b. Separable
d. Linear differential equation

31. In mathematics, an ordinary differential equation of the form

$$y' + P(x)y = Q(x)y^n$$

is called a _____ when n≠1, 0. Bernoulli equations are special because they are nonlinear differential equations with known exact solutions. Dividing by y^n yields

$$\frac{y'}{y^n} + \frac{P(x)}{y^{n-1}} = Q(x).$$

A change of variables is made to transform into a linear first-order differential equation.

a. Separation of variables
b. Bernoulli equation
c. Growth curve
d. Spectral theory of ordinary differential equations

32. The _____ are a pair of first order, non-linear, differential equations frequently used to describe the dynamics of biological systems in which two species interact, one a predator and one its prey. They were proposed independently by Alfred J. Lotka in 1925 and Vito Volterra in 1926.

where

- y is the number of some predator;
- x is the number of its prey;
- dy/dt and dx/dt represents the growth of the two populations against time;
- t represents the time; and
- >α, >β, >γ and >δ are parameters representing the interaction of the two species.

When multiplied out, the equations take a form useful for physical interpretation. Their origin should be considered from a more general framework,

where both functions represent per capita growth rates of the prey and predator, respectively.

a. Lotka-Volterra equations
b. BIBO stability
c. 15 theorem
d. BDDC

33. In mathematics, the point $\tilde{x} \in \mathbb{R}^n$ is an _____ for the differential equation

$$\frac{d\mathbf{x}}{dt} = \mathbf{f}(t, \mathbf{x})$$

if $\mathbf{f}(t, \tilde{\mathbf{x}}) = 0$ for all t.

Similarly, the point $\tilde{\mathbf{x}} \in \mathbb{R}^n$ is an _____ (or fixed point) for the difference equation

$$\mathbf{x}_{k+1} = \mathbf{f}(k, \mathbf{x}_k)$$

if $\mathbf{f}(k, \tilde{\mathbf{x}}) = \tilde{\mathbf{x}}$ for $k = 0, 1, 2, \ldots$.

Equilibria can be classified by looking at the signs of the eigenvalues of the linearization of the equations about the equilibria.

- a. Equilibrium point
- b. ALGOR
- c. ACTRAN
- d. AUSM

34. A _____ is a visual display of certain characteristics of certain kinds of differential equations.

Phase planes are useful in visualizing the behavior of physical systems; in particular, of oscillatory systems such as predator-prey models These models can 'spiral in' towards zero, 'spiral out' towards infinity, or reach neutrally stable situations called centres where the path traced out can be either circular, elliptical, or ovoid, or some variant thereof.

- a. Frobenius method
- b. Phase plane
- c. Separation of variables
- d. Power series method

35. A _____ is a geometric representation of the trajectories of a dynamical system in the phase plane. Each set of initial conditions is represented by a different curve, or point.

they are an invaluable tool in studying dynamical systems.

- a. BIBO stability
- b. BDDC
- c. 15 theorem
- d. Phase portrait

36. In physics, and more specifically kinematics, _____ is the change in velocity over time. Because velocity is a vector, it can change in two ways: a change in magnitude and/or a change in direction. In one dimension, _____ is the rate at which something speeds up or slows down.
- a. Acceleration
- b. AUSM
- c. ACTRAN
- d. ALGOR

Chapter 11. Parametric Equations and Polar Coordinates

1. In mathematics, _____ are a method of defining a curve. A simple kinematical example is when one uses a time parameter to determine the position, velocity, and other information about a body in motion.

Abstractly, a relation is given in the form of an equation, and it is shown also to be the image of functions from items such as R^n.

- a. Multivariable calculus
- b. Laplace operator
- c. Parametric equations
- d. Differential operator

2. In mathematics, a (topological) _____ is defined as follows: let I be an interval of real numbers (i.e. a non-empty connected subset of $\mathbb{R}$); then a _____ γ is a continuous mapping $\gamma : I \to X$, where X is a topological space. The _____ γ is said to be simple if it is injective, i.e. if for all x, y in I, we have $\gamma(x) = \gamma(y) \implies x = y$. If I is a closed bounded interval $[a, b]$, we also allow the possibility $\gamma(a) = \gamma(b)$ (this convention makes it possible to talk about closed simple _____.)

- a. Tractrix
- b. Closed curve
- c. Prolate cycloid
- d. Curve

3. In geometry, a _____ is a special plane curve generated by the trace of a fixed point on a small circle that rolls within a larger circle. It is comparable to the cycloid but instead of the circle rolling along a line, it rolls within a circle. The red curve is a _____ traced as the smaller black circle rolls around inside the larger blue circle (parameters are R=3.0, r=1.0, and so k=3), giving a deltoid.

If the smaller circle has radius r, and the larger circle has radius R = kr, then the parametric equations for the curve can be given by either:

$$x(\theta) = (R - r)\cos\theta + r\cos\left(\frac{R-r}{r}\theta\right)$$
$$y(\theta) = (R - r)\sin\theta - r\sin\left(\frac{R-r}{r}\theta\right),$$

or:

$$x(\theta) = r(k-1)\cos\theta + r\cos((k-1)\theta)$$
$$y(\theta) = r(k-1)\sin\theta - r\sin((k-1)\theta).$$

If k is an integer, then the curve is closed, and has k cusps (i.e., sharp corners, where the curve is not differentiable.)

- a. Bullet-nose curve
- b. Kappa curve
- c. Closed curve
- d. Hypocycloid

4. In economics, the _____ functional form of production functions is widely used to represent the relationship of an output to inputs. It was proposed by Knut Wicksell (1851-1926), and tested against statistical evidence by Charles Cobb and Paul Douglas in 1900-1928.

For production, the function is

$$Y = AL^\alpha K^\beta,$$

where:

- Y = total production (the monetary value of all goods produced in a year)
- L = labor input
- K = capital input
- A = total factor productivity
- α and β are the output elasticities of labor and capital, respectively. These values are constants determined by available technology.

Output elasticity measures the responsiveness of output to a change in levels of either labor or capital used in production, ceteris paribus. For example if α = 0.15, a 1% increase in labor would lead to approximately a 0.15% increase in output.

a. BDDC
b. Cobb-Douglas
c. 15 theorem
d. BIBO stability

5. A _____ is a reference from which measurements are made. In surveying and geodesy, a datum is a set of reference points on the earth's surface against which position measurements are made, and (often) an associated model of the shape of the earth (reference ellipsoid) to define a geographic coordinate system. Horizontal datums are used for describing a point on the earth's surface, in latitude and longitude or another coordinate system.

a. Geodetic datum
b. BIBO stability
c. 15 theorem
d. BDDC

6. In mathematics, _____, first defined by the mathematician Daniel Bernoulli and generalized by Friedrich Bessel, are canonical solutions y(x) of Bessel's differential equation:

$$x^2 \frac{d^2 y}{dx^2} + x \frac{dy}{dx} + (x^2 - \alpha^2)y = 0$$

for an arbitrary real or complex number α (the order of the Bessel function.) The most common and important special case is where α is an integer n.

Although α and −α produce the same differential equation, it is conventional to define different _____ for these two orders (e.g., so that the _____ are mostly smooth functions of α.)

a. Bessel functions
b. 15 theorem
c. Logarithmic integral function
d. Multiplication theorem

Chapter 11. Parametric Equations and Polar Coordinates   105

7. A _____ is the curve defined by the path of a point on the edge of circular wheel as the wheel rolls along a straight line. It is an example of a roulette, a curve generated by a curve rolling on another curve.

The _____ is the solution to the brachistochrone problem (i.e. it is the curve of fastest descent under gravity) and the related tautochrone problem (i.e. the period of a ball rolling back and forth inside it does not depend on the ball's starting position.)

a. Prolate cycloid
b. Cycloid
c. Curtate cycloid
d. Tractrix

8. A _____ is the curve between two points that is covered in the least time by a body that starts at the first point with zero speed and is constrained to move along the curve to the second point, under the action of constant gravity and assuming no friction.

Given two points A and B, with A not lower than B, there is just one upside down cycloid that passes through A with infinite slope, passes also through B and does not have maximum points between A and B. This particular inverted cycloid is a _____. The curve does not depend on the body's mass or on the strength of the gravitational constant.

a. Prolate cycloid
b. Space curve
c. Closed curve
d. Brachistochrone curve

9. A tautochrone or isochrone curve is the curve for which the time taken by an object sliding without friction in uniform gravity to its lowest point is independent of its starting point. The curve is a cycloid, and the time is equal to >π times the square root of the radius over the acceleration of gravity.

The _____, the attempt to identify this curve, was solved by Christiaan Huygens in 1659. He proved geometrically in his Horologium oscillatorium (The Pendulum Clock, 1673) that the curve was a cycloid. This solution was later used to attack the problem of the brachistochrone curve. Jakob Bernoulli solved the problem using calculus in a paper (Acta Eruditorum, 1690) that saw the first published use of the term integral.

a. Hypocycloid
b. Folium of Descartes
c. Space curve
d. Tautochrone problem

10. _____ is the word created by Gilles de Roberval for the curve described by a fixed point as a circle rolls along a straight line. As a circle of radius a rolls without slipping along a line L, the center C moves parallel to L, and every other point P in the rotating plane rigidly attached to the circle traces the curve called the _____. Let CP = b. If P lies inside the circle (b < a), on its circumference (b = a), or outside (b > a), the _____ is described as being curtate, common, or prolate, respectively.

a. Trochoid
b. Witch of Agnesi
c. Hypocycloid
d. Kappa curve

11. In mathematics, the _____ , is the curve defined as follows.

Starting with a fixed circle, a point O on the circle is chosen. For any other point A on the circle, the secant line OA is drawn. The point M is diametrically opposite O. The line OA intersects the tangent at M at the point N. The line parallel to OM through N, and the line perpendicular to OM through A intersect at P. As the point A is varied, the path of P is the witch.

a. Cochleoid
b. Folium of Descartes
c. Witch of Agnesi
d. Closed curve

12. In mathematics, an _____ is a particular type of curve: a hypocycloid with four cusps. Astroids are also superellipses: all astroids are scaled versions of the curve specified by the equation

$$x^{2/3} + y^{2/3} = 1.$$

Its modern name comes from the Greek word for 'star'.

a. Epicycloid
b. ALGOR
c. Astroid
d. ACTRAN

13. In geometry, an _____ is a plane curve produced by tracing the path of a chosen point of a circle -- called epicycle -- which rolls without slipping around a fixed circle. It is a particular kind of roulette.

If the smaller circle has radius r, and the larger circle has radius R = kr, then the parametric equations for the curve can be given by either:

$$x(\theta) = (R+r)\cos\theta - r\cos\left(\frac{R+r}{r}\theta\right)$$
$$y(\theta) = (R+r)\sin\theta - r\sin\left(\frac{R+r}{r}\theta\right),$$

or:

$$x(\theta) = r(k+1)\cos\theta - r\cos((k+1)\theta)$$
$$y(\theta) = r(k+1)\sin\theta - r\sin((k+1)\theta).$$

If k is an integer, then the curve is closed, and has k cusps (i.e., sharp corners, where the curve is not differentiable.)

a. Asymptotic curve
b. ACTRAN
c. ALGOR
d. Epicycloid

14. In mathematics, a _____ is the graph of the system of parametric equations

Chapter 11. Parametric Equations and Polar Coordinates

$$x = A\sin(at + \delta), \quad y = B\sin(bt),$$

which describes complex harmonic motion. This family of curves was investigated by Nathaniel Bowditch in 1815, and later in more detail by Jules Antoine Lissajous in 1857.

The appearance of the figure is highly sensitive to the ratio a/b.

- a. BDDC
- b. 15 theorem
- c. BIBO stability
- d. Lissajous curve

15. In geometry, the _____ (or simply the tangent) to a curve at a given point is the straight line that 'just touches' the curve at that point (in the sense explained more precisely below.) As it passes through the point of tangency, the _____ is 'going in the same direction' as the curve, and in this sense it is the best straight-line approximation to the curve at that point. The same definition applies to space curves and curves in n-dimensional Euclidean space.
    - a. Minimal surface
    - b. Lie derivative
    - c. Sphere
    - d. Tangent line

16. For some curves there is a smallest number L that is an upper bound on the length of any polygonal approximation. If such a number exists, then the curve is said to be rectifiable and the curve is defined to have _____ L.

Let C be a curve in Euclidean (or, generally, a metric) space X = R^n, so C is the image of a continuous function f : [a, b] → X of the interval [a, b] into X.

- a. Integrand
- b. Order of integration
- c. Integration by parametric derivatives
- d. Arc length

17. Determining the _____ segment -- also called rectification of a curve -- was historically difficult. Although many methods were used for specific curves, the advent of calculus led to a general formula that provides closed-form solutions in some cases.

A curve in, say, the plane can be approximated by connecting a finite number of points on the curve using line segments to create a polygonal path. Since it is straightforward to calculate the length of each linear segment (using the theorem of Pythagoras in Euclidean space, for example), the total length of the approximation can be found by summing the lengths of each linear segment.

- a. Nonelementary integral
- b. Surface of revolution
- c. Riemann sum
- d. Length of an irregular arc

18. _____ is how much exposed area an object has. It is expressed in square units. If an object has flat faces, its _____ can be calculated by adding together the areas of its faces.
    - a. Gyroid
    - b. Plane curve
    - c. Lipschitz domain
    - d. Surface Area

Chapter 11. Parametric Equations and Polar Coordinates

19. In mathematics, _____ refers to any of a number of loosely related concepts in different areas of geometry. Intuitively, _____ is the amount by which a geometric object deviates from being flat, or straight in the case of a line, but this is defined in different ways depending on the context. There is a key distinction between extrinsic _____, which is defined for objects embedded in another space (usually a Euclidean space) in a way that relates to the radius of _____ of circles that touch the object, and intrinsic _____, which is defined at each point in a differential manifold.

   a. Tangent line   b. Tortuosity
   c. Lie derivative   d. Curvature

20. In mathematics, the _____ is a two-dimensional coordinate system in which each point on a plane is determined by an angle and a distance. The _____ is especially useful in situations where the relationship between two points is most easily expressed in terms of angles and distance; in the more familiar Cartesian or rectangular coordinate system, such a relationship can only be found through trigonometric formulation.

As the coordinate system is two-dimensional, each point is determined by two polar coordinates: the radial coordinate and the angular coordinate.

   a. BIBO stability   b. Polar coordinate system
   c. 15 theorem   d. BDDC

21. In complex analysis, a mathematical discipline, a _____ of a meromorphic function is a certain type of singularity that behaves like the singularity of $\frac{1}{z^n}$ at z = 0. This means that, in particular, a _____ of the function f(z) is a point z = a such that f(z) approaches infinity uniformly as z approaches a.

Formally, suppose U is an open subset of the complex plane C, a is an element of U and f : U {a} → C is a function which is holomorphic over its domain.

   a. Holomorphic function   b. Removable singularity
   c. Pole   d. Regular part

22. In mathematics and its applications, a _____ system is a system for assigning an n-tuple of numbers or scalars to each point in an n-dimensional space. This concept is part of the theory of manifolds. 'Scalars' in many cases means real numbers, but, depending on context, can mean complex numbers or elements of some other commutative ring.

   a. Cylindrical coordinate system   b. Spherical coordinate system
   c. Coordinate   d. 15 theorem

23. A _____ is one of the most curvilinear basic geometric shapes: It has two faces, zero vertices, and zero edges. The surface formed by the points at a fixed distance from a given straight line, the axis of the _____. The solid enclosed by this surface and by two planes perpendicular to the axis is also called a _____.

   a. 15 theorem   b. Right circular cylinder
   c. BDDC   d. Cylinder

24. A _____ is closed curve with one cusp.

In geometry, the _____ is an epicycloid with one cusp.

Rolling circle around another fixed circle produces _____ (red curve) Conformal mapping from circle to _____

- epicycloid produced as the path (or locus) of a point on the circumference of a circle as that circle rolls around another fixed circle with the same radius.

- limaçon with one cusp. The cusp is formed when the ratio of a to b in the equation is equal to one.

a. Cardioid
c. 15 theorem
b. BIBO stability
d. BDDC

25. In mathematics, a _____ or rhodonea curve is a sinusoid plotted in polar coordinates. Up to similarity, these curves can all be expressed by a polar equation of the form

$$r = \cos(k\theta).$$

If k is an integer, the curve will be _____ shaped with

- 2k petals if k is even, and
- k petals if k is odd.

When k is even, the entire graph of the _____ will be traced out exactly once when the value of θ changes from 0 to 2π. When k is odd, this will happen on the interval between 0 and π. (More generally, this will happen on any interval of length 2π for k even, and π for k odd.)

a. Curtate cycloid
c. Space curve
b. Cochleoid
d. Rose

26. _____ generally conveys two primary meanings. The first is an imprecise sense of harmonious or aesthetically-pleasing proportionality and balance; such that it reflects beauty or perfection. The second meaning is a precise and well-defined concept of balance or 'patterned self-similarity' that can be demonstrated or proved according to the rules of a formal system: by geometry, through physics or otherwise.

a. Symmetry
c. BDDC
b. BIBO stability
d. 15 theorem

27. In mathematics, the _____ is used to determine each point uniquely in a plane through two numbers, usually called the x-coordinate or abscissa and the y-coordinate or ordinate of the point. To define the coordinates, two perpendicular directed lines, are specified, as well as the unit length, which is marked off on the two axes Cartesian coordinate systems are also used in space and in higher dimensions.

a. 15 theorem
c. Cartesian coordinate system
b. Coordinate
d. Spherical coordinate system

Chapter 11. Parametric Equations and Polar Coordinates

28. In mathematics, a _____ is a set (or locus) of points in the plane such that each point p on the oval bears a special relation to two other, fixed points q_1 and q_2: the product of the distance from p to q_1 and the distance from p to q_2 is constant. That is, if we define the function dist(x,y) to be the distance from a point x to a point y, then all points p on a _____ satisfy the equation

$$\text{dist}(q_1, p) \times \text{dist}(q_2, p) = b^2$$

where b is a constant.

The points q_1 and q_2 are called the foci of the oval.

  a. Secant line
  c. Folium of Descartes
  b. Tractrix
  d. Cassini oval

29. A _____ is a cubic curve generated by increasing or diminishing the radius vector of a variable point P on a straight line by the distance PA of the point from the foot of the perpendicular drawn from the origin to the fixed line.

The polar equation is

$$r = a\ \cos 2\theta \sec \theta.$$

The Cartesian equation is

$$y^2 = x^2\,/,$$

where a is the distance of the line from the origin.

  a. Tschirnhausen cubic
  c. Macbeath surface
  b. Kampyle of Eudoxus
  d. Strophoid

30. In mathematics, a _____ (or just conic) is a curve obtained by intersecting a cone (more precisely, a circular conical surface) with a plane. A _____ is therefore a restriction of a quadric surface to the plane. The conic sections were named and studied as long ago as 200 BC, when Apollonius of Perga undertook a systematic study of their properties.

  a. 15 theorem
  c. BDDC
  b. Foci
  d. Conic section

31. The concept of _____ in mathematics evolved from the concept of _____ in physics. The nth _____ of a real-valued function f(x) of a real variable about a value c is

$$\mu'_n = \int_{-\infty}^{\infty} (x-c)^n\, f(x)\, dx.$$

It is possible to define moments for random variables in a more general fashion than moments for real values. See Moments in metric spaces.

Chapter 11. Parametric Equations and Polar Coordinates

a. Standard deviation
b. Linear regression
c. Poisson distribution
d. Moment

32. The _____ is an important family of continuous probability distributions, applicable in many fields. Each member of the family may be defined by two parameters, location and scale: the mean and variance respectively. The standard _____ is the _____ with a mean of zero and a variance of one.
   a. Poisson distribution
   b. Continuous random variable
   c. Linear regression
   d. Normal distribution

33. In mathematics, the _____ is a conic section, the intersection of a right circular conical surface and a plane parallel to a generating straight line of that surface. Given a point (the focus) and a line (the directrix) that lie in a plane, the locus of points in that plane that are equidistant to them is a _____.

A particular case arises when the plane is tangent to the conical surface of a circle.

   a. BDDC
   b. 15 theorem
   c. BIBO stability
   d. Parabola

34. In physics, and more specifically kinematics, _____ is the change in velocity over time. Because velocity is a vector, it can change in two ways: a change in magnitude and/or a change in direction. In one dimension, _____ is the rate at which something speeds up or slows down.
   a. Acceleration
   b. ALGOR
   c. AUSM
   d. ACTRAN

35. In infinitesimal calculus, a _____ is traditionally an infinitesimally small change in a variable. For example, if x is a variable, then a change in the value of x is often denoted Δx (or δx when this change is considered to be small.) The _____ dx represents such a change, but is infinitely small.
   a. Continuous function
   b. Dirichlet integral
   c. Differential
   d. Related rates

36. In mathematics, an _____, is the apparent shape of a circle viewed obliquely from outside it, as distinct from a hyperbola which is the shape seen from inside. It is the finite or bounded case of a conic section as a shape cut in a cone by a plane, the unbounded cases being the parabola, which like the _____ remains connected, and the hyperbola, which separates into two connected components or branches.

Equivalently an _____ can be defined as the locus of points, or path traced out, in a plane such that the sum of the distances from the moving point to two fixed points remains constant.

   a. AUSM
   b. ALGOR
   c. ACTRAN
   d. Ellipse

37. In geometry, the _____ (also semimajor axis) is used to describe the dimensions of ellipses and hyperbolae.

The major axis of an ellipse is its longest diameter, a line that runs through the centre and both foci, its ends being at the widest points of the shape. The _____ is one half of the major axis, and thus runs from the centre, through a focus, and to the edge of the ellipse.

a. Semi-major axis
c. BIBO stability

b. 15 theorem
d. BDDC

38. In geometry, the _____, pronounced , are a pair of special points used in describing conic sections. The four types of conic sections are the circle, parabola, ellipse, and hyperbola.

The focus has two equivalent defining properties; and they always fall on the major axis of symmetry of the conic.

a. Latus rectum
c. 15 theorem

b. BDDC
d. Foci

39. In the various subfields of physics, there exist two common usages of the term _____, both with rigorous mathematical frameworks.

- In the study of transport phenomena (heat transfer, mass transfer and fluid dynamics), _____ is defined as the amount that flows through a unit area per unit time. _____ in this definition is a vector.
- In the field of electromagnetism and mathematics, _____ is usually the integral of a vector quantity over a finite surface. The result of this integration is a scalar quantity. The magnetic _____ is thus the integral of the magnetic vector field B over a surface, and the electric _____ is defined similarly. Using this definition, the _____ of the Poynting vector over a specified surface is the rate at which electromagnetic energy flows through that surface. Confusingly, the Poynting vector is sometimes called the power _____, which is an example of the first usage of _____, above. It has units of watts per square metre (WÂ·m^{-2})

One could argue, based on the work of James Clerk Maxwell, that the transport definition precedes the more recent way the term is used in electromagnetism. The specific quote from Maxwell is 'In the case of fluxes, we have to take the integral, over a surface, of the _____ through every element of the surface. The result of this operation is called the surface integral of the _____.

a. 15 theorem
c. BIBO stability

b. BDDC
d. Flux

40. An _____ of a real-valued function y = f(x) is a curve which describes the behavior of f as either x or y tends to infinity.

In other words, as one moves along the graph of f(x) in some direction, the distance between it and the _____ eventually becomes smaller than any distance that one may specify.

a. Asymptote
c. AUSM

b. ALGOR
d. ACTRAN

41. In mathematics, the _____ of a power series is a non-negative quantity, either a real number or ∞, that represents a domain (within the radius) in which the series will converge. Within the _____, a power series converges absolutely and uniformly on compacta as well. If the series converges, it is the Taylor series of the analytic function to which it converges inside its _____.

Chapter 11. Parametric Equations and Polar Coordinates 113

a. Principal values
b. Motor variable
c. Movable singularity
d. Radius of convergence

42. In mathematics, the _____ of a function y = f(x) is a function that, in some fashion, 'undoes' the effect of f The _____ of f is denoted f^{-1}. The statements y=f(x) and x=f^{-1}(y) are equivalent.
   a. ACTRAN
   b. AUSM
   c. Inverse
   d. ALGOR

43. In mathematics, the _____ are analogs of the ordinary trigonometric or circular functions. The basic _____ are the hyperbolic sine 'sinh', and the hyperbolic cosine 'cosh', from which are derived the hyperbolic tangent 'tanh', etc., in analogy to the derived trigonometric functions. The inverse _____ are the area hyperbolic sine 'arsinh' (also called 'asinh', or sometimes by the misnomer of 'arcsinh') and so on.
   a. Hyperbolic functions
   b. Hyperbolic sine
   c. Step function
   d. Hyperbolic tangent

44. In mathematics, a _____ is a quadric surface of special kind. There are two kinds of paraboloids: elliptic and hyperbolic. The elliptic _____ is shaped like an oval cup and can have a maximum or minimum point.
   a. Normal vector
   b. Parametric surface
   c. Paraboloid
   d. Normal line

45. In physics, _____ is defined as the rate of change of position. it is vector physical quantity; both speed and direction are required to define it. In the SI (metric) system, it is measured in meters per second: (m/s) or ms^{-1}.
   a. BDDC
   b. BIBO stability
   c. Velocity
   d. 15 theorem

46. Integration is an important concept in mathematics, specifically in the field of calculus and, more broadly, mathematical analysis. Given a function f of a real variable x and an interval [a, b] of the real line, the _____

$$\int_a^b f(x)\,dx,$$

is defined informally to be the net signed area of the region in the xy-plane bounded by the graph of f, the x-axis, and the vertical lines x = a and x = b.

The term '_____' may also refer to the notion of antiderivative, a function F whose derivative is the given function f.

   a. Integral
   b. Integral test for convergence
   c. Integrand
   d. Indefinite integral

47. The _____ of a material is defined as its mass per unit volume. The symbol of _____ is ρ '>rho.)

Mathematically:

$$d = \frac{m}{V}$$

where:

        d is the _____,
        m is the mass,
        V is the volume.

a. Density
c. BIBO stability
b. BDDC
d. 15 theorem

48. Derivative terms are used to identify the body being orbited. The most common are perigee and apogee, referring to orbits around the Earth , and perihelion and _____, referring to orbits around the Sun . During the Apollo program, the terms pericynthion and apocynthion were used when referring to the moon.
a. ACTRAN
c. AUSM
b. Aphelion
d. ALGOR

49. A _____ is a snail-shaped curve similar to a strophoid which can be represented by the polar equation

$$r = \frac{a \sin \theta}{\theta}$$

the Cartesian equation

$$(x^2 + y^2) \arctan \frac{y}{x} = ay$$

or the parametric equations

$$x = \frac{a \sin t \cos t}{t}$$
$$y = \frac{a \sin^2 t}{t}$$

a. Secant line
c. Cochleoid
b. Hypocycloid
d. Tautochrone problem

50. In Geometry, the _____ is an algebraic curve defined by the equation

$$x^3 + y^3 - 3axy = 0$$

It forms a loop in the first quadrant with a double point at the origin and asymptote

$$x + y + a = 0$$

It is symmetrical about y = x.

a. Prolate cycloid
c. Folium of Descartes

b. Cochleoid
d. Curve

Chapter 12. Infinite Sequences and Series

1. In mathematics a _____ is a construction in vector calculus which associates a vector to every point in a (locally) Euclidean space.

Vector fields are often used in physics to model, for example, the speed and direction of a moving fluid throughout space, or the strength and direction of some force, such as the magnetic or gravitational force, as it changes from point to point.

In the rigorous mathematical treatment, (tangent) vector fields are defined on manifolds as sections of a manifold's tangent bundle.

    a. 15 theorem
    b. BDDC
    c. Vector field
    d. BIBO stability

2. In infinitesimal calculus, a _____ is traditionally an infinitesimally small change in a variable. For example, if x is a variable, then a change in the value of x is often denoted Δx (or δx when this change is considered to be small.) The _____ dx represents such a change, but is infinitely small.

    a. Related rates
    b. Continuous function
    c. Differential
    d. Dirichlet integral

3. A _____ is a mathematical equation for an unknown function of one or several variables that relates the values of the function itself and of its derivatives of various orders. they play a prominent role in engineering, physics, economics and other disciplines.

A simplified real world example of a _____ is modeling the acceleration of a ball falling through the air (considering only gravity and air resistance.)

    a. Differential equation
    b. Petrovsky lacuna
    c. Structural stability
    d. Lax pair

4. In mathematics, a _____ is an ordered list of objects (or events). Like a set, it contains members (also called elements or terms), and the number of terms (possibly infinite) is called the length of the _____. Unlike a set, order matters, and the exact same elements can appear multiple times at different positions in the _____.

    a. BDDC
    b. 15 theorem
    c. Y-intercept
    d. Sequence

5. In mathematics, the concept of a '_____' is used to describe the behavior of a function as its argument or input either 'gets close' to some point, or as the argument becomes arbitrarily large; or the behavior of a sequence's elements as their index increases indefinitely. Limits are used in calculus and other branches of mathematical analysis to define derivatives and continuity.

In formulas, _____ is usually abbreviated as lim

    a. Limit
    b. 15 theorem
    c. BIBO stability
    d. BDDC

Chapter 12. Infinite Sequences and Series

6. In vector calculus, the _____ is an operator that measures the magnitude of a vector field's source or sink at a given point; the _____ of a vector field is a (signed) scalar. For example, consider air as it is heated or cooled. The relevant vector field for this example is the velocity of the moving air at a point.
   a. Divergence
   b. Divergence Theorem
   c. Triple product
   d. Gradient theorem

7. The _____ is one of the oldest concepts in mathematical analysis. It provides a rigorous definition of the idea of a sequence converging towards a point called the limit.

Intuitively, suppose we have a sequence of points (i.e. an infinite set of points labelled using the natural numbers) in some sort of mathematical object (for example the real numbers or a vector space) which has a concept of nearness (such as 'all points within a given distance of a fixed point'.)

   a. Table of limits
   b. Squeeze Theorem
   c. 15 theorem
   d. Limit of a sequence

8. In calculus, an _____ is the limit of a definite integral as an endpoint of the interval of integration approaches either a specified real number or ∞ or −∞ or, in some cases, as both endpoints approach limits.

Specifically, an _____ is a limit of the form

$$\lim_{b \to \infty} \int_a^b f(x)\,dx, \qquad \lim_{a \to -\infty} \int_a^b f(x)\,dx,$$

or of the form

$$\lim_{c \to b^-} \int_a^c f(x)\,dx, \qquad \lim_{c \to a^+} \int_c^b f(x)\,dx,$$

in which one takes a limit in one or the other (or sometimes both) endpoints . Improper integrals may also occur at an interior point of the domain of integration, or at multiple such points.

   a. Improper integral
   b. AUSM
   c. ACTRAN
   d. ALGOR

9. Integration is an important concept in mathematics, specifically in the field of calculus and, more broadly, mathematical analysis. Given a function f of a real variable x and an interval [a, b] of the real line, the _____

$$\int_a^b f(x)\,dx,$$

is defined informally to be the net signed area of the region in the xy-plane bounded by the graph of f, the x-axis, and the vertical lines x = a and x = b.

The term '_____' may also refer to the notion of antiderivative, a function F whose derivative is the given function f.

a. Indefinite integral
b. Integral test for convergence
c. Integrand
d. Integral

10. When a linear asymptote is not parallel to the x- or y-axis, it is called either an oblique asymptote or equivalently a _____. The function f(x) is asymptotic to y = mx + b if

$$\lim_{x \to \infty} f(x) - (mx + b) = 0 \quad \text{or} \quad \lim_{x \to -\infty} f(x) - (mx + b) = 0$$

Note that y = mx + b is never a vertical asymptote, but can be a horizontal asymptote if m=0 (in which case it is not an oblique asymptote.)

An example is $f(x)=(x^2-1)/x$ which has an oblique asymptote of y=x (m=1, b=0) as seen in the limit

$$\lim_{x \to \infty} f(x) - x$$
$$= \lim_{x \to \infty} \frac{x^2 - 1}{x} - x$$
$$= \lim_{x \to \infty} (x - 1/x) - x$$
$$= \lim_{x \to \infty} -1/x = 0$$

Computationally identifying an oblique asymptote can be more difficult than a horizontal or vertical asymptote, in particular because the m and b might not be known.

a. Slant asymptote
b. Horizontal asymptote
c. Second derivative
d. Geometric function theory

11. An _____ of a real-valued function y = f(x) is a curve which describes the behavior of f as either x or y tends to infinity.

In other words, as one moves along the graph of f(x) in some direction, the distance between it and the _____ eventually becomes smaller than any distance that one may specify.

a. ACTRAN
b. Asymptote
c. AUSM
d. ALGOR

12. In mathematics, a function f defined on some set X with real or complex values is a _____ function, if the set of its values is _____. In other words, there exists a number M>0 such that

$$|f(x)| \leq M$$

for all x in X.

Sometimes, if $f(x) \leq A$ for all x in X, then the function is said to be _____ above by A.

- a. Differential calculus
- b. Stationary phase approximation
- c. Caccioppoli set
- d. Bounded

13. In mathematics, a _____ is a function which preserves the given order. This concept first arose in calculus, and was later generalized to the more abstract setting of order theory.

In calculus, a function f defined on a subset of the real numbers with real values is called monotonic (also monotonically increasing or non-decreasing), if for all x and y such that x >≤ y one has f(x) >≤ f(y), so f preserves the order.

- a. Monotonic function
- b. 15 theorem
- c. Pettis integral
- d. Pseudo-differential operator

14. In mathematics, the trigonometric integrals are a family of integrals which involve trigonometric functions. A number of the basic trigonometric integrals are discussed at the list of integrals of trigonometric functions. Plot of Si(x) for 0 ≤ x ≤ 8π.

The different _____ definitions are:

$$\text{Si}(x) = \int_0^x \frac{\sin t}{t} dt$$

$$\text{si}(x) = -\int_x^\infty \frac{\sin t}{t} dt$$

Si(x) is the primitive of sinx / x which is zero for x = 0; si(x) is the primitive of sinx / x which is zero for $x = \infty$.

- a. Trigonometric
- b. 15 theorem
- c. Sine integral
- d. Trigonometric integrals

15. In mathematics, given a subset S of a partially ordered set T, the _____ (sup) of S, if it exists, is the least element of T that is greater than or equal to each element of S. Consequently, the _____ is also referred to as the least upper bound, lub or LUB. If the _____ exists, it may or may not belong to S.

- a. BDDC
- b. 15 theorem
- c. BIBO stability
- d. Supremum

16. _____ is a method of mathematical proof typically used to establish that a given statement is true of all natural numbers. It is done by proving that the first statement in the infinite sequence of statements is true, and then proving that if any one statement in the infinite sequence of statements is true, then so is the next one.

The method can be extended to prove statements about more general well-founded structures, such as trees; this generalization, known as structural induction, is used in mathematical logic and computer science.

a. 15 theorem
c. BDDC
b. Mathematical induction
d. BIBO stability

17. In mathematics, the _____ of two positive real numbers x and y is defined as follows:

First compute the arithmetic mean of x and y and call it a_1. Next compute the geometric mean of x and y and call it g_1; this is the square root of the product xy:

$$a_1 = \frac{x+y}{2}$$

$$g_1 = \sqrt{xy}.$$

Then iterate this operation with a_1 taking the place of x and g_1 taking the place of y. In this way, two sequences (a_n) and (g_n) are defined:

$$a_{n+1} = \frac{a_n + g_n}{2}$$

$$g_{n+1} = \sqrt{a_n g_n}.$$

These two sequences converge to the same number, which is the _____ of x and y; it is denoted by M(x, y), or sometimes by agm(x, y.)

a. ACTRAN
c. ALGOR
b. Arithmetic-geometric mean
d. AUSM

18. In mathematics, a _____ is an expression such as

Chapter 12. Infinite Sequences and Series

$$x = a_0 + \cfrac{1}{a_1 + \cfrac{1}{a_2 + \cfrac{1}{a_3 + \cfrac{1}{\ddots}}}}$$

where a_0 is an integer and all the other numbers a_i ($i \neq 0$) are positive integers. Longer expressions are defined analogously. If the partial numerators and partial denominators are allowed to assume arbitrary values, which may in some contexts include functions, the resulting expression is a generalized _____.

a. Stern-Brocot tree
c. Periodic continued fraction
b. Restricted partial quotients
d. Continued fraction

19. In probability theory and statistics, the _____ (or expectation value or mean and for continuous random variables with a density function it is the probability density -weighted integral of the possible values.

The term '_____' can be misleading.

a. ACTRAN
c. Expected value
b. ALGOR
d. AUSM

20. The largest and the smallest element of a set are called extreme values, absolute extrema, or extreme records.

For a differentiable function f, if $f(x_0)$ is an _____ for the set of all values f(x), and if x_0 is in the interior of the domain of f, then x_0 is a critical point, by Fermat's theorem.

In the case of a general partial order one should not confuse a least element (smaller than all other) and a minimal element (nothing is smaller.)

a. Infinitesimal
c. Extreme Value Theorem
b. Integration by substitution
d. Extreme Value

21. In calculus, the _____ states that if a real-valued function f is continuous in the closed and bounded interval [a,b], then f must attain its maximum and minimum value, each at least once. That is, there exist numbers c and d in [a,b] such that:

$$f(c) \geq f(x) \geq f(d) \quad \text{for all } x \in [a, b].$$

A related theorem is the boundedness theorem which states that a continuous function f in the closed interval [a,b] is bounded on that interval. That is, there exist real numbers m and M such that:

$$m \leq f(x) \leq M \quad \text{for all } x \in [a, b].$$

The _____ enriches the boundedness theorem by saying that not only is the function bounded, but it also attains its least upper bound as its maximum and its greatest lower bound as its minimum.

- a. Extreme Value Theorem
- b. Integral of secant cubed
- c. Infinitesimal
- d. Uniform convergence

22. Cantor defined two kinds of _____ numbers, the ordinal numbers and the cardinal numbers. Ordinal numbers may be identified with well-ordered sets, or counting carried on to any stopping point, including points after an _____ number have already been counted. Generalizing finite and the ordinary _____ sequences which are maps from the positive integers leads to mappings from ordinal numbers, and transfinite sequences.
- a. AUSM
- b. Infinite
- c. ACTRAN
- d. ALGOR

23. In mathematics, a _____ is an infinite series that is not convergent, meaning that the infinite sequence of the partial sums of the series does not have a limit.

If a series converges, the individual terms of the series must approach zero. Thus any series in which the individual terms do not approach zero diverges.

- a. BIBO stability
- b. BDDC
- c. 15 theorem
- d. Divergent series

24. In mathematics, a _____ is a series with a constant ratio between successive terms. For example, the series

$$\frac{1}{2} + \frac{1}{4} + \frac{1}{8} + \frac{1}{16} + \cdots$$

is geometric, because each term is equal to half of the previous term. The sum of this series is 1, as illustrated in the following picture:

_____ are one of the simplest examples of infinite series with finite sums.

- a. Telescoping series
- b. Sequence transformation
- c. Converge absolutely
- d. Geometric series

25. Call S_N the _____ to N of the sequence {a_n}, or _____ of the series. A series is the sequence of partial sums, {S_N}.

Chapter 12. Infinite Sequences and Series

When talking about series, one can refer either to the sequence {S$_N$} of the partial sums, or to the sum of the series,

$$\sum_{n=0}^{\infty} a_n$$

i.e., the limit of the sequence of partial sums - it is clear which one is meant from context.

- a. Periodic function
- b. Partial sum
- c. Root test
- d. Minimum

26. In mathematics, a _____ (or direction field) is a graphical representation of the solutions of a first-order differential equation. It is achieved without solving the differential equation analytically, and thence it is useful. The representation may be used to qualitatively visualise solutions, or to numerically approximate them.
    - a. Fresnel integrals
    - b. The Method of Mechanical Theorems
    - c. Slope field
    - d. Standard part function

27. A plane curve is a curve for which X is the Euclidean plane -- these are the examples first encountered -- or in some cases the projective plane. A _____ is a curve for which X is of three dimensions, usually Euclidean space; a skew curve is a _____ which lies in no plane. These definitions also apply to algebraic curves
    - a. Folium of Descartes
    - b. Hypocycloid
    - c. Curtate cycloid
    - d. Space curve

28. A _____ is perfectly round geometrical object in three-dimensional space, such as the shape of a round ball. Like a circle in two dimensions, a perfect _____ is completely symmetrical around its center, with all points on the surface lying the same distance r from the center point. This distance r is known as the radius of the _____.
    - a. Differentiable manifold
    - b. Minimal surface
    - c. Tortuosity
    - d. Sphere

29. In mathematics, a (topological) _____ is defined as follows: let I be an interval of real numbers (i.e. a non-empty connected subset of $\mathbb{R}$); then a _____ γ is a continuous mapping $\gamma : I \to X$, where X is a topological space. The _____ γ is said to be simple if it is injective, i.e. if for all x, y in I, we have $\gamma(x) = \gamma(y) \implies x = y$. If I is a closed bounded interval $[a, b]$, we also allow the possibility $\gamma(a) = \gamma(b)$ (this convention makes it possible to talk about closed simple _____.)
    - a. Closed curve
    - b. Prolate cycloid
    - c. Tractrix
    - d. Curve

30. The terms of the series are often produced according to a certain rule, such as by a formula, by an algorithm, by a sequence of measurements, or even by a random number generator. As there are an infinite number of terms, this notion is often called an _____. Unlike finite summations, series need tools from mathematical analysis to be fully understood and manipulated.

a. Infinite series
b. Extreme Value Theorem
c. Integration by substitution
d. Extreme value

31. In a totally ordered set all elements are mutually comparable, so such a set can have at most one minimal element and at most one maximal element. Then, due to mutual comparability, the minimal element will also be the least element and the maximal element will also be the greatest element. Thus in a totally ordered set we can simply use the terms minimum and _____.

a. Dirichlet integral
b. Hyperbolic angle
c. Complex analysis
d. Maximum

32. In a totally ordered set all elements are mutually comparable, so such a set can have at most one minimal element and at most one maximal element. Then, due to mutual comparability, the minimal element will also be the least element and the maximal element will also be the greatest element. Thus in a totally ordered set we can simply use the terms _____ and maximum.

a. Calculus controversy
b. Periodic function
c. Taylor's theorem
d. Minimum

33. In acoustics and telecommunication, a _____ of a wave is a component frequency of the signal that is an integer multiple of the fundamental frequency. For example, if the fundamental frequency is f, the harmonics have frequencies f, 2f, 3f, 4f, etc. The harmonics have the property that they are all periodic at the fundamental frequency, therefore the sum of harmonics is also periodic at that frequency.

a. 15 theorem
b. BDDC
c. BIBO stability
d. Harmonic

34. In mathematics, the _____ is the infinite series

$$\sum_{k=1}^{\infty} \frac{1}{k} = 1 + \frac{1}{2} + \frac{1}{3} + \frac{1}{4} + \cdots.$$

Its name derives from the concept of overtones, or harmonics, in music: the wavelengths of the overtones of a vibrating string are 1/2, 1/3, 1/4, etc., of the string's fundamental wavelength. Every term of the series after the first is the harmonic mean of the neighboring terms; the term harmonic mean likewise derives from music.

The _____ diverges to infinity, albeit rather slowly (the first 10^{43} terms sum to less than 100 .)

a. BDDC
b. Harmonic series
c. 15 theorem
d. BIBO stability

35. In mathematics, a _____ is an informal expression referring to a series whose sum can be found by exploiting the circumstance that nearly every term cancels with either a succeeding or preceding term. Such a technique is also known as the method of differences.

For example, the series

$$\sum_{n=1}^{\infty} \frac{1}{n(n+1)}$$

simplifies as

$$\sum_{n=1}^{\infty} \frac{1}{n(n+1)} = \sum_{n=1}^{\infty} \left(\frac{1}{n} - \frac{1}{n+1}\right)$$

$$= \left(1 - \frac{1}{2}\right) + \left(\frac{1}{2} - \frac{1}{3}\right) + \cdots$$

$$= 1 + \left(-\frac{1}{2} + \frac{1}{2}\right) + \left(-\frac{1}{3} + \frac{1}{3}\right) + \cdots = 1.$$

Although telescoping can be a useful technique, there are pitfalls to watch out for:

$$0 = \sum_{n=1}^{\infty} 0 = \sum_{n=1}^{\infty} (1-1) = 1 + \sum_{n=1}^{\infty} (-1+1) = 1$$

is not correct because regrouping of terms is invalid unless the individual terms converge to 0; see Grandi's series.

a. Telescoping series
b. Geometric series
c. Sequence transformation
d. Converge absolutely

36. In mathematics, the nth term _____ is a simple test for the divergence of an infinite series:

- If $\lim_{n \to \infty} a_n \neq 0$ or if the limit does not exist, then $\sum_{n=1}^{\infty} a_n$ diverges.

Many authors do not name this test or give it a shorter name.

Unlike stronger convergence tests, the term test cannot prove by itself that a series converges. In particular, the converse to the test is not true; instead all one can say is:

- If $\lim_{n \to \infty} a_n = 0$, then $\sum_{n=1}^{\infty} a_n$ may or may not converge. In other words, if $\lim_{n \to \infty} a_n = 0$, the test is inconclusive.

The harmonic series is a classic example of a divergent series whose terms limit to zero. The more general class of p-series,

$$\sum_{n=1}^{\infty} \frac{1}{n^p},$$

exemplifies the possible results of the test:

- If p ≤ 0, then the term test identifies the series as divergent.
- If 0 < p ≤ 1, then the term test is inconclusive, but the series is divergent by the integral test for convergence.
- If 1 < p, then the term test is inconclusive, but the series is convergent, again by the integral test for convergence.

The test is typically proved in contrapositive form:

- If $\sum_{n=1}^{\infty} a_n$ converges, then $\lim_{n \to \infty} a_n = 0.$

If s_n are the partial sums of the series, then the assumption that the series converges means that

$$\lim_{n \to \infty} s_n = s$$

for some number s. Then

$$\lim_{n \to \infty} a_n = \lim_{n \to \infty} (s_n - s_{n-1}) = s - s = 0.$$

The assumption that the series converges means that it passes Cauchy's convergence test: for every $\varepsilon > 0$ there is a number N such that

$$|a_{n+1} + a_{n+2} + \ldots + a_{n+p}| < \varepsilon$$

holds for all n > N and p ≥ 1. Setting p = 1 recovers the definition of the statement

$$\lim_{n \to \infty} a_n = 0.$$

The simplest version of the term test applies to infinite series of real numbers.

Chapter 12. Infinite Sequences and Series

a. First derivative test
b. Visual Calculus
c. Nth term
d. Test for Divergence

37. In mathematics, a _____ (in one variable) is an infinite series of the form

$$f(x) = \sum_{n=0}^{\infty} a_n (x - c)^n = a_0 + a_1(x - c)^1 + a_2(x - c)^2 + a_3(x - c)^3 + \cdots$$

where a_n represents the coefficient of the nth term, c is a constant, and x varies around c (for this reason one sometimes speaks of the series as being centered at c

In many situations c is equal to zero, for instance when considering a Maclaurin series.

a. Caccioppoli set
b. Mountain pass theorem
c. Power series
d. Differential calculus

38. In mathematics, the _____, introduced by German mathematician Georg Cantor in 1883 (but discovered in 1875 by Henry John Stephen Smith), is a set of points lying on a single line segment that has a number of remarkable and deep properties. Through consideration of it, Cantor and others helped lay the foundations of modern general topology. Although Cantor himself defined the set in a general, abstract way, the most common modern construction is the Cantor ternary set, built by removing the middle thirds of a line segment.

a. 15 theorem
b. Cantor set
c. Planar Lamina
d. BDDC

39. The _____ is a plane fractal first described by Waclaw Sierpinski in 1916. The carpet is a generalization of the Cantor set to two dimensions (another is Cantor dust.) Sierpinski demonstrated that this fractal is a universal curve, in that any possible one-dimensional graph, projected onto the two-dimensional plane, is homeomorphic to a subset of the _____.

a. BDDC
b. Siegel disc
c. 15 theorem
d. Sierpinski carpet

40. In mathematics, an _____ is an infinite series of the form

$$\sum_{n=0}^{\infty} (-1)^n a_n,$$

with $a_n \geq 0$ (or $a_n \leq 0$) for all n. A finite sum of this kind is an alternating sum. An _____ converges if the terms a_n converge to 0 monotonically.

a. Uniform convergence
b. Extreme value
c. Infinite series
d. Alternating Series

41. The _____ converges:

$$\sum_{k=1}^{\infty} \frac{(-1)^{k+1}}{k} = 1 - \frac{1}{2} + \frac{1}{3} - \frac{1}{4} + \cdots = \ln 2 = 0.693\,147\,180\ldots.$$

This equality is a consequence of the Mercator series, the Taylor series for the natural logarithm. Another equality, similar in form to Mercator's series, is:

$$\sum_{k=0}^{\infty} \frac{(-1)^k}{2k+1} = 1 - \frac{1}{3} + \frac{1}{5} - \frac{1}{7} + \cdots = \arctan(1) = \frac{\pi}{4}.$$

This is a consequence of the Taylor series representation of the inverse tangent function (which has a radius of convergence of 1.)

The nth partial sum of the diverging harmonic series,

$$H_n = \sum_{k=1}^{n} \frac{1}{k},$$

is called the nth harmonic number.

a. ACTRAN
b. ALGOR
c. AUSM
d. Alternating harmonic series

42. In calculus, a branch of mathematics, the _____ is a measurement of how a function changes when its input changes. Loosely speaking, a _____ can be thought of as how much a quantity is changing at some given point. For example, the _____ of the position (or distance) of a vehicle with respect to time is the instantaneous velocity (respectively, instantaneous speed) at which the vehicle is traveling.

The process of finding a _____ is called differentiation. The fundamental theorem of calculus states that differentiation is the reverse process to integration.

a. Derivative
b. Mountain pass theorem
c. Ramp function
d. Concave upwards

43. In mathematics, a series or integral is said to be _____ if it converges, but it does not converge absolutely.

More precisely, a series $\sum_{n=0}^{\infty} a_n$ is said to converge conditionally if $\lim_{m \to \infty} \sum_{n=0}^{m} a_n$ exists and is a finite number (not ∞ or −∞), but $\sum_{n=0}^{\infty} |a_n| = \infty$.

A classical example is given by

$$1 - \frac{1}{2} + \frac{1}{3} - \frac{1}{4} + \frac{1}{5} - \cdots = \sum_{n=1}^{\infty} \frac{(-1)^{n+1}}{n}$$

which converges to ln 2 , but is not absolutely convergent

The simplest examples of _____ series (including the one above) are the alternating series.

a. Geometric series
b. Telescoping series
c. Conditionally convergent
d. Converge absolutely

44. In mathematics, a series (or sometimes also an integral) is said to _____ if the sum (or integral) of the absolute value of the summand or integrand is finite.

More precisely, a real or complex-valued series $\sum_{n=0}^{\infty} a_n$ is said to _____ if $\sum_{n=0}^{\infty} |a_n| < \infty$.

Absolute convergence is vitally important to the study of infinite series because on the one hand, it is strong enough that such series retain certain basic properties of finite sums -- the most important ones being rearrangement of the terms and convergence of products of two infinite series -- that are unfortunately not possessed by all convergent series. On the other hand absolute convergence is weak enough to occur very often in practice.

a. Converge absolutely
b. Sequence transformation
c. Geometric series
d. Telescoping series

45. A _____ is an expression which compares quantities relative to each other. The most common examples involve two quantities, but in theory any number of quantities can be compared. In mathematical terms, they are represented by separating each quantity with a colon, for example the _____ 2:3, which is read as the _____ 'two to three'.
a. Sequence
b. Ratio
c. BDDC
d. 15 theorem

46. In mathematics, the _____ is a criterion for the convergence (a convergence test) of an infinite series

$$\sum_{n=1}^{\infty} a_n.$$

It is particularly useful in connection with power series.

The _____ was developed first by Cauchy and so is sometimes known as the Cauchy _____ or Cauchy's radical test.
The _____ uses the number

$$C = \limsup_{n \to \infty} \sqrt[n]{|a_n|},$$

where 'lim sup' denotes the limit superior, possibly ∞.

a. Dirichlet integral
c. Related rates
b. Binomial series
d. Root Test

47. In mathematics, a _____ is a constant multiplicative factor of a certain object. For example, in the expression 9x², the _____ of x² is 9.

The object can be such things as a variable, a vector, a function, etc.

a. Leading coefficient
c. Coefficient
b. Difference polynomial
d. Degree of the polynomial

48. Trigonometry is a branch of mathematics that deals with triangles, particularly those plane triangles in which one angle has 90 degrees (right triangles.) Trigonometry deals with relationships between the sides and the angles of triangles and with the _____ functions, which describe those relationships.

Trigonometry has applications in both pure mathematics and in applied mathematics, where it is essential in many branches of science and technology.

a. Trigonometric functions
c. Trigonometric integrals
b. 15 theorem
d. Trigonometric

49. In mathematics, a _____ is any series of the form:

$$\frac{1}{2}A_o + \sum_{n=1}^{\infty}(A_n \cos nx + B_n \sin nx).$$

It is called a Fourier series when the terms A_n and B_n have the form:

$$A_n = \frac{1}{\pi}\int_0^{2\pi} f(x) \cos nx\, dx \qquad (n = 0, 1, 2, \ldots)$$

$$B_n = \frac{1}{\pi}\int_0^{2\pi} f(x) \sin nx\, dx \qquad (n = 1, 2, 3, \ldots)$$

where f is an integrable function.

It is not that case that every _____ is a Fourier Series. A particular question of interest is given a _____, for which values of x does the series converge.

a. Nash-Moser theorem
b. P-Laplacian
c. Trigonometric series
d. Palais-Smale compactness condition

50. In mathematics, _____, first defined by the mathematician Daniel Bernoulli and generalized by Friedrich Bessel, are canonical solutions y(x) of Bessel's differential equation:

$$x^2 \frac{d^2y}{dx^2} + x\frac{dy}{dx} + (x^2 - \alpha^2)y = 0$$

for an arbitrary real or complex number α (the order of the Bessel function.) The most common and important special case is where α is an integer n.

Although α and −α produce the same differential equation, it is conventional to define different _____ for these two orders (e.g., so that the _____ are mostly smooth functions of α.)

a. Logarithmic integral function
b. Multiplication theorem
c. 15 theorem
d. Bessel functions

51. In mathematics, the _____ of a power series is a non-negative quantity, either a real number or ∞, that represents a domain (within the radius) in which the series will converge. Within the _____, a power series converges absolutely and uniformly on compacta as well. If the series converges, it is the Taylor series of the analytic function to which it converges inside its _____.

a. Motor variable
b. Principal values
c. Movable singularity
d. Radius of convergence

52. A _____ is a model used within physics to explain how gravity exists in the universe. In its original concept, gravity was a force between point masses. Following Newton, Laplace attempted to model gravity as some kind of radiation field or fluid, and since the 19th century explanations for gravity have usually been sought in terms of a field model, rather than a point attraction.

a. BDDC
b. BIBO stability
c. 15 theorem
d. Gravitational field

53. Continuous functions are of utmost importance in mathematics and applications. However, not all functions are continuous. If a function is not continuous at a point in its domain, one says that it has a _____ there. The set of all points of _____ of a function may be a discrete set, a dense set, or even the entire domain of the function.

a. BDDC
b. Discontinuity
c. 15 theorem
d. BIBO stability

54. In mathematics, the _____ is a representation of a function as an infinite sum of terms calculated from the values of its derivatives at a single point. It may be regarded as the limit of the Taylor polynomials. If the series is centered at zero, the series is also called a Maclaurin series.

a. BIBO stability
b. BDDC
c. 15 theorem
d. Taylor series

55. In geometry, a _____ is a three-dimensional figure formed by six parallelograms. It is to a parallelogram as a cube is to a square: Euclidean geometry supports all four notions but affine geometry admits only parallelograms and parallelepipeds. Three equivalent definitions of _____ are

- a polyhedron with six faces (hexahedron), each of which is a parallelogram,
- a hexahedron with three pairs of parallel faces, and
- a prism of which the base is a parallelogram.

The cuboid (six rectangular faces), cube (six square faces), and the rhombohedron (six rhombus faces) are all specific cases of _____.

Parallelepipeds are a subclass of the prismatoids.

a. Parallelepiped
b. 15 theorem
c. BIBO stability
d. BDDC

56. In calculus, _____ gives a sequence of approximations of a differentiable function around a given point by polynomials (the Taylor polynomials of that function) whose coefficients depend only on the derivatives of the function at that point. The theorem also gives precise estimates on the size of the error in the approximation. The theorem is named after the mathematician Brook Taylor, who stated it in 1712, though the result was first discovered 41 years earlier in 1671 by James Gregory.

a. Taylor's theorem
b. Continuous function
c. Leibniz differential
d. Complex analysis

57. In elementary algebra, a _____ is a polynomial with two terms--the sum of two monomials--often bound by parenthesis or brackets when operated upon. It is the simplest kind of polynomial other than monomials.

- The _____ $a^2 - b^2$ can be factored as the product of two other binomials:

    $a^2 - b^2 = (a + b)(a - b.)$

    This is a special case of the more general formula:

    $$a^{n+1} - b^{n+1} = (a - b) \sum_{k=0}^{n} a^k b^{n-k}$$

- The product of a pair of linear binomials (ax + b) and (cx + d) is:

    $(ax + b)(cx + d) = acx^2 + axd + bcx + bd.$

- A _____ raised to the nth power, represented as

    $(a + b)^n$

    can be expanded by means of the _____ theorem or, equivalently, using Pascal's triangle. Taking a simple example, the perfect square _____ $(p + q)^2$ can be found by squaring the first digit, adding twice the product of the first and second digit and finally adding the square of the second digit, to give $p^2 + 2pq + q^2$.

a. Partial fractions
b. Multinomial theorem
c. Completing the square
d. Binomial

58. In mathematics, the _____ is an important formula giving the expansion of powers of sums. Its simplest version states that

$$(x + y)^n = \sum_{k=0}^{n} \binom{n}{k} x^{n-k} y^k \qquad (1)$$

for any real or complex numbers x and y, and any non-negative integer n. The binomial coefficient appearing in (1) may be defined in terms of the factorial function n!:

$$\binom{n}{k} = \frac{n!}{k!\,(n-k)!}.$$

For example, here are the cases where 2 ≤ n ≤ 5:

$$(x+y)^2 = x^2 + 2xy + y^2$$
$$(x+y)^3 = x^3 + 3x^2y + 3xy^2 + y^3$$
$$(x+y)^4 = x^4 + 4x^3y + 6x^2y^2 + 4xy^3 + y^4$$
$$(x+y)^5 = x^5 + 5x^4y + 10x^3y^2 + 10x^2y^3 + 5xy^4 + y^5.$$

Formula (1) is valid more generally for any elements x and y of a semiring as long as xy = yx.

a. Binomial Theorem
b. Stirling transform
c. Lah numbers
d. Trinomial expansion

59. In mathematics, the _____ generalizes the purely algebraic formula of the binomial theorem to complex values of α. It is also a special case of a Newton series. The _____ is the series

$$(1+x)^\alpha = \sum_{k=0}^{\infty} \binom{\alpha}{k} x^k = \sum_{k=0}^{\infty} \frac{\prod_{a=0}^{k-1}(\alpha - a)\, x^k}{k!}$$

where α is a complex number and

$$\binom{\alpha}{k} = \frac{\alpha(\alpha-1)(\alpha-2)\cdots(\alpha-k+1)}{k!}$$

is the (generalized) binomial coefficient (if α is a non negative integer, then the (α + 1) th term and all later terms in the series are zero, since each one contains a factor equal to (α − α): thus, in that case, the summation reduces to the algebraic binomial formula.)

a. Taylor's theorem
b. Leibniz formula
c. Fundamental Theorem of Calculus
d. Binomial series

60. The _____ is a function in mathematics. The application of this function to a value x is written as exp(x). Equivalently, this can be written in the form e^x, where e is a mathematical constant, the base of the natural logarithm, which equals approximately 2.718281828, and is also known as Euler's number.

a. ACTRAN
b. Area hyperbolic functions
c. Integral part
d. Exponential function

Chapter 13. Vectors and the Geometry of Space

1. In mathematics and its applications, a _____ system is a system for assigning an n-tuple of numbers or scalars to each point in an n-dimensional space. This concept is part of the theory of manifolds. 'Scalars' in many cases means real numbers, but, depending on context, can mean complex numbers or elements of some other commutative ring.
   a. Spherical coordinate system
   b. 15 theorem
   c. Cylindrical coordinate system
   d. Coordinate

2. In mathematics a _____ is a construction in vector calculus which associates a vector to every point in a (locally) Euclidean space.

   Vector fields are often used in physics to model, for example, the speed and direction of a moving fluid throughout space, or the strength and direction of some force, such as the magnetic or gravitational force, as it changes from point to point.

   In the rigorous mathematical treatment, (tangent) vector fields are defined on manifolds as sections of a manifold's tangent bundle.

   a. 15 theorem
   b. BIBO stability
   c. BDDC
   d. Vector field

3. In mathematics, the _____ is used to determine each point uniquely in a plane through two numbers, usually called the x-coordinate or abscissa and the y-coordinate or ordinate of the point. To define the coordinates, two perpendicular directed lines, are specified, as well as the unit length, which is marked off on the two axes Cartesian coordinate systems are also used in space and in higher dimensions.
   a. Cartesian coordinate system
   b. Coordinate
   c. 15 theorem
   d. Spherical coordinate system

4. In mathematics, the _____ is a conic section, the intersection of a right circular conical surface and a plane parallel to a generating straight line of that surface. Given a point (the focus) and a line (the directrix) that lie in a plane, the locus of points in that plane that are equidistant to them is a _____.

   A particular case arises when the plane is tangent to the conical surface of a circle.

   a. BIBO stability
   b. 15 theorem
   c. BDDC
   d. Parabola

5. In mathematics, _____ and minima, known collectively as extrema, are the largest value (maximum) or smallest value (minimum), that a function takes in a point either within a given neighbourhood (local extremum) or on the function domain in its entirety (global extremum.)

   Throughout, a point refers to an input (x), while a value refers to an output (y): one distinguishing between the maximum value and the point (or points) at which it occurs.

   A real-valued function f defined on the real line is said to have a local maximum point at the point x^*, if there exists some $\varepsilon > 0$, such that $f(x^*) \geq f(x)$ when $|x - x^*| < \varepsilon$.

a. Fundamental Theorem of Calculus
b. Partial sum
c. Standard part function
d. Maxima

6. A _____ is perfectly round geometrical object in three-dimensional space, such as the shape of a round ball. Like a circle in two dimensions, a perfect _____ is completely symmetrical around its center, with all points on the surface lying the same distance r from the center point. This distance r is known as the radius of the _____.
   a. Sphere
   b. Tortuosity
   c. Differentiable manifold
   d. Minimal surface

7. In mathematics, a _____ (or direction field) is a graphical representation of the solutions of a first-order differential equation. It is achieved without solving the differential equation analytically, and thence it is useful. The representation may be used to qualitatively visualise solutions, or to numerically approximate them.
   a. The Method of Mechanical Theorems
   b. Standard part function
   c. Fresnel integrals
   d. Slope field

8. In linear algebra, the null vector or _____ is the vector (0, 0, â€¦, 0) in Euclidean space, all of whose components are zero. It is usually written $\vec{0}$ or 0 or simply 0. A _____ has no direction.
   a. Dot product
   b. Scalar multiplication
   c. Direction vector
   d. Zero vector

9. In mathematics, a (topological) _____ is defined as follows: let I be an interval of real numbers (i.e. a non-empty connected subset of $\mathbb{R}$); then a _____ γ is a continuous mapping $\gamma : I \to X$, where X is a topological space. The _____ γ is said to be simple if it is injective, i.e. if for all x, y in I, we have $\gamma(x) = \gamma(y) \implies x = y$. If I is a closed bounded interval $[a, b]$, we also allow the possibility $\gamma(a) = \gamma(b)$ (this convention makes it possible to talk about closed simple _____.)
   a. Closed curve
   b. Tractrix
   c. Prolate cycloid
   d. Curve

10. In physics, _____ is defined as the rate of change of position. it is vector physical quantity; both speed and direction are required to define it. In the SI (metric) system, it is measured in meters per second: (m/s) or ms^{-1}.
    a. BDDC
    b. BIBO stability
    c. Velocity
    d. 15 theorem

11. Determining the _____ segment -- also called rectification of a curve -- was historically difficult. Although many methods were used for specific curves, the advent of calculus led to a general formula that provides closed-form solutions in some cases.

A curve in, say, the plane can be approximated by connecting a finite number of points on the curve using line segments to create a polygonal path. Since it is straightforward to calculate the length of each linear segment (using the theorem of Pythagoras in Euclidean space, for example), the total length of the approximation can be found by summing the lengths of each linear segment.

   a. Surface of revolution
   b. Nonelementary integral
   c. Riemann sum
   d. Length of an irregular arc

12. The _____ is an important second-order linear partial differential equation that describes the propagation of a variety of waves, such as sound waves, light waves and water waves. It arises in fields such as acoustics, electromagnetics, and fluid dynamics. Historically, the problem of a vibrating string such as that of a musical instrument was studied by Jean le Rond d'Alembert, Leonhard Euler, Daniel Bernoulli, and Joseph-Louis Lagrange.
   a. Klein-Gordon equation
   b. Dirac equation
   c. Wave equation
   d. Moment of Inertia

13. In vector calculus, there are two ways of multiplying three vectors together, to make a _____ of vectors. Three vectors defining a parallelepiped

The scalar _____ is defined as the dot product of one of the vectors with the cross product of the other two.

Geometrically, the scalar _____

$$\mathbf{a} \cdot (\mathbf{b} \times \mathbf{c})$$

is the (signed) volume of the parallelepiped defined by the three vectors given.

   a. Triple product
   b. Divergence
   c. Gradient theorem
   d. Divergence Theorem

14. In mathematics, a _____ in a normed vector space is a vector (often a spatial vector) whose length is 1 (the unit length.) A _____ is often denoted by a lowercase letter with a superscribed caret or e;hate;, like this: $\hat{\imath}$.

In Euclidean space, the dot product of two unit vectors is simply the cosine of the angle between them.

   a. ACTRAN
   b. Overdetermined
   c. Unit vector
   d. ALGOR

15. The line x = a is a _____ of a curve y=f(x) if at least one of the following statements is true:

1. $\lim_{x \to a} f(x) = \pm \infty$
2. $\lim_{x \to a^-} f(x) = \pm \infty$
3. $\lim_{x \to a^+} f(x) = \pm \infty$

Intuitively, if x = a is an asymptote of f, then, if we imagine x approaching a from one side, the value of f(x) grows without bound; i.e., f(x) becomes large (positively or negatively), and, in fact, becomes larger than any finite value.

Note that f(x) may or may not be defined at a: what the function is doing precisely at x = a does not affect the asymptote. For example, consider the function

$$f(x) = \begin{cases} \frac{1}{x} & \text{if } x > 0, \\ 5 & \text{if } x \leq 0 \end{cases}$$

As $\lim_{x \to 0+} f(x) = \infty$, f(x) has a _____ at 0, even though f(0) = 5.

Another example is $f(x) = 1/(x-1)$ which has a _____ of x=1 as shown by the limit

$$\lim_{x \to 1+} \frac{1}{x-1} = \infty$$

In the graph of $f(x) = x + \frac{1}{x}$, the y-axis (x = 0) and the line y = x are both asymptotes.

When a linear asymptote is not parallel to the x- or y-axis, it is called either an oblique asymptote or equivalently a slant asymptote.

    a. Vertical asymptote   b. Geometric function theory
    c. Fractional calculus   d. Semi-differentiability

16. In mathematics, the _____ , is the curve defined as follows.

Starting with a fixed circle, a point O on the circle is chosen. For any other point A on the circle, the secant line OA is drawn. The point M is diametrically opposite O. The line OA intersects the tangent at M at the point N. The line parallel to OM through N, and the line perpendicular to OM through A intersect at P. As the point A is varied, the path of P is the witch.

    a. Cochleoid   b. Witch of Agnesi
    c. Closed curve   d. Folium of Descartes

17. An _____ of a real-valued function y = f(x) is a curve which describes the behavior of f as either x or y tends to infinity.

In other words, as one moves along the graph of f(x) in some direction, the distance between it and the _____ eventually becomes smaller than any distance that one may specify.

    a. AUSM   b. ACTRAN
    c. Asymptote   d. ALGOR

18. In mathematics, the _____ of two monic polynomials P and Q over a field k is defined as the product

$$\operatorname{res}(P,Q) = \prod_{(x,y):\, P(x)=0,\, Q(y)=0} (x-y),$$

of the differences of their roots, where x and y take on values in the algebraic closure of k. For non-monic polynomials with leading coefficients p and q, respectively, the above product is multiplied by

$$p^{\deg Q} q^{\deg P}.$$

- The _____ is the determinant of the Sylvester matrix (and of the Bezout matrix.)

- When Q is separable, the above product can be rewritten to

$$\operatorname{res}(P,Q) = \prod_{P(x)=0} Q(x)$$

and this expression remains unchanged if Q is reduced modulo P. Note that, when non-monic, this includes the factor $q^{\deg P}$ but still needs the factor $p^{\deg Q}$.

- Let $P' = P \mod Q$. The above idea can be continued by swapping the roles of P' and Q. However, P' has a set of roots different from that of P. This can be resolved by writing $\prod_{Q(y)=0} P'(y)$ as a determinant again, where P' has leading zero coefficients. This determinant can now be simplified by iterative expansion with respect to the column, where only the leading coefficient q of Q appears.

$$\operatorname{res}(P,Q) = q^{\deg P - \deg P'} \cdot \operatorname{res}(P',Q)$$

Continuing this procedure ends up in a variant of the Euclidean algorithm. This procedure needs quadratic runtime.

a. Leading coefficient
b. Resultant
c. Difference polynomial
d. Coefficient

19. A _____, $F_{net} = F_1 + F_2 + …$ (also known as a resultant force) is a vector produced when two or more forces { F_1, F_2, … } act upon a single object. It is calculated by vector addition of the force vectors acting upon the object. A _____ can also be defined as the overall force acting on an object, when all the individual forces acting on the object are added together.
   a. 15 theorem
   b. Net force
   c. BDDC
   d. BIBO stability

20. In mathematics, an _____ is an infinite series of the form

Chapter 13. Vectors and the Geometry of Space

$$\sum_{n=0}^{\infty} (-1)^n a_n,$$

with $a_n \geq 0$ (or $a_n \leq 0$) for all n. A finite sum of this kind is an alternating sum. An _____ converges if the terms a_n converge to 0 monotonically.

a. Extreme value
b. Alternating Series
c. Infinite series
d. Uniform convergence

21. In mathematics, the _____ is an operation which takes two vectors over the real numbers R and returns a real-valued scalar quantity. It is the standard inner product of the orthonormal Euclidean space. It contrasts with the cross product which produces a vector result.

a. Dot product
b. Vector-valued function
c. Homogeneous function
d. Direction vector

22. In mathematics, the _____ is a special function defined on the complex plane given the symbol Ei.

For real, nonzero values of x, the _____ Ei(x) can be defined as

$$\mathrm{Ei}(x) = \int_{-\infty}^{x} \frac{e^t}{t}\, dt.$$

The definition above can be used for positive values of x, but the integral has to be understood in terms of the Cauchy principal value, due to the singularity in the integrand at zero. For complex values of the argument, the definition becomes ambiguous due to branch points at 0 and ∞. In general, a branch cut is taken on the negative real axis and Ei can be defined by analytic continuation elsewhere on the complex plane.

a. Exponential sum
b. ACTRAN
c. ALGOR
d. Exponential integral

23. Integration is an important concept in mathematics, specifically in the field of calculus and, more broadly, mathematical analysis. Given a function f of a real variable x and an interval [a, b] of the real line, the _____

$$\int_a^b f(x)\, dx,$$

is defined informally to be the net signed area of the region in the xy-plane bounded by the graph of f, the x-axis, and the vertical lines x = a and x = b.

The term '_____' may also refer to the notion of antiderivative, a function F whose derivative is the given function f.

Chapter 13. Vectors and the Geometrq of Space

a. Indefinite integral
b. Integrand
c. Integral test for convergence
d. Integral

24. When a unit vector in space is expressed, with Cartesian notation, as a linear combination of i, j, k, its three scalar components can be referred to as '_____'. The value of each component is equal to the cosine of the angle formed by the unit vector with the respective basis vector. This is one of the methods used to describe the orientation (angular position) of a straight line, segment of straight line, oriented axis, or segment of oriented axis (vector.)

a. Direction cosines
b. Dot product
c. Vector-valued function
d. Zero vector

25. In mathematics, two vectors are _____ if they are perpendicular, i.e., they form a right angle. For example, a subway and the street above, although they do not physically intersect, are _____ if they cross at a right angle.

a. AUSM
b. ALGOR
c. ACTRAN
d. Orthogonal

26. _____ is a means of calculating the volume of a solid of revolution, when integrating along the axis of revolution. This method models the generated 3 dimensional shape as a 'stack' of an infinite number of disks of infinitesimal thickness. It is possible to use 'washers' instead of 'disks' (the washer method) to obtain 'hollow' solids of revolutions, and uses the same principles that underlie _____.

a. Multiple integral
b. Shell integration
c. Surface of revolution
d. Disk integration

27. In geometry, a _____ is a three-dimensional figure formed by six parallelograms. It is to a parallelogram as a cube is to a square: Euclidean geometry supports all four notions but affine geometry admits only parallelograms and parallelepipeds. Three equivalent definitions of _____ are

- a polyhedron with six faces (hexahedron), each of which is a parallelogram,
- a hexahedron with three pairs of parallel faces, and
- a prism of which the base is a parallelogram.

The cuboid (six rectangular faces), cube (six square faces), and the rhombohedron (six rhombus faces) are all specific cases of _____.

Parallelepipeds are a subclass of the prismatoids.

a. BIBO stability
b. 15 theorem
c. BDDC
d. Parallelepiped

28. _____ is the tendency of a force to rotate an object about an axis (or fulcrum or pivot.) Just as a force is a push or a pull, a _____ can be thought of as a twist. The symbol for _____ is τ, the Greek letter tau.

a. 15 theorem
b. BIBO stability
c. Torque
d. BDDC

29. In mathematics, _____ is the process of constructing new data points outside a discrete set of known data points. It is similar to the process of interpolation, which constructs new points between known points, but the results of extrapolations are often less meaningful, and are subject to greater uncertainty. Example illustration of the _____ problem, consisting of assigning a meaningful value at the blue box, at x = 7, given the red data points.

A sound choice of which _____ method to apply relies on a prior knowledge of the process that created the existing data points.

a. ALGOR
b. ACTRAN
c. AUSM
d. Extrapolation

30. A surface normal to a flat surface is a vector which is perpendicular to that surface. A normal to a non-flat surface at a point P on the surface is a vector perpendicular to the tangent plane to that surface at P. The word 'normal' is also used as an adjective: a line normal to a plane, the normal component of a force, the _____, etc. The concept of normality generalizes to orthogonality.

a. Normal vector
b. Paraboloid
c. Hyperbolic paraboloid
d. PDE surfaces

31. In numerical analysis, _____ constitutes a broad family of algorithms for calculating the numerical value of a definite integral, and by extension, the term is also sometimes used to describe the numerical solution of differential equations The term numerical quadrature is more or less a synonym for _____, especially as applied to one-dimensional integrals.

a. Galerkin methods
b. Multigrid method
c. Meshfree methods
d. Numerical integration

32. In geometry, a _____ is a special plane curve generated by the trace of a fixed point on a small circle that rolls within a larger circle. It is comparable to the cycloid but instead of the circle rolling along a line, it rolls within a circle. The red curve is a _____ traced as the smaller black circle rolls around inside the larger blue circle (parameters are R=3.0, r=1.0, and so k=3), giving a deltoid.

If the smaller circle has radius r, and the larger circle has radius R = kr, then the parametric equations for the curve can be given by either:

$$x(\theta) = (R-r)\cos\theta + r\cos\left(\frac{R-r}{r}\theta\right)$$
$$y(\theta) = (R-r)\sin\theta - r\sin\left(\frac{R-r}{r}\theta\right),$$

or:

$$x(\theta) = r(k-1)\cos\theta + r\cos((k-1)\theta)$$
$$y(\theta) = r(k-1)\sin\theta - r\sin((k-1)\theta).$$

Chapter 13. Vectors and the Geometry of Space

If k is an integer, then the curve is closed, and has k cusps (i.e., sharp corners, where the curve is not differentiable.)

  a. Hypocycloid
  b. Bullet-nose curve
  c. Closed curve
  d. Kappa curve

33. In mathematics, _____ are a method of defining a curve. A simple kinematical example is when one uses a time parameter to determine the position, velocity, and other information about a body in motion.

Abstractly, a relation is given in the form of an equation, and it is shown also to be the image of functions from items such as R^n.

  a. Differential operator
  b. Parametric equations
  c. Multivariable calculus
  d. Laplace operator

34. A _____ is an algebraic equation in which each term is either a constant or the product of a constant and (the first power of) a single variable. Linear equations can have one, two, three or more variables. Linear equations occur with great regularity in applied mathematics.
  a. Linear equation
  b. Cubic function
  c. 15 theorem
  d. BDDC

35. _____ is a term in geometry and in everyday life that refers to a property in Euclidean space of two or more lines or planes, or a combination of these. The existence and properties of parallel lines are the basis of Euclid's parallel postulate. Two lines parallel would be denoted as ABC DEF.
  a. BIBO stability
  b. 15 theorem
  c. BDDC
  d. Parallelism

36. A _____ is one of the most curvilinear basic geometric shapes:It has two faces, zero vertices, and zero edges. The surface formed by the points at a fixed distance from a given straight line, the axis of the _____. The solid enclosed by this surface and by two planes perpendicular to the axis is also called a _____.
  a. Cylinder
  b. BDDC
  c. Right circular cylinder
  d. 15 theorem

37. An _____ is a type of quadric surface that is a higher dimensional analogue of an ellipse. The equation of a standard axis-aligned _____ body in an xyz-Cartesian coordinate system is

$$\frac{x^2}{a^2} + \frac{y^2}{b^2} + \frac{z^2}{c^2} = 1$$

where a and b are the equatorial radii (along the x and y axes) and c is the polar radius (along the z-axis), all of which are fixed positive real numbers determining the shape of the _____.

More generally, a not-necessarily-axis-aligned _____ is defined by the equation

$$\mathbf{x}^T A \mathbf{x} = 1$$

where A is a symmetric positive definite matrix and x is a vector.

a. ACTRAN
b. ALGOR
c. AUSM
d. Ellipsoid

38. In mathematics, a _____ is a quadric surface of special kind. There are two kinds of paraboloids: elliptic and hyperbolic. The elliptic _____ is shaped like an oval cup and can have a maximum or minimum point.

a. Normal vector
b. Normal line
c. Parametric surface
d. Paraboloid

39. The _____ is a doubly ruled surface shaped like a saddle. In a suitable coordinate system, it can be represented by the equation

$$z = \frac{x^2}{a^2} - \frac{y^2}{b^2}.$$

This is a _____ that opens up along the x-axis and down along the y-axis.

Paraboloid of revolution

With a = b an elliptic paraboloid is a paraboloid of revolution: a surface obtained by revolving a parabola around its axis.

a. PDE surfaces
b. Prolate
c. Parametric surface
d. Hyperbolic paraboloid

40. In mathematics, a _____ is a constant multiplicative factor of a certain object. For example, in the expression $9x^2$, the _____ of x^2 is 9.

The object can be such things as a variable, a vector, a function, etc.

a. Degree of the polynomial
b. Leading coefficient
c. Difference polynomial
d. Coefficient

Chapter 14. Vector Functions

1. A _____ is a surface in the Euclidean space R^3 which is defined by a parametric equation with two parameters. Parametric representation is the most general way to specify a surface. Surfaces that occur in two of the main theorems of vector calculus, Stokes' theorem and divergence theorem, are frequently given in a parametric form.
   a. Normal line
   b. Paraboloid
   c. PDE surfaces
   d. Parametric surface

2. In economics, the _____ functional form of production functions is widely used to represent the relationship of an output to inputs. It was proposed by Knut Wicksell (1851-1926), and tested against statistical evidence by Charles Cobb and Paul Douglas in 1900-1928.

For production, the function is

$$Y = AL^{\alpha}K^{\beta},$$

where:

- Y = total production (the monetary value of all goods produced in a year)
- L = labor input
- K = capital input
- A = total factor productivity
- α and β are the output elasticities of labor and capital, respectively. These values are constants determined by available technology.

Output elasticity measures the responsiveness of output to a change in levels of either labor or capital used in production, ceteris paribus. For example if α = 0.15, a 1% increase in labor would lead to approximately a 0.15% increase in output.

   a. BDDC
   b. Cobb-Douglas
   c. 15 theorem
   d. BIBO stability

3. In mathematics, a (topological) _____ is defined as follows: let I be an interval of real numbers (i.e. a non-empty connected subset of $\mathbb{R}$); then a _____ γ is a continuous mapping $\gamma : I \to X$, where X is a topological space. The _____ γ is said to be simple if it is injective, i.e. if for all x, y in I, we have $\gamma(x) = \gamma(y) \implies x = y$. If I is a closed bounded interval $[a, b]$, we also allow the possibility $\gamma(a) = \gamma(b)$ (this convention makes it possible to talk about closed simple _____.)
   a. Prolate cycloid
   b. Tractrix
   c. Closed curve
   d. Curve

4. In acoustics and telecommunication, a _____ of a wave is a component frequency of the signal that is an integer multiple of the fundamental frequency. For example, if the fundamental frequency is f, the harmonics have frequencies f, 2f, 3f, 4f, etc. The harmonics have the property that they are all periodic at the fundamental frequency, therefore the sum of harmonics is also periodic at that frequency.
   a. BDDC
   b. BIBO stability
   c. 15 theorem
   d. Harmonic

5. In mathematics, mathematical physics and the theory of stochastic processes, a _____ is a twice continuously differentiable function f : U → R (where U is an open subset of Rⁿ) which satisfies Laplace's equation, i.e.

$$\frac{\partial^2 f}{\partial x_1^2} + \frac{\partial^2 f}{\partial x_2^2} + \cdots + \frac{\partial^2 f}{\partial x_n^2} = 0$$

everywhere on U. This is also often written as

$$\nabla^2 f = 0 \quad \text{or} \quad \Delta f = 0.$$

There also exists a seemingly weaker definition that is equivalent. Indeed a function is harmonic if and only if it is weakly harmonic.

Harmonic functions can be defined on an arbitrary Riemannian manifold, using the Laplace-de Rham operator Δ.

a. Harmonic function
b. Hilbert transform
c. Newtonian potential
d. Maximum principle

6. In mathematics, the concept of a '_____' is used to describe the behavior of a function as its argument or input either 'gets close' to some point, or as the argument becomes arbitrarily large; or the behavior of a sequence's elements as their index increases indefinitely. Limits are used in calculus and other branches of mathematical analysis to define derivatives and continuity.

In formulas, _____ is usually abbreviated as lim

a. BIBO stability
b. BDDC
c. 15 theorem
d. Limit

7. A plane curve is a curve for which X is the Euclidean plane -- these are the examples first encountered -- or in some cases the projective plane. A _____ is a curve for which X is of three dimensions, usually Euclidean space; a skew curve is a _____ which lies in no plane. These definitions also apply to algebraic curves

a. Hypocycloid
b. Folium of Descartes
c. Curtate cycloid
d. Space curve

8. A _____ is a mathematical function that maps real numbers to vectors. Vector-valued functions can be defined as:

- $\mathbf{r}(t) = f(t)\hat{\mathbf{i}} + g(t)\hat{\mathbf{j}}$ or
- $\mathbf{r}(t) = f(t)\hat{\mathbf{i}} + g(t)\hat{\mathbf{j}} + h(t)\hat{\mathbf{k}}$

where f(t), g(t) and h(t) are the coordinate functions of the parameter t, and $\hat{\mathbf{i}}, \hat{\mathbf{j}},$ and $\hat{\mathbf{k}}$ are unit vectors. r(t) is a vector which has its tail at the origin and its head at the coordinates evaluated by the function.

Chapter 14. Vector Functions

The vector shown in the graph to the right is the evaluation of the function near t=19.5 (between 6π and 6.5π; i.e., somewhat more than 3 rotations.)

- a. Zero vector
- b. Direction vector
- c. Vector-valued function
- d. Dot product

9. In mathematics, a _____ is a function which preserves the given order. This concept first arose in calculus, and was later generalized to the more abstract setting of order theory.

In calculus, a function f defined on a subset of the real numbers with real values is called monotonic (also monotonically increasing or non-decreasing), if for all x and y such that x >≤ y one has f(x) >≤ f(y), so f preserves the order.

- a. Pseudo-differential operator
- b. 15 theorem
- c. Pettis integral
- d. Monotonic function

10. In mathematics, _____ are a method of defining a curve. A simple kinematical example is when one uses a time parameter to determine the position, velocity, and other information about a body in motion.

Abstractly, a relation is given in the form of an equation, and it is shown also to be the image of functions from items such as R^n.

- a. Parametric equations
- b. Multivariable calculus
- c. Differential operator
- d. Laplace operator

11. In mathematics, a _____ is an ordered list of objects (or events). Like a set, it contains members (also called elements or terms), and the number of terms (possibly infinite) is called the length of the _____. Unlike a set, order matters, and the exact same elements can appear multiple times at different positions in the _____.

- a. BDDC
- b. Y-intercept
- c. Sequence
- d. 15 theorem

12. In geometry, a _____ is a special plane curve generated by the trace of a fixed point on a small circle that rolls within a larger circle. It is comparable to the cycloid but instead of the circle rolling along a line, it rolls within a circle. The red curve is a _____ traced as the smaller black circle rolls around inside the larger blue circle (parameters are R=3.0, r=1.0, and so k=3), giving a deltoid.

If the smaller circle has radius r, and the larger circle has radius R = kr, then the parametric equations for the curve can be given by either:

$$x(\theta) = (R-r)\cos\theta + r\cos\left(\frac{R-r}{r}\theta\right)$$
$$y(\theta) = (R-r)\sin\theta - r\sin\left(\frac{R-r}{r}\theta\right),$$

or:

$$x(\theta) = r(k-1)\cos\theta + r\cos((k-1)\theta)$$
$$y(\theta) = r(k-1)\sin\theta - r\sin((k-1)\theta).$$

If k is an integer, then the curve is closed, and has k cusps (i.e., sharp corners, where the curve is not differentiable.)

a. Closed curve
c. Kappa curve
b. Hypocycloid
d. Bullet-nose curve

13. A _____ is a special kind of space curve, i.e. a smooth curve in three-space. As a mental image of a _____ one may take the spring (although the spring is not a curve, and so is technically not a _____, it does give a convenient mental picture.) A _____ is characterised by the fact that the tangent line at any point makes a constant angle with a fixed line.

a. Helix
c. BIBO stability
b. 15 theorem
d. BDDC

14. In calculus, a branch of mathematics, the _____ is a measurement of how a function changes when its input changes. Loosely speaking, a _____ can be thought of as how much a quantity is changing at some given point. For example, the _____ of the position (or distance) of a vehicle with respect to time is the instantaneous velocity (respectively, instantaneous speed) at which the vehicle is traveling.

The process of finding a _____ is called differentiation. The fundamental theorem of calculus states that differentiation is the reverse process to integration.

a. Ramp function
c. Mountain pass theorem
b. Derivative
d. Concave upwards

15. In mathematics, an _____ is a generalization for the concept of a function in which the dependent variable has not been given 'explicitly' in terms of the independent variable. To give a function f explicitly is to provide a prescription for determining the output value of the function y in terms of the input value x:

y = f(x.)

By contrast, the function is implicit if the value of y is obtained from x by solving an equation of the form:

$$R(x,y) = 0.$$

a. Implicit function
c. Automatic differentiation
b. Ordinary differential equation
d. Implicit differentiation

16. In geometry, the _____ (or simply the tangent) to a curve at a given point is the straight line that 'just touches' the curve at that point (in the sense explained more precisely below.) As it passes through the point of tangency, the _____ is 'going in the same direction' as the curve, and in this sense it is the best straight-line approximation to the curve at that point. The same definition applies to space curves and curves in n-dimensional Euclidean space.

a. Tangent line
c. Sphere
b. Lie derivative
d. Minimal surface

17. The first Frenet vector $e_1(t)$ is the _____ in the same direction, defined at each regular point of γ:

$$\mathbf{e}_1(t) = \frac{\gamma'(t)}{\|\gamma'(t)\|}.$$

If t = s is the natural parameter then the tangent vector has unit length, so that the formula simplifies:

$$\mathbf{e}_1(s) = \gamma'(s).$$

The _____ determines the orientation of the curve, or the forward direction, corresponding to the increasing values of the parameter.

The normal vector, sometimes called the curvature vector, indicates the deviance of the curve from being a straight line.

It is defined as

$$\overline{\mathbf{e}_2}(t) = \gamma''(t) - \langle \gamma''(t), \mathbf{e}_1(t) \rangle \mathbf{e}_1(t).$$

Its normalized form, the unit normal vector, is the second Frenet vector $e_2(t)$ and defined as

$$\mathbf{e}_2(t) = \frac{\overline{\mathbf{e}_2}(t)}{\|\overline{\mathbf{e}_2}(t)\|}.$$

The tangent and the normal vector at point t define the osculating plane at point t.

a. Invariant differential operator
b. ACTRAN
c. Isothermal coordinates
d. Unit tangent vector

18. In physics, _____ is defined as the rate of change of position. it is vector physical quantity; both speed and direction are required to define it. In the SI (metric) system, it is measured in meters per second: (m/s) or ms^{-1}.
    a. Velocity
    b. BIBO stability
    c. 15 theorem
    d. BDDC

19. Let f be a differentiable function, and let f'(x) be its derivative. The derivative of f'(x) (if it has one) is written f''(x) and is called the _____ of f. Similarly, the derivative of a _____, if it exists, is written f'''(x) and is called the third derivative of f.
    a. Ramp function
    b. Stationary phase approximation
    c. Horizontal asymptote
    d. Second derivative

20. A _____ is a type of manifold that is locally similar enough to Euclidean space to allow one to do calculus Any manifold can be described by a collection of charts, also known as an atlas.
    a. Minimal surface
    b. Differentiable manifold
    c. Lie derivative
    d. Tortuosity

21. In mathematics, the _____ of a function y = f(x) is a function that, in some fashion, 'undoes' the effect of f The _____ of f is denoted f^{-1}. The statements y=f(x) and x=f^{-1}(y) are equivalent.
    a. ACTRAN
    b. ALGOR
    c. Inverse
    d. AUSM

22. Integration is an important concept in mathematics, specifically in the field of calculus and, more broadly, mathematical analysis. Given a function f of a real variable x and an interval [a, b] of the real line, the _____

$$\int_a^b f(x)\, dx,$$

is defined informally to be the net signed area of the region in the xy-plane bounded by the graph of f, the x-axis, and the vertical lines x = a and x = b.

The term '_____' may also refer to the notion of antiderivative, a function F whose derivative is the given function f.

a. Integrand
b. Integral test for convergence
c. Indefinite integral
d. Integral

23. For some curves there is a smallest number L that is an upper bound on the length of any polygonal approximation. If such a number exists, then the curve is said to be rectifiable and the curve is defined to have _____ L.

Let C be a curve in Euclidean (or, generally, a metric) space X = R^n, so C is the image of a continuous function f : [a, b] → X of the interval [a, b] into X.

Chapter 14. Vector Functions

a. Integration by parametric derivatives
c. Arc length
b. Integrand
d. Order of integration

24. Determining the _____ segment -- also called rectification of a curve -- was historically difficult. Although many methods were used for specific curves, the advent of calculus led to a general formula that provides closed-form solutions in some cases.

A curve in, say, the plane can be approximated by connecting a finite number of points on the curve using line segments to create a polygonal path. Since it is straightforward to calculate the length of each linear segment (using the theorem of Pythagoras in Euclidean space, for example), the total length of the approximation can be found by summing the lengths of each linear segment.

a. Nonelementary integral
c. Surface of revolution
b. Riemann sum
d. Length of an irregular arc

25. In vector calculus, the _____ of a scalar field is a vector field which points in the direction of the greatest rate of increase of the scalar field, and whose magnitude is the greatest rate of change.

A generalization of the _____ for functions on a Euclidean space which have values in another Euclidean space is the Jacobian. A further generalization for a function from one Banach space to another is the Fréchet derivative.

a. Leibniz's notation
c. Smooth function
b. Parametric derivative
d. Gradient

26. In mathematics, _____ refers to any of a number of loosely related concepts in different areas of geometry. Intuitively, _____ is the amount by which a geometric object deviates from being flat, or straight in the case of a line, but this is defined in different ways depending on the context. There is a key distinction between extrinsic _____, which is defined for objects embedded in another space (usually a Euclidean space) in a way that relates to the radius of _____ of circles that touch the object, and intrinsic _____, which is defined at each point in a differential manifold.

a. Tortuosity
c. Tangent line
b. Lie derivative
d. Curvature

27. A surface normal to a flat surface is a vector which is perpendicular to that surface. A normal to a non-flat surface at a point P on the surface is a vector perpendicular to the tangent plane to that surface at P. The word 'normal' is also used as an adjective: a line normal to a plane, the normal component of a force, the _____, etc. The concept of normality generalizes to orthogonality.

a. PDE surfaces
c. Normal vector
b. Paraboloid
d. Hyperbolic paraboloid

28. In mathematics, a _____ in a normed vector space is a vector (often a spatial vector) whose length is 1 (the unit length.) A _____ is often denoted by a lowercase letter with a superscribed caret or e;hate;, like this: $\hat{\imath}$.

In Euclidean space, the dot product of two unit vectors is simply the cosine of the angle between them.

a. Overdetermined
b. ACTRAN
c. ALGOR
d. Unit vector

29. The _____ is a test to determine if a relation or its graph is a function or not. For a relation or graph to be a function, it can have at most a single y-value for each x-value. Thus, a vertical line drawn at any x-position on the graph of a function will intersect the graph at most once.
    a. BDDC
    b. 15 theorem
    c. BIBO stability
    d. Vertical Line Test

30. In physics, and more specifically kinematics, _____ is the change in velocity over time. Because velocity is a vector, it can change in two ways: a change in magnitude and/or a change in direction. In one dimension, _____ is the rate at which something speeds up or slows down.
    a. AUSM
    b. Acceleration
    c. ALGOR
    d. ACTRAN

31. A _____ is the path a moving object follows through space. The object might be a projectile or a satellite, for example. It thus includes the meaning of orbit - the path of a planet, an asteroid or a comet as it travels around a central mass.
    a. 15 theorem
    b. BDDC
    c. BIBO stability
    d. Trajectory

32. _____ was a German mathematician, astronomer and astrologer, and key figure in the 17th century scientific revolution. He is best known for his eponymous laws of planetary motion, codified by later astronomers based on his works Astronomia nova, Harmonices Mundi, and Epitome of Copernican Astronomy. They also provided one of the foundations for Isaac Newton's theory of universal gravitation.
    a. Robin K. Bullough
    b. Nicolaus Copernicus
    c. MÄ dhava of Sangamagrama
    d. Johannes Kepler

33. In metric topology and related fields of mathematics, a set U is called _____ if, intuitively speaking, starting from any point x in U one can move by a small amount in any direction and still be in the set U. In other words, the distance between any point x in U and the edge of U is always greater than zero.

As an example, consider the _____ interval (0, 1) consisting of all real numbers x with 0 < x < 1. Here, the topology is the usual topology on the real line. We can look at this in two ways.

    a. Open
    b. AUSM
    c. ACTRAN
    d. ALGOR

34. _____ is a PDE solver of Maxwell's equations based on the method of moments. It is a 3-D planar electromagnetic (EM) simulator used for passive circuit analysis. It is presently marketed by Agilent Technologies EEsof division, but the tool was original developed by a Belgian company, Alphabit, a spinoff from IMEC, which was acquired by Hewlett-Packard and later spun out as part of Agilent.
    a. Trefftz method
    b. Partial Element Equivalent Circuit
    c. Stencil
    d. Momentum

35. _____ is the tendency of a force to rotate an object about an axis (or fulcrum or pivot.) Just as a force is a push or a pull, a _____ can be thought of as a twist. The symbol for _____ is τ, the Greek letter tau.
   a. BIBO stability
   b. Torque
   c. BDDC
   d. 15 theorem

Chapter 15. Partial Derivatives

1. In mathematics, the _____ is a fundamental concept in calculus and analysis concerning the behavior of that function near a particular input. Informally, a function assigns an output f(x) to every input x. The function has a limit L at an input p if f(x) is 'close' to L whenever x is 'close' to p.

   a. Table of limits
   b. Limit of a sequence
   c. 15 theorem
   d. Limit of a function

2. In economics, the _____ functional form of production functions is widely used to represent the relationship of an output to inputs. It was proposed by Knut Wicksell (1851-1926), and tested against statistical evidence by Charles Cobb and Paul Douglas in 1900-1928.

   For production, the function is

   $$Y = AL^{\alpha}K^{\beta},$$

   where:

   - Y = total production (the monetary value of all goods produced in a year)
   - L = labor input
   - K = capital input
   - A = total factor productivity
   - α and β are the output elasticities of labor and capital, respectively. These values are constants determined by available technology.

   Output elasticity measures the responsiveness of output to a change in levels of either labor or capital used in production, ceteris paribus. For example if α = 0.15, a 1% increase in labor would lead to approximately a 0.15% increase in output.

   a. BDDC
   b. BIBO stability
   c. 15 theorem
   d. Cobb-Douglas

3. The terms '_____' and 'independent variable' are used in similar but subtly different ways in mathematics and statistics as part of the standard terminology in those subjects. They are used to distinguish between two types of quantities being considered, separating them into those available at the start of a process and those being created by it, where the latter (dependent variables) are dependent on the former (independent variables.)

   In traditional calculus, a function is defined as a relation between two terms called variables because their values vary.

   a. BDDC
   b. 15 theorem
   c. BIBO stability
   d. Dependent variable

4. The _____ of a quantity whose value decreases with time is the interval required for the quantity to decay to half of its initial value. The concept originated in describing how long it takes atoms to undergo radioactive decay but also applies in a wide variety of other situations.

   The term '_____' dates to 1907.

Chapter 15. Partial Derivatives

    a. BDDC
    b. 15 theorem
    c. BIBO stability
    d. Half-life

5. The terms 'dependent variable' and '_____' are used in similar but subtly different ways in mathematics and statistics as part of the standard terminology in those subjects. They are used to distinguish between two types of quantities being considered, separating them into those available at the start of a process and those being created by it, where the latter (dependent variables) are dependent on the former (independent variables.)

In traditional calculus, a function is defined as a relation between two terms called variables because their values vary.

    a. ALGOR
    b. ACTRAN
    c. AUSM
    d. Independent variable

6. In mathematics, the _____ of a function is the set of all 'output' values produced by that function. Sometimes it is called the image, or more precisely, the image of the domain of the function. If a function is a surjection then its _____ is equal to its codomain.

    a. Constant function
    b. Range
    c. Piecewise-defined function
    d. Surjective

7. In mathematics, the _____ (or replacement set) of a given function is the set of 'input' values for which the function is defined. For instance, the _____ of cosine would be all real numbers, while the _____ of the square root would be only numbers greater than or equal to 0 (ignoring complex numbers in both cases.) In a representation of a function in a xy Cartesian coordinate system, the _____ is represented on the x axis (or abscissa.)

    a. BDDC
    b. Domain
    c. BIBO stability
    d. 15 theorem

8. In mathematics, the _____ is a conic section, the intersection of a right circular conical surface and a plane parallel to a generating straight line of that surface. Given a point (the focus) and a line (the directrix) that lie in a plane, the locus of points in that plane that are equidistant to them is a _____.

A particular case arises when the plane is tangent to the conical surface of a circle.

    a. BDDC
    b. BIBO stability
    c. 15 theorem
    d. Parabola

9. In mathematics, a (topological) _____ is defined as follows: let I be an interval of real numbers (i.e. a non-empty connected subset of $\mathbb{R}$); then a _____ γ is a continuous mapping $\gamma : I \to X$, where X is a topological space. The _____ γ is said to be simple if it is injective, i.e. if for all x, y in I, we have $\gamma(x) = \gamma(y) \implies x = y$. If I is a closed bounded interval $[a, b]$, we also allow the possibility $\gamma(a) = \gamma(b)$ (this convention makes it possible to talk about closed simple _____.)

    a. Tractrix
    b. Closed curve
    c. Prolate cycloid
    d. Curve

Chapter 15. Partial Derivatives

10. An _____ process is a change in which the temperature of the system stays constant: ΔT = 0. This typically occurs when a system is in contact with an outside thermal reservoir (heat bath), and the change occurs slowly enough to allow the system to continually adjust to the temperature of the reservoir through heat exchange. An alternative special case in which a system exchanges no heat with its surroundings (Q = 0) is called an adiabatic process.

    a. AUSM
    c. ALGOR
    b. ACTRAN
    d. Isothermal

11. In probability theory and statistics, the _____ (or expectation value or mean and for continuous random variables with a density function it is the probability density -weighted integral of the possible values.

The term '_____' can be misleading.

    a. AUSM
    c. ACTRAN
    b. ALGOR
    d. Expected value

12. In vector calculus, the _____ of a scalar field is a vector field which points in the direction of the greatest rate of increase of the scalar field, and whose magnitude is the greatest rate of change.

A generalization of the _____ for functions on a Euclidean space which have values in another Euclidean space is the Jacobian. A further generalization for a function from one Banach space to another is the Fréchet derivative.

    a. Parametric derivative
    c. Smooth function
    b. Leibniz's notation
    d. Gradient

13. _____ or isopotential in mathematics and physics (especially electronics) refers to a region in space where every point in it is at the same potential. This usually refers to a scalar potential, although it can also be applied to vector potentials. Often, _____ surfaces are used to visualize an (n)-dimensional scalar potential function in (n-1) dimensional space.

    a. Inverse function theorem
    c. Upper convected time derivative
    b. Implicit function theorem
    d. Equipotential

14. In mathematics, the _____ is the surface defined by the equation

$$z = x^3 - 3xy^2.$$

It belongs to the class of saddle surfaces and its name derives from the observation that a saddle for a monkey requires three depressions: two for the legs, and one for the tail. The point (0,0,0) on the _____ corresponds to a degenerate critical point of the function z(x,y) at (0, 0.) The _____ has an isolated umbilic point with zero Gaussian curvature at the origin, while the curvature is strictly negative at all other points.

    a. Level set
    c. Symmetry of second derivatives
    b. Vector Laplacian
    d. Monkey saddle

Chapter 15. Partial Derivatives

15. In mathematics, the concept of a '_____' is used to describe the behavior of a function as its argument or input either 'gets close' to some point, or as the argument becomes arbitrarily large; or the behavior of a sequence's elements as their index increases indefinitely. Limits are used in calculus and other branches of mathematical analysis to define derivatives and continuity.

In formulas, _____ is usually abbreviated as lim

- a. Limit
- b. 15 theorem
- c. BIBO stability
- d. BDDC

16. In mathematics, a _____ or rhodonea curve is a sinusoid plotted in polar coordinates. Up to similarity, these curves can all be expressed by a polar equation of the form

$$r = \cos(k\theta).$$

If k is an integer, the curve will be _____ shaped with

- 2k petals if k is even, and
- k petals if k is odd.

When k is even, the entire graph of the _____ will be traced out exactly once when the value of θ changes from 0 to 2π. When k is odd, this will happen on the interval between 0 and π. (More generally, this will happen on any interval of length 2π for k even, and π for k odd.)

- a. Rose
- b. Curtate cycloid
- c. Space curve
- d. Cochleoid

17. In mathematics, a _____ is any function which can be written as the ratio of two polynomial functions.

$$y = \frac{x^2 - 3x - 2}{x^2 - 4}$$

In the case of one variable, x, a _____ is a function of the form

$$f(x) = \frac{P(x)}{Q(x)}$$

where P and Q are polynomial function in x and Q is not the zero polynomial. The domain of f is the set of all points x for which the denominator Q(x) is not zero.

- a. BDDC
- b. 15 theorem
- c. BIBO stability
- d. Rational function

Chapter 15. Partial Derivatives

18. In calculus, a branch of mathematics, the _____ is a measurement of how a function changes when its input changes. Loosely speaking, a _____ can be thought of as how much a quantity is changing at some given point. For example, the _____ of the position (or distance) of a vehicle with respect to time is the instantaneous velocity (respectively, instantaneous speed) at which the vehicle is traveling.

The process of finding a _____ is called differentiation. The fundamental theorem of calculus states that differentiation is the reverse process to integration.

    a. Mountain pass theorem   b. Derivative
    c. Concave upwards   d. Ramp function

19. In mathematics, a _____ of a function of several variables is its derivative with respect to one of those variables with the others held constant (as opposed to the total derivative, in which all variables are allowed to vary.) Partial derivatives are useful in vector calculus and differential geometry.

The _____ of a function f with respect to the variable x is written as f'$_x$, ∂_xf, or ∂f/∂x.

    a. Shift theorem   b. Partial derivative
    c. Second partial derivatives test   d. Monkey saddle

20. In calculus, a method called _____ can be applied to implicitly defined functions. This method is an application of the chain rule allowing one to calculate the derivative of a function given implicitly.

As explained in the introduction, y can be given as a function of x implicitly rather than explicitly. When we have an equation R (x,y) = 0, we may be able to solve it for y and then differentiate. However, sometimes it is simpler to differentiate R(x,y) with respect to x and then solve for dy / dx.

    a. Implicit differentiation   b. Ordinary differential equation
    c. Automatic differentiation   d. Implicit function

21. In acoustics and telecommunication, a _____ of a wave is a component frequency of the signal that is an integer multiple of the fundamental frequency. For example, if the fundamental frequency is f, the harmonics have frequencies f, 2f, 3f, 4f, etc. The harmonics have the property that they are all periodic at the fundamental frequency, therefore the sum of harmonics is also periodic at that frequency.

    a. 15 theorem   b. BDDC
    c. BIBO stability   d. Harmonic

22. In mathematics, mathematical physics and the theory of stochastic processes, a _____ is a twice continuously differentiable function f : U → R (where U is an open subset of R^n) which satisfies Laplace's equation, i.e.

$$\frac{\partial^2 f}{\partial x_1^2} + \frac{\partial^2 f}{\partial x_2^2} + \cdots + \frac{\partial^2 f}{\partial x_n^2} = 0$$

everywhere on U. This is also often written as

$$\nabla^2 f = 0 \quad \text{or} \quad \Delta f = 0.$$

There also exists a seemingly weaker definition that is equivalent. Indeed a function is harmonic if and only if it is weakly harmonic.

Harmonic functions can be defined on an arbitrary Riemannian manifold, using the Laplace-de Rham operator Δ.

- a. Maximum principle
- c. Newtonian potential
- b. Hilbert transform
- d. Harmonic function

23. The _____ is an important second-order linear partial differential equation that describes the propagation of a variety of waves, such as sound waves, light waves and water waves. It arises in fields such as acoustics, electromagnetics, and fluid dynamics. Historically, the problem of a vibrating string such as that of a musical instrument was studied by Jean le Rond d'Alembert, Leonhard Euler, Daniel Bernoulli, and Joseph-Louis Lagrange.

- a. Dirac equation
- c. Klein-Gordon equation
- b. Moment of Inertia
- d. Wave equation

24. In infinitesimal calculus, a _____ is traditionally an infinitesimally small change in a variable. For example, if x is a variable, then a change in the value of x is often denoted Δx (or δx when this change is considered to be small.) The _____ dx represents such a change, but is infinitely small.

- a. Differential
- c. Dirichlet integral
- b. Continuous function
- d. Related rates

25. A _____ is a mathematical equation for an unknown function of one or several variables that relates the values of the function itself and of its derivatives of various orders. they play a prominent role in engineering, physics, economics and other disciplines.

A simplified real world example of a _____ is modeling the acceleration of a ball falling through the air (considering only gravity and air resistance.)

- a. Petrovsky lacuna
- c. Lax pair
- b. Structural stability
- d. Differential equation

26. The _____ is an important partial differential equation which describes the distribution of heat (or variation in temperature) in a given region over time. For a function u(x,y,z,t) of three spatial variables (x,y,z) and the time variable t, the _____ is

$$\frac{\partial u}{\partial t} - k\left(\frac{\partial^2 u}{\partial x^2} + \frac{\partial^2 u}{\partial y^2} + \frac{\partial^2 u}{\partial z^2}\right) = 0$$

or equivalently

$$\frac{\partial u}{\partial t} = k\nabla^2 u$$

where k is a constant.

The _____ is of fundamental importance in diverse scientific fields.

- a. 15 theorem
- b. BIBO stability
- c. BDDC
- d. Heat equation

27. In mathematics, a _____ is an approximation of a general function using a linear function (more precisely, an affine function.)

Given a differentiable function f of one real variable, Taylor's theorem for n=1 states that

$$f(x) = f(a) + f\,'(a)(x-a) + R_2$$

where R_2 is the remainder term. The _____ is obtained by dropping the remainder:

$$f(x) \approx f(a) + f\,'(a)(x-a)$$

which is true for x close to a.

- a. Differentiation of trigonometric functions
- b. Linear approximation
- c. Smooth function
- d. Linearity of differentiation

28. In geometry, the _____ (or simply the tangent) to a curve at a given point is the straight line that 'just touches' the curve at that point (in the sense explained more precisely below.) As it passes through the point of tangency, the _____ is 'going in the same direction' as the curve, and in this sense it is the best straight-line approximation to the curve at that point. The same definition applies to space curves and curves in n-dimensional Euclidean space.
- a. Sphere
- b. Lie derivative
- c. Minimal surface
- d. Tangent line

29. In mathematics and its applications, _____ refers to finding the linear approximation to a function at a given point. In the study of dynamical systems, _____ is a method for assessing the local stability of an equilibrium point of a system of nonlinear differential equations or discrete dynamical systems. This method is used in fields such as engineering, physics, economics, and ecology.
- a. Point of inflection
- b. Stationary point
- c. Symmetrically continuous
- d. Linearization

30. In a totally ordered set all elements are mutually comparable, so such a set can have at most one minimal element and at most one maximal element. Then, due to mutual comparability, the minimal element will also be the least element and the maximal element will also be the greatest element. Thus in a totally ordered set we can simply use the terms minimum and _____.

a. Hyperbolic angle
b. Complex analysis
c. Dirichlet integral
d. Maximum

31. In calculus, the _____ is a formula for the derivative of the composite of two functions.

In intuitive terms, if a variable, y, depends on a second variable, u, which in turn depends on a third variable, x, then the rate of change of y with respect to x can be computed as the rate of change of y with respect to u multiplied by the rate of change of u with respect to x. Schematically,

$$\frac{dy}{dx} = \frac{dy}{du} \cdot \frac{du}{dx}.$$

a. Reciprocal Rule
b. Differentiation rules
c. Chain Rule
d. Quotient Rule

32. In mathematics, an _____ is a generalization for the concept of a function in which the dependent variable has not been given 'explicitly' in terms of the independent variable. To give a function f explicitly is to provide a prescription for determining the output value of the function y in terms of the input value x:

y = f(x.)

By contrast, the function is implicit if the value of y is obtained from x by solving an equation of the form:

R(x,y) = 0.

a. Ordinary differential equation
b. Automatic differentiation
c. Implicit differentiation
d. Implicit Function

33. In the branch of mathematics called multivariable calculus, the _____ is a tool which allows relations to be converted to functions. It does this by representing the relation as the graph of a function. There may not be a single function whose graph is the entire relation, but there may be such a function on a restriction of the domain of the relation.

a. Implicit Function Theorem
b. Isoperimetric inequality
c. Upper convected time derivative
d. Inverse function theorem

34. In mathematics, the _____ of a multivariate differentiable function along a given vector V at a given point P intuitively represents the instantaneous rate of change of the function, moving through P, in the direction of V. It therefore generalizes the notion of a partial derivative, in which the direction is always taken parallel to one of the coordinate axes.

The _____ is a special case of the Gâteaux derivative.

The _____ of a scalar function $f(\vec{x}) = f(x_1, x_2, \ldots, x_n)$ along a vector $\vec{v} = (v_1, \ldots, v_n)$ is the function defined by the limit

<_____>
$$\nabla_{\vec{v}} f(\vec{x}) = \lim_{h \to 0} \frac{f(\vec{x} + h\vec{v}) - f(\vec{x})}{h}.$$

Sometimes authors write D_v instead of ∇_v.

a. Reduced derivative
b. Symmetric derivative
c. Directional derivative
d. Difference quotient

35. In vector calculus, _____ is a vector differential operator represented by the nabla symbol: ∇.

_____ is a mathematical tool serving primarily as a convention for mathematical notation; it makes many equations easier to comprehend, write, and remember. Depending on the way _____ is applied, it can describe the gradient (slope), divergence (degree to which something converges or diverges) or curl (rotational motion at points in a fluid.)

a. Del
b. Divergence
c. Gradient theorem
d. Divergence Theorem

36. In mathematics, an _____ on a real vector space is a choice of which ordered bases are 'positively' oriented and which are 'negatively' oriented. In the three-dimensional Euclidean space, the two possible basis orientations are called right-handed and left-handed (or right-chiral and left-chiral), respectively. However, the choice of _____ is independent of the handedness or chirality of the bases (although right-handed bases are typically declared to be positively oriented, they may also be assigned a negative _____.)

a. Unit vector
b. ACTRAN
c. ALGOR
d. Orientation

37. In the two-dimensional case, a _____ perpendicularly intersects the tangent line to a curve at a given point.

The _____ is often used in computer graphics to determine a surface's orientation toward a light source for flat shading, or the orientation of each of the corners (vertices) to mimic a curved surface with Phong shading.

For a polygon (such as a triangle), a surface normal can be calculated as the vector cross product of two (non-parallel) edges of the polygon.

a. Prolate
b. PDE surfaces
c. Parametric surface
d. Normal line

38. In mathematics, two vectors are _____ if they are perpendicular, i.e., they form a right angle. For example, a subway and the street above, although they do not physically intersect, are _____ if they cross at a right angle.

Chapter 15. Partial Derivatives

a. ACTRAN
b. ALGOR
c. Orthogonal
d. AUSM

39. In a totally ordered set all elements are mutually comparable, so such a set can have at most one minimal element and at most one maximal element. Then, due to mutual comparability, the minimal element will also be the least element and the maximal element will also be the greatest element. Thus in a totally ordered set we can simply use the terms _____ and maximum.
    a. Periodic function
    b. Taylor's theorem
    c. Calculus controversy
    d. Minimum

40. In mathematics, a _____ (or critical number) is a point on the domain of a function where:

    - one dimension: the derivative (or slope of the line when visualized) is equal to zero or a point where the function ceases to be differentiable.
    - in general: there are two distinct concepts: either the derivative (Jacobian) vanishes, or it is not of full rank (or, in either case, the function is not differentiable); these agree in one dimension.

    Note that in one dimension, a critical value or critical number x of function f is the domain element at which the derivative is zero or undefined, whereas the associated ordered pair (x, y) is the _____. In higher dimensions a critical value is in the range whereas a _____ is in the domain.

    There are two situations in which a point becomes a _____ of a function of one variable. The first of which is that the value of the first derivative is equal to zero.

    a. Differentiation operator
    b. Shift theorem
    c. Differential operator
    d. Critical point

41. Let f be a differentiable function, and let f'(x) be its derivative. The derivative of f'(x) (if it has one) is written f''(x) and is called the _____ of f. Similarly, the derivative of a _____, if it exists, is written f'''(x) and is called the third derivative of f.
    a. Stationary phase approximation
    b. Ramp function
    c. Horizontal asymptote
    d. Second Derivative

42. In mathematics, a _____ is a point in the domain of a function of two variables which is a stationary point but not a local extremum. At such a point, in general, the surface resembles a saddle that curves up in one direction, and curves down in a different direction (like a mountain pass.) In terms of contour lines, a _____ can be recognized, in general, by a contour that appears to intersect itself.
    a. BDDC
    b. 15 theorem
    c. BIBO stability
    d. Saddle point

43. In mathematics, a function f defined on some set X with real or complex values is a _____ function, if the set of its values is _____. In other words, there exists a number M>0 such that

$$|f(x)| \leq M$$

for all x in X.

Sometimes, if $f(x) \leq A$ for all x in X, then the function is said to be _____ above by A.

a. Bounded
b. Differential calculus
c. Caccioppoli set
d. Stationary phase approximation

44. The largest and the smallest element of a set are called extreme values, absolute extrema, or extreme records.

For a differentiable function f, if f(x_0) is an _____ for the set of all values f(x), and if x_0 is in the interior of the domain of f, then x_0 is a critical point, by Fermat's theorem.

In the case of a general partial order one should not confuse a least element (smaller than all other) and a minimal element (nothing is smaller.)

a. Integration by substitution
b. Extreme Value
c. Extreme Value Theorem
d. Infinitesimal

45. In calculus, the _____ states that if a real-valued function f is continuous in the closed and bounded interval [a,b], then f must attain its maximum and minimum value, each at least once. That is, there exist numbers c and d in [a,b] such that:

$$f(c) \geq f(x) \geq f(d) \quad \text{for all } x \in [a, b].$$

A related theorem is the boundedness theorem which states that a continuous function f in the closed interval [a,b] is bounded on that interval. That is, there exist real numbers m and M such that:

$$m \leq f(x) \leq M \quad \text{for all } x \in [a, b].$$

The _____ enriches the boundedness theorem by saying that not only is the function bounded, but it also attains its least upper bound as its maximum and its greatest lower bound as its minimum.

a. Integral of secant cubed
b. Infinitesimal
c. Extreme Value Theorem
d. Uniform convergence

46. The method of _____ or ordinary _____ is used to solve overdetermined systems. _____ is often applied in statistical contexts, particularly regression analysis.

_____ can be interpreted as a method of fitting data. The best fit in the _____ sense is that instance of the model for which the sum of squared residuals has its least value, a residual being the difference between an observed value and the value given by the model.

a. 15 theorem	b. BIBO stability
c. BDDC	d. Least squares

47. In calculus, _____ gives a sequence of approximations of a differentiable function around a given point by polynomials (the Taylor polynomials of that function) whose coefficients depend only on the derivatives of the function at that point. The theorem also gives precise estimates on the size of the error in the approximation. The theorem is named after the mathematician Brook Taylor, who stated it in 1712, though the result was first discovered 41 years earlier in 1671 by James Gregory.

a. Complex analysis	b. Leibniz differential
c. Continuous function	d. Taylor's theorem

48. In mathematical optimization, the method of Lagrange multipliers provides a strategy for finding the maximum/minimum of a function subject to constraints.

For example, consider the optimization problem

$$\text{maximize } f(x,y)$$
$$\text{subject to } g(x,y) = c.$$

We introduce a new variable (λ) called a _____, and study the Lagrange function defined by

$$\Lambda(x,y,\lambda) = f(x,y) - \lambda\big(g(x,y) - c\big).$$

If (x,y) is a maximum for the original constrained problem, then there exists a λ such that (x,y,λ) is a stationary point for the Lagrange function (stationary points are those points where the partial derivatives of Λ are zero.) However, not all stationary points yield a solution of the original problem.

a. BIBO stability	b. 15 theorem
c. BDDC	d. Lagrange multiplier

49. In mathematics, the simplest case of _____ refers to the study of problems in which one seeks to minimize or maximize a real function by systematically choosing the values of real or integer variables from within an allowed set. This (a scalar real valued objective function) is actually a small subset of this field which comprises a large area of applied mathematics and generalizes to study of means to obtain 'best available' values of some objective function given a defined domain where the elaboration is on the types of functions and the conditions and nature of the objects in the problem domain.

The first _____ technique, which is known as steepest descent, goes back to Gauss.

a. ALGOR	b. Optimization
c. AUSM	d. ACTRAN

Chapter 16. Multiple Integrals

1. In mathematics, the _____ of a function y = f(x) is a function that, in some fashion, 'undoes' the effect of f The _____ of f is denoted f^{-1}. The statements y=f(x) and $x=f^{-1}(y)$ are equivalent.
   - a. ALGOR
   - b. ACTRAN
   - c. AUSM
   - d. Inverse

2. Just as the definite integral of a positive function of one variable represents the area of the region between the graph of the function and the x-axis, the _____ of a positive function of two variables represents the volume of the region between the surface defined by the function (on the three dimensional Cartesian plane where z = f(x,y)) and the plane which contains its domain. (Note that the same volume can be obtained via the triple integral -- the integral of a function in three variables -- of the constant function f(x, y, z) = 1 over the above-mentioned region between the surface and the plane.) If there are more variables, a multiple integral will yield hypervolumes of multi-dimensional functions.
   - a. Double integral
   - b. Nonelementary integral
   - c. Linearity of integration
   - d. Sum rule in integration

3. Integration is an important concept in mathematics, specifically in the field of calculus and, more broadly, mathematical analysis. Given a function f of a real variable x and an interval [a, b] of the real line, the _____

$$\int_a^b f(x)\,dx,$$

is defined informally to be the net signed area of the region in the xy-plane bounded by the graph of f, the x-axis, and the vertical lines x = a and x = b.

The term '_____' may also refer to the notion of antiderivative, a function F whose derivative is the given function f.

   - a. Integral test for convergence
   - b. Integrand
   - c. Indefinite integral
   - d. Integral

4. In mathematics, a _____ is a method for approximating the total area underneath a curve on a graph, otherwise known as an integral. It may also be used to define the integration operation.

Consider a function $f: D \longrightarrow \mathbf{R}$, where D is a subset of the real numbers $\mathbf{R}$, and let I = [a, b] be a closed interval contained in D. A finite set of points $\{x_0, x_1, x_2, \ldots x_n\}$ such that $a = x_0 < x_1 < x_2 \ldots < x_n = b$ creates a partition

$$P = \{[x_0, x_1), [x_1, x_2), \ldots [x_{n-1}, x_n]\}$$

of I.

   - a. Surface of revolution
   - b. Disk integration
   - c. Riemann sum
   - d. Signed measure

5. The _____ is a type of definite integral extended to functions of more than one real variable, for example, f(x, y) or f(x, y, z.)

Chapter 16. Multiple Integrals

Introduction

Just as the definite integral of a positive function of one variable represents the area of the region between the graph of the function and the x-axis, the double integral of a positive function of two variables represents the volume of the region between the surface defined by the function (on the three dimensional Cartesian plane where z = f(x,y)) and the plane which contains its domain. (Note that the same volume can be obtained via the triple integral -- the integral of a function in three variables -- of the constant function f(x, y, z) = 1 over the above-mentioned region between the surface and the plane.)

- a. Constant of integration
- b. Multiple integral
- c. Disk integration
- d. Risch algorithm

6. In geometry, a _____ is a special plane curve generated by the trace of a fixed point on a small circle that rolls within a larger circle. It is comparable to the cycloid but instead of the circle rolling along a line, it rolls within a circle. The red curve is a _____ traced as the smaller black circle rolls around inside the larger blue circle (parameters are R=3.0, r=1.0, and so k=3), giving a deltoid.

If the smaller circle has radius r, and the larger circle has radius R = kr, then the parametric equations for the curve can be given by either:

$$x(\theta) = (R - r)\cos\theta + r\cos\left(\frac{R-r}{r}\theta\right)$$
$$y(\theta) = (R - r)\sin\theta - r\sin\left(\frac{R-r}{r}\theta\right),$$

or:

$$x(\theta) = r(k-1)\cos\theta + r\cos((k-1)\theta)$$
$$y(\theta) = r(k-1)\sin\theta - r\sin((k-1)\theta).$$

If k is an integer, then the curve is closed, and has k cusps (i.e., sharp corners, where the curve is not differentiable.)

- a. Bullet-nose curve
- b. Kappa curve
- c. Closed curve
- d. Hypocycloid

7. The terms 'dependent variable' and '_____' are used in similar but subtly different ways in mathematics and statistics as part of the standard terminology in those subjects. They are used to distinguish between two types of quantities being considered, separating them into those available at the start of a process and those being created by it, where the latter (dependent variables) are dependent on the former (independent variables.)

In traditional calculus, a function is defined as a relation between two terms called variables because their values vary.

a. ALGOR
b. AUSM
c. Independent variable
d. ACTRAN

8. In mathematics, the _____ of a non-negative integer n, denoted by n!, is the product of all positive integers less than or equal to n. For example,

$$5! = 1 \times 2 \times 3 \times 4 \times 5 = 120$$

and

$$6! = 1 \times 2 \times 3 \times 4 \times 5 \times 6 = 720.$$

The notation n! was introduced by Christian Kramp in 1808.

The _____ function is formally defined by

$$n! = \prod_{k=1}^{n} k \qquad \forall n \in \mathbb{N}$$

or recursively defined by

$$n! = \begin{cases} n \leq 1 & 1 \\ n > 1 & n(n-1)! \end{cases} \qquad \forall n \in \mathbb{N}.$$

Both of the above definitions incorporate the instance

$$0! = 1$$

as an instance of the fact that the product of no numbers at all is 1.

a. 15 theorem
b. BDDC
c. Constraint counting
d. Factorial

9. In calculus, interchange of the _____ is a methodology that transforms multiple integrations of functions into other, hopefully simpler, integrals by changing the order in which the integrations are performed.

Chapter 16. Multiple Integrals

The problem for examination is evaluation of an integral of the form:

$$\iint_D dxdy\ f(x,y),$$

where D is some two-dimensional area in the xy-plane. For some functions f straightforward integration is feasible, but where that is not true, the integral can sometimes be reduced to simpler form by changing the _____.

a. Integration by parts
c. Arc length
b. Order of integration
d. Indefinite integral

10. In mathematics and its applications, a _____ system is a system for assigning an n-tuple of numbers or scalars to each point in an n-dimensional space. This concept is part of the theory of manifolds. 'Scalars' in many cases means real numbers, but, depending on context, can mean complex numbers or elements of some other commutative ring.

a. Cylindrical coordinate system
c. Spherical coordinate system
b. 15 theorem
d. Coordinate

11. In mathematics, the _____ is a two-dimensional coordinate system in which each point on a plane is determined by an angle and a distance. The _____ is especially useful in situations where the relationship between two points is most easily expressed in terms of angles and distance; in the more familiar Cartesian or rectangular coordinate system, such a relationship can only be found through trigonometric formulation.

As the coordinate system is two-dimensional, each point is determined by two polar coordinates: the radial coordinate and the angular coordinate.

a. 15 theorem
c. BDDC
b. BIBO stability
d. Polar coordinate system

12. In mathematics, a _____ is a basic technique used to simplify problems in which the original variables are replaced with new ones; the new and old variables being related in some specified way. The intent is that the problem expressed in new variables may be simpler, or else equivalent to a better understood problem.

A very simple example of a useful variable change can be seen in the problem of finding the roots of the eighth order polynomial:

$$x^8 + 3x^4 + 2 = 0$$

Eighth order polynomial equations are generally impossible to solve in terms of elementary functions.

a. BDDC
c. Cubic function
b. 15 theorem
d. Change of variables

13. The _____ of a material is defined as its mass per unit volume. The symbol of _____ is ρ '>rho.)

Mathematically:

$$d = \frac{m}{V}$$

where:

    d is the _____,
    m is the mass,
    V is the volume.

a. Density
b. BIBO stability
c. 15 theorem
d. BDDC

14. The concept of _____ in mathematics evolved from the concept of _____ in physics. The nth _____ of a real-valued function f(x) of a real variable about a value c is

$$\mu'_n = \int_{-\infty}^{\infty} (x - c)^n f(x)\, dx.$$

It is possible to define moments for random variables in a more general fashion than moments for real values. See Moments in metric spaces.

a. Standard deviation
b. Linear regression
c. Poisson distribution
d. Moment

15. The _____ is an important family of continuous probability distributions, applicable in many fields. Each member of the family may be defined by two parameters, location and scale: the mean and variance respectively. The standard _____ is the _____ with a mean of zero and a variance of one.

a. Linear regression
b. Normal distribution
c. Continuous random variable
d. Poisson distribution

16. In mathematics, a _____ is a quadric surface of special kind. There are two kinds of paraboloids: elliptic and hyperbolic. The elliptic _____ is shaped like an oval cup and can have a maximum or minimum point.

a. Paraboloid
b. Parametric surface
c. Normal line
d. Normal vector

17. A _____ is one of the most curvilinear basic geometric shapes:It has two faces, zero vertices, and zero edges. The surface formed by the points at a fixed distance from a given straight line, the axis of the _____. The solid enclosed by this surface and by two planes perpendicular to the axis is also called a _____.

a. BDDC
b. 15 theorem
c. Right circular cylinder
d. Cylinder

Chapter 16. Multiple Integrals

18. _____, also called mass _____ or the angular mass, (SI units kg m^2) is a measure of an object's resistance to changes in its rotation rate. It is the rotational analog of mass. That is, it is the inertia of a rigid rotating body with respect to its rotation.

   a. Moment of Inertia
   b. Klein-Gordon equation
   c. Wave equation
   d. Dirac equation

19. In geometry, a _____ is a three-dimensional figure formed by six parallelograms. It is to a parallelogram as a cube is to a square: Euclidean geometry supports all four notions but affine geometry admits only parallelograms and parallelepipeds. Three equivalent definitions of _____ are

   - a polyhedron with six faces (hexahedron), each of which is a parallelogram,
   - a hexahedron with three pairs of parallel faces, and
   - a prism of which the base is a parallelogram.

The cuboid (six rectangular faces), cube (six square faces), and the rhombohedron (six rhombus faces) are all specific cases of _____.

Parallelepipeds are a subclass of the prismatoids.

   a. BDDC
   b. 15 theorem
   c. BIBO stability
   d. Parallelepiped

20. In economics, the _____ functional form of production functions is widely used to represent the relationship of an output to inputs. It was proposed by Knut Wicksell (1851-1926), and tested against statistical evidence by Charles Cobb and Paul Douglas in 1900-1928.

For production, the function is

$$Y = AL^{\alpha}K^{\beta},$$

where:

   - Y = total production (the monetary value of all goods produced in a year)
   - L = labor input
   - K = capital input
   - A = total factor productivity
   - α and β are the output elasticities of labor and capital, respectively. These values are constants determined by available technology.

Output elasticity measures the responsiveness of output to a change in levels of either labor or capital used in production, ceteris paribus. For example if α = 0.15, a 1% increase in labor would lead to approximately a 0.15% increase in output.

a. 15 theorem b. Cobb-Douglas
c. BIBO stability d. BDDC

21. In mathematics, a _____ (pdf) is a function that represents a probability distribution in terms of integrals.

Formally, a probability distribution has density f, if f is a non-negative Lebesgue-integrable function $\mathbb{R} \to \mathbb{R}$ such that the probability of the interval [a, b] is given by

$$\int_a^b f(x)\,dx$$

for any two numbers a and b. This implies that the total integral of f must be 1.

a. Probability density function b. 15 theorem
c. BDDC d. BIBO stability

22. _____ is the name of several related measures of the size of an object, a surface, or an ensemble of points. It is calculated as the root mean square distance of the objects' parts from either its center of gravity or an axis.

In structural engineering, the two-dimensional _____ is used to describe the distribution of cross sectional area in a beam around its centroidal axis.

a. 15 theorem b. BDDC
c. BIBO stability d. Radius of gyration

23. In mathematics, a _____ is an ordered list of objects (or events). Like a set, it contains members (also called elements or terms), and the number of terms (possibly infinite) is called the length of the _____. Unlike a set, order matters, and the exact same elements can appear multiple times at different positions in the _____.

a. 15 theorem b. Y-intercept
c. BDDC d. Sequence

24. In probability theory and statistics, the _____ (or expectation value or mean and for continuous random variables with a density function it is the probability density -weighted integral of the possible values.

The term '_____' can be misleading.

a. ACTRAN b. ALGOR
c. Expected value d. AUSM

25. The _____ is a test to determine if a relation or its graph is a function or not. For a relation or graph to be a function, it can have at most a single y-value for each x-value. Thus, a vertical line drawn at any x-position on the graph of a function will intersect the graph at most once.

a. BIBO stability b. Vertical Line Test
c. 15 theorem d. BDDC

26. _____ is how much exposed area an object has. It is expressed in square units. If an object has flat faces, its _____ can be calculated by adding together the areas of its faces.
  a. Surface area
  b. Lipschitz domain
  c. Plane curve
  d. Gyroid

27. In mathematics, a function f defined on some set X with real or complex values is a _____ function, if the set of its values is _____. In other words, there exists a number M>0 such that

$$|f(x)| \leq M$$

for all x in X.

Sometimes, if $f(x) \leq A$ for all x in X, then the function is said to be _____ above by A.

  a. Caccioppoli set
  b. Differential calculus
  c. Stationary phase approximation
  d. Bounded

28. _____ is a term in geometry and in everyday life that refers to a property in Euclidean space of two or more lines or planes, or a combination of these. The existence and properties of parallel lines are the basis of Euclid's parallel postulate. Two lines parallel would be denoted as ABC DEF.
  a. 15 theorem
  b. BDDC
  c. BIBO stability
  d. Parallelism

29. In mathematics, a _____ is a unicursal quartic curve with three inflection points, given by the equation

$$a^2 y^2 - b^2 x^2 = x^2 y^2$$

The bullet curve has three double points in the real projective plane, at x=0 and y=0, x=0 and z=0, and y=0 and z=0, and is therefore a unicursal (rational) curve of genus zero.

If

$$f(z) = \sum_{n=0}^{\infty} \binom{2n}{n} z^{2n+1} = z + 2z^3 + 6z^5 + 20z^7 + \cdots$$

then

$$y = f\left(\frac{x}{2a}\right) \pm 2b$$

are the two branches of the bullet curve at the origin.

Chapter 16. Multiple Integrals

a. Closed curve
b. Folium of Descartes
c. Hypocycloid
d. Bullet-nose curve

30. In vector calculus, the _____ is shorthand for either the _____ matrix or its determinant, the _____ determinant.

In algebraic geometry the _____ of a curve means the _____ variety: a group variety associated to the curve, in which the curve can be embedded.

These concepts are all named after the mathematician Carl Gustav Jacob Jacobi.

a. Partial derivative
b. Contact
c. Symmetry of second derivatives
d. Jacobian

31. An injective function is called an injection, and is also said to be a _____ function (not to be confused with _____ correspondence, i.e. a bijective function.)

A function f that is not injective is sometimes called many-to-one. (However, this terminology is also sometimes used to mean 'single-valued', i.e. each argument is mapped to at most one value.)

a. Onto
b. Injective function
c. One-to-one function
d. One-to-one

32. In mathematics, a (topological) _____ is defined as follows: let I be an interval of real numbers (i.e. a non-empty connected subset of $\mathbb{R}$); then a _____ γ is a continuous mapping $\gamma : I \to X$, where X is a topological space. The _____ γ is said to be simple if it is injective, i.e. if for all x, y in I, we have $\gamma(x) = \gamma(y) \implies x = y$. If I is a closed bounded interval $[a, b]$, we also allow the possibility $\gamma(a) = \gamma(b)$ (this convention makes it possible to talk about closed simple _____.)

a. Curve
b. Tractrix
c. Prolate cycloid
d. Closed curve

33. _____ generally conveys two primary meanings. The first is an imprecise sense of harmonious or aesthetically-pleasing proportionality and balance; such that it reflects beauty or perfection. The second meaning is a precise and well-defined concept of balance or 'patterned self-similarity' that can be demonstrated or proved according to the rules of a formal system: by geometry, through physics or otherwise.

a. 15 theorem
b. BIBO stability
c. BDDC
d. Symmetry

34. The largest and the smallest element of a set are called extreme values, absolute extrema, or extreme records.

For a differentiable function f, if $f(x_0)$ is an _____ for the set of all values f(x), and if x_0 is in the interior of the domain of f, then x_0 is a critical point, by Fermat's theorem.

In the case of a general partial order one should not confuse a least element (smaller than all other) and a minimal element (nothing is smaller.)

a. Extreme Value
b. Extreme Value Theorem
c. Infinitesimal
d. Integration by substitution

35. In calculus, the _____ states that if a real-valued function f is continuous in the closed and bounded interval [a,b], then f must attain its maximum and minimum value, each at least once. That is, there exist numbers c and d in [a,b] such that:

$$f(c) \geq f(x) \geq f(d) \quad \text{for all } x \in [a, b].$$

A related theorem is the boundedness theorem which states that a continuous function f in the closed interval [a,b] is bounded on that interval. That is, there exist real numbers m and M such that:

$$m \leq f(x) \leq M \quad \text{for all } x \in [a, b].$$

The _____ enriches the boundedness theorem by saying that not only is the function bounded, but it also attains its least upper bound as its maximum and its greatest lower bound as its minimum.

a. Uniform convergence
b. Infinitesimal
c. Integral of secant cubed
d. Extreme Value Theorem

36. In calculus, the _____ states, roughly, that given a section of a smooth curve, there is at least one point on that section at which the derivative (slope) of the curve is equal (parallel) to the 'average' derivative of the section. It is used to prove theorems that make global conclusions about a function on an interval starting from local hypotheses about derivatives at points of the interval.

This theorem can be understood concretely by applying it to motion: If a car travels one hundred miles in one hour, so its average speed during that time was 100 miles per hour.

a. Mean Value Theorem
b. First derivative test
c. Fresnel integrals
d. Leibniz differential

Chapter 17. Vector Calculus

1. In mathematics a _____ is a construction in vector calculus which associates a vector to every point in a (locally) Euclidean space.

Vector fields are often used in physics to model, for example, the speed and direction of a moving fluid throughout space, or the strength and direction of some force, such as the magnetic or gravitational force, as it changes from point to point.

In the rigorous mathematical treatment, (tangent) vector fields are defined on manifolds as sections of a manifold's tangent bundle.

    a. Vector field   b. BDDC
    c. 15 theorem   d. BIBO stability

2. In physics, _____ is defined as the rate of change of position. it is vector physical quantity; both speed and direction are required to define it. In the SI (metric) system, it is measured in meters per second: (m/s) or ms^{-1}.

    a. 15 theorem   b. BDDC
    c. BIBO stability   d. Velocity

3. _____ or isopotential in mathematics and physics (especially electronics) refers to a region in space where every point in it is at the same potential. This usually refers to a scalar potential, although it can also be applied to vector potentials. Often, _____ surfaces are used to visualize an (n)-dimensional scalar potential function in (n-1) dimensional space.

    a. Implicit function theorem   b. Upper convected time derivative
    c. Inverse function theorem   d. Equipotential

4. In mathematics and physics, a _____ associates a scalar value, which can be either mathematical in definition to every point in space. Scalar fields are often used in physics, for instance to indicate the temperature distribution throughout space or more specifically, differential geometry, the set of functions defined on a manifold define the commutative ring of functions.

    a. Differential operator   b. Jacobian
    c. Shift theorem   d. Scalar field

5. In mathematics, a (topological) _____ is defined as follows: let I be an interval of real numbers (i.e. a non-empty connected subset of $\mathbb{R}$); then a _____ γ is a continuous mapping $\gamma : I \to X$, where X is a topological space. The _____ γ is said to be simple if it is injective, i.e. if for all x, y in I, we have $\gamma(x) = \gamma(y) \implies x = y$. If I is a closed bounded interval $[a, b]$, we also allow the possibility $\gamma(a) = \gamma(b)$ (this convention makes it possible to talk about closed simple _____.)

    a. Curve   b. Prolate cycloid
    c. Tractrix   d. Closed curve

Chapter 17. Vector Calculus

6. In the various subfields of physics, there exist two common usages of the term _____, both with rigorous mathematical frameworks.

    - In the study of transport phenomena (heat transfer, mass transfer and fluid dynamics), _____ is defined as the amount that flows through a unit area per unit time. _____ in this definition is a vector.
    - In the field of electromagnetism and mathematics, _____ is usually the integral of a vector quantity over a finite surface. The result of this integration is a scalar quantity. The magnetic _____ is thus the integral of the magnetic vector field B over a surface, and the electric _____ is defined similarly. Using this definition, the _____ of the Poynting vector over a specified surface is the rate at which electromagnetic energy flows through that surface. Confusingly, the Poynting vector is sometimes called the power _____, which is an example of the first usage of _____, above. It has units of watts per square metre (W·m⁻²)

One could argue, based on the work of James Clerk Maxwell, that the transport definition precedes the more recent way the term is used in electromagnetism. The specific quote from Maxwell is 'In the case of fluxes, we have to take the integral, over a surface, of the _____ through every element of the surface. The result of this operation is called the surface integral of the _____.

   a. 15 theorem
   c. BDDC
   b. Flux
   d. BIBO stability

7. In mathematics, the point $\tilde{\mathbf{x}} \in \mathbb{R}^n$ is an _____ for the differential equation

$$\frac{d\mathbf{x}}{dt} = \mathbf{f}(t, \mathbf{x})$$

if $\mathbf{f}(t, \tilde{\mathbf{x}}) = 0$ for all t.

Similarly, the point $\tilde{\mathbf{x}} \in \mathbb{R}^n$ is an _____ (or fixed point) for the difference equation

$$\mathbf{x}_{k+1} = \mathbf{f}(k, \mathbf{x}_k)$$

if $\mathbf{f}(k, \tilde{\mathbf{x}}) = \tilde{\mathbf{x}}$ for $k = 0, 1, 2, \ldots$.

Equilibria can be classified by looking at the signs of the eigenvalues of the linearization of the equations about the equilibria.

   a. ALGOR
   c. AUSM
   b. ACTRAN
   d. Equilibrium point

8. A _____, sometimes known as an energy shield, force shield typically made of energy or charged particles, that protects a person, area or object from attacks or intrusions.

A University of Washington in Seattle group has been experimenting with using a bubble of charged plasma to surround a spacecraft, contained by a fine mesh of superconducting wire. This would protect the spacecraft from interstellar radiation and some particles without needing physical shielding.

a. Force field
c. 15 theorem
b. BIBO stability
d. BDDC

9. In vector calculus, the _____ of a scalar field is a vector field which points in the direction of the greatest rate of increase of the scalar field, and whose magnitude is the greatest rate of change.

A generalization of the _____ for functions on a Euclidean space which have values in another Euclidean space is the Jacobian. A further generalization for a function from one Banach space to another is the Fréchet derivative.

a. Smooth function
c. Parametric derivative
b. Gradient
d. Leibniz's notation

10. A _____ is a model used within physics to explain how gravity exists in the universe. In its original concept, gravity was a force between point masses. Following Newton, Laplace attempted to model gravity as some kind of radiation field or fluid, and since the 19th century explanations for gravity have usually been sought in terms of a field model, rather than a point attraction.

a. BDDC
c. BIBO stability
b. 15 theorem
d. Gravitational field

11. In linear algebra, the null vector or _____ is the vector (0, 0, …, 0) in Euclidean space, all of whose components are zero. It is usually written $\vec{0}$ or 0 or simply 0. A _____ has no direction.

a. Direction vector
c. Scalar multiplication
b. Zero vector
d. Dot product

12. In economics, the _____ functional form of production functions is widely used to represent the relationship of an output to inputs. It was proposed by Knut Wicksell (1851-1926), and tested against statistical evidence by Charles Cobb and Paul Douglas in 1900-1928.

For production, the function is

$$Y = AL^{\alpha}K^{\beta},$$

Chapter 17. Vector Calculus

where:

- Y = total production (the monetary value of all goods produced in a year)
- L = labor input
- K = capital input
- A = total factor productivity
- α and β are the output elasticities of labor and capital, respectively. These values are constants determined by available technology.

Output elasticity measures the responsiveness of output to a change in levels of either labor or capital used in production, ceteris paribus. For example if α = 0.15, a 1% increase in labor would lead to approximately a 0.15% increase in output.

a. Cobb-Douglas
c. 15 theorem
b. BIBO stability
d. BDDC

13. In mathematics, a _____ is an integral where the function to be integrated is evaluated along a curve. Various different line integrals are in use. A specific case of an integration along a closed curve in two dimensions or the complex plane is the contour integral.

a. Nevanlinna theory
c. Line integral
b. Regular part
d. Radius of convergence

14. Integration is an important concept in mathematics, specifically in the field of calculus and, more broadly, mathematical analysis. Given a function f of a real variable x and an interval [a, b] of the real line, the _____

$$\int_a^b f(x)\, dx,$$

is defined informally to be the net signed area of the region in the xy-plane bounded by the graph of f, the x-axis, and the vertical lines x = a and x = b.

The term '_____' may also refer to the notion of antiderivative, a function F whose derivative is the given function f.

a. Integral
c. Integrand
b. Indefinite integral
d. Integral test for convergence

15. A _____ is a type of manifold that is locally similar enough to Euclidean space to allow one to do calculus Any manifold can be described by a collection of charts, also known as an atlas.

a. Tortuosity
c. Minimal surface
b. Lie derivative
d. Differentiable manifold

16. For some curves there is a smallest number L that is an upper bound on the length of any polygonal approximation. If such a number exists, then the curve is said to be rectifiable and the curve is defined to have _____ L.

Chapter 17. Vector Calculus

Let C be a curve in Euclidean (or, generally, a metric) space X = R^n, so C is the image of a continuous function f : [a, b] → X of the interval [a, b] into X.

a. Order of integration
b. Integrand
c. Integration by parametric derivatives
d. Arc length

17. In mathematics, an _____ on a real vector space is a choice of which ordered bases are 'positively' oriented and which are 'negatively' oriented. In the three-dimensional Euclidean space, the two possible basis orientations are called right-handed and left-handed (or right-chiral and left-chiral), respectively. However, the choice of _____ is independent of the handedness or chirality of the bases (although right-handed bases are typically declared to be positively oriented, they may also be assigned a negative _____.)

a. Unit vector
b. ACTRAN
c. ALGOR
d. Orientation

18. A _____ is one of the most curvilinear basic geometric shapes:It has two faces, zero vertices, and zero edges. The surface formed by the points at a fixed distance from a given straight line, the axis of the _____. The solid enclosed by this surface and by two planes perpendicular to the axis is also called a _____.

a. 15 theorem
b. BDDC
c. Right circular cylinder
d. Cylinder

19. The concept of _____ in mathematics evolved from the concept of _____ in physics. The nth _____ of a real-valued function f(x) of a real variable about a value c is

$$\mu'_n = \int_{-\infty}^{\infty} (x - c)^n f(x)\, dx.$$

It is possible to define moments for random variables in a more general fashion than moments for real values. See Moments in metric spaces.

a. Linear regression
b. Poisson distribution
c. Standard deviation
d. Moment

20. _____, also called mass _____ or the angular mass, (SI units kg m^2) is a measure of an object's resistance to changes in its rotation rate. It is the rotational analog of mass. That is, it is the inertia of a rigid rotating body with respect to its rotation.

a. Klein-Gordon equation
b. Dirac equation
c. Wave equation
d. Moment of Inertia

21. In metric topology and related fields of mathematics, a set U is called _____ if, intuitively speaking, starting from any point x in U one can move by a small amount in any direction and still be in the set U. In other words, the distance between any point x in U and the edge of U is always greater than zero.

As an example, consider the _____ interval (0, 1) consisting of all real numbers x with 0 < x < 1. Here, the topology is the usual topology on the real line. We can look at this in two ways.

a. ALGOR
c. ACTRAN
b. Open
d. AUSM

22. A curve γ is said to be closed or a loop if $I = [a, b]$ and if $\gamma(a) = \gamma(b)$. A _____ is thus a continuous mapping of the circle S¹; a simple _____ is also called a Jordan curve or a Jordan arc. The Jordan curve theorem states that such curves divide the plane into an 'interior' and an 'exterior'.
   a. Closed Curve
   b. Bullet-nose curve
   c. Kappa curve
   d. Curve

23. A quantity is said to be subject to _____ if it decreases at a rate proportional to its value. Symbolically, this can be expressed as the following differential equation, where N is the quantity and λ is a positive number called the decay constant.

$$\frac{dN}{dt} = -\lambda N.$$

The solution to this equation is:

$$N(t) = N_0 e^{-\lambda t}.$$

Here N(t) is the quantity at time t, and $N_0 = N(0)$ is the initial quantity, i.e. the quantity at time t = 0.

   a. ACTRAN
   b. Exponential sum
   c. ALGOR
   d. Exponential decay

24. The _____ of an object is the extra energy which it possesses due to its motion. It is defined as the work needed to accelerate a body of a given mass from rest to its current velocity. Having gained this energy during its acceleration, the body maintains this _____ unless its speed changes.
   a. 15 theorem
   b. Kinetic energy
   c. Potential energy
   d. BDDC

25. The _____ states that the total amount of energy in an isolated system remains constant. A consequence of this law is that energy cannot be created or destroyed. The only thing that can happen with energy in an isolated system is that it can change form, that is to say for instance kinetic energy can become thermal energy.
   a. Potential energy
   b. 15 theorem
   c. Law of Conservation of Energy
   d. BDDC

26. _____ can be thought of as energy stored within a physical system. It is called _____ because it has the potential to be converted into other forms of energy, such as kinetic energy, and to do work in the process. The standard (SI) unit of measure for _____ is the joule, the same as for work or energy in general.
   a. 15 theorem
   b. Law of Conservation of Energy
   c. BDDC
   d. Potential energy

Chapter 17. Vector Calculus

27. In vector calculus, the _____ is an operator that measures the magnitude of a vector field's source or sink at a given point; the _____ of a vector field is a (signed) scalar. For example, consider air as it is heated or cooled. The relevant vector field for this example is the velocity of the moving air at a point.
   a. Divergence
   b. Triple product
   c. Gradient theorem
   d. Divergence Theorem

28. In calculus, an _____ is the limit of a definite integral as an endpoint of the interval of integration approaches either a specified real number or ∞ or −∞ or, in some cases, as both endpoints approach limits.

Specifically, an _____ is a limit of the form

$$\lim_{b \to \infty} \int_a^b f(x)\, dx, \qquad \lim_{a \to -\infty} \int_a^b f(x)\, dx,$$

or of the form

$$\lim_{c \to b^-} \int_a^c f(x)\, dx, \qquad \lim_{c \to a^+} \int_c^b f(x)\, dx,$$

in which one takes a limit in one or the other (or sometimes both) endpoints . Improper integrals may also occur at an interior point of the domain of integration, or at multiple such points.

   a. ACTRAN
   b. Improper integral
   c. AUSM
   d. ALGOR

29. In vector calculus a conservative vector field is a vector field which is the gradient of a scalar potential. There are two closely related concepts: path independence and _____ vector fields. Every conservative vector field has zero curl (and is thus _____), and every conservative vector field has the path independence property.
   a. AUSM
   b. Irrotational
   c. ACTRAN
   d. ALGOR

30. In mathematics and physics, the _____ or Laplacian, denoted by Δ or ∇^2 and named after Pierre-Simon de Laplace, is a differential operator, specifically an important case of an elliptic operator, with many applications. In physics, it is used in modeling of wave propagation, heat flow and forming the Helmholtz equation. It is central in electrostatics and fluid mechanics, anchoring in Laplace's equation and Poisson's equation.
   a. Partial derivative
   b. Vector Laplacian
   c. Differentiation operator
   d. Laplace operator

31. In calculus, a branch of mathematics, the _____ is a measurement of how a function changes when its input changes. Loosely speaking, a _____ can be thought of as how much a quantity is changing at some given point. For example, the _____ of the position (or distance) of a vehicle with respect to time is the instantaneous velocity (respectively, instantaneous speed) at which the vehicle is traveling.

The process of finding a _____ is called differentiation. The fundamental theorem of calculus states that differentiation is the reverse process to integration.

a. Derivative
c. Ramp function
b. Concave upwards
d. Mountain pass theorem

32. A _____ is a surface in the Euclidean space R^3 which is defined by a parametric equation with two parameters. Parametric representation is the most general way to specify a surface. Surfaces that occur in two of the main theorems of vector calculus, Stokes' theorem and divergence theorem, are frequently given in a parametric form.

a. Parametric surface
c. Paraboloid
b. PDE surfaces
d. Normal line

33. In geometry, a _____ is a special plane curve generated by the trace of a fixed point on a small circle that rolls within a larger circle. It is comparable to the cycloid but instead of the circle rolling along a line, it rolls within a circle. The red curve is a _____ traced as the smaller black circle rolls around inside the larger blue circle (parameters are R=3.0, r=1.0, and so k=3), giving a deltoid.

If the smaller circle has radius r, and the larger circle has radius R = kr, then the parametric equations for the curve can be given by either:

$$x(\theta) = (R - r)\cos\theta + r\cos\left(\frac{R-r}{r}\theta\right)$$
$$y(\theta) = (R - r)\sin\theta - r\sin\left(\frac{R-r}{r}\theta\right),$$

or:

$$x(\theta) = r(k-1)\cos\theta + r\cos((k-1)\theta)$$
$$y(\theta) = r(k-1)\sin\theta - r\sin((k-1)\theta).$$

If k is an integer, then the curve is closed, and has k cusps (i.e., sharp corners, where the curve is not differentiable.)

a. Kappa curve
c. Bullet-nose curve
b. Closed curve
d. Hypocycloid

34. A _____ is a surface created by rotating a curve lying on some plane (the generatrix) around a straight line (the axis of rotation) that lies on the same plane.

Examples of surfaces generated by a straight line are the cylindrical and conical surfaces. A circle that is rotated about a (coplanar) axis through the center generates a sphere.

a. Nonelementary integral
c. Surface of revolution
b. Solid of revolution
d. Disk integration

35. In geometry, the _____ (or simply the tangent) to a curve at a given point is the straight line that 'just touches' the curve at that point (in the sense explained more precisely below.) As it passes through the point of tangency, the _____ is 'going in the same direction' as the curve, and in this sense it is the best straight-line approximation to the curve at that point. The same definition applies to space curves and curves in n-dimensional Euclidean space.

a. Minimal surface
c. Lie derivative
b. Sphere
d. Tangent line

36. _____ is how much exposed area an object has. It is expressed in square units. If an object has flat faces, its _____ can be calculated by adding together the areas of its faces.

a. Plane curve
c. Surface area
b. Lipschitz domain
d. Gyroid

37. A _____ is perfectly round geometrical object in three-dimensional space, such as the shape of a round ball. Like a circle in two dimensions, a perfect _____ is completely symmetrical around its center, with all points on the surface lying the same distance r from the center point. This distance r is known as the radius of the _____.

a. Sphere
c. Minimal surface
b. Tortuosity
d. Differentiable manifold

38. The _____, after the plane and the catenoid, is the third minimal surface to be known. It was first discovered by Jean Baptiste Meusnier in 1776. Its name derives from its similarity to the helix: for every point on the _____ there is a helix contained in the _____ which passes through that point.

a. Scherk surface
c. 15 theorem
b. Helicoid
d. BDDC

39. In mathematics, a _____ is a definite integral taken over a surface (which may be a curved set in space); it can be thought of as the double integral analog of the line integral. Given a surface, one may integrate over it scalar fields (that is, functions which return numbers as values), and vector fields (that is, functions which return vectors as values.)

Surface integrals have applications in physics, particularly with the classical theory of electromagnetism.

a. Second partial derivatives test
c. Surface integral
b. Hessian matrix
d. Jacobian

40. In geometry, a _____ (pl. tori) is a surface of revolution generated by revolving a circle in three dimensional space about an axis coplanar with the circle, which does not touch the circle. Examples of tori include the surfaces of doughnuts and inner tubes.

a. Torus
c. Normal vector
b. PDE surfaces
d. Prolate

41. In vector calculus, the _____ Ostrogradskye;s theorem the _____ states that the outward flux of a vector field through a surface is equal to the triple integral of the divergence on the region inside the surface. Intuitively, it states that the sum of all sources minus the sum of all sinks gives the net flow out of a region.

a. Gradient theorem
c. Triple product
b. Divergence Theorem
d. Divergence

42. The _____ is an important partial differential equation which describes the distribution of heat (or variation in temperature) in a given region over time. For a function u(x,y,z,t) of three spatial variables (x,y,z) and the time variable t, the _____ is

$$\frac{\partial u}{\partial t} - k\left(\frac{\partial^2 u}{\partial x^2} + \frac{\partial^2 u}{\partial y^2} + \frac{\partial^2 u}{\partial z^2}\right) = 0$$

or equivalently

$$\frac{\partial u}{\partial t} = k\nabla^2 u$$

where k is a constant.

The _____ is of fundamental importance in diverse scientific fields.

a. 15 theorem
c. Heat equation
b. BIBO stability
d. BDDC

Chapter 18. Second-Order Differential Equations

1. In mathematics, _____ are a concept central to linear algebra and related fields of mathematics

   Suppose that K is a field and V is a vector space over K. As usual, we call elements of V vectors and call elements of K scalars.

   a. 15 theorem
   b. Linear combinations
   c. Permutation
   d. BDDC

2. In mathematics, a _____ is a differential equation of the form

$$Ly = f$$

   where the differential operator L is a linear operator, y is the unknown function, and the right hand side f is a given function (called the source term.) The linearity condition on L rules out operations such as taking the square of the derivative of y; but permits, for example, taking the second derivative of y. Therefore a fairly general form of such an equation would be

$$a_n(x)D^n y(x) + a_{n-1}(x)D^{n-1}y(x) + \cdots + a_1(x)Dy(x) + a_0(x)y(x) = f(x)$$

   where D is the differential operator d/dx (i.e. Dy = y' , D²y = y',...), and the a_i are given functions.

   a. Nullcline
   b. Linear differential equation
   c. Separable
   d. Petrovsky lacuna

3. In infinitesimal calculus, a _____ is traditionally an infinitesimally small change in a variable. For example, if x is a variable, then a change in the value of x is often denoted Δx (or δx when this change is considered to be small.) The _____ dx represents such a change, but is infinitely small.

   a. Related rates
   b. Differential
   c. Dirichlet integral
   d. Continuous function

4. A _____ is a mathematical equation for an unknown function of one or several variables that relates the values of the function itself and of its derivatives of various orders. they play a prominent role in engineering, physics, economics and other disciplines.

   A simplified real world example of a _____ is modeling the acceleration of a ball falling through the air (considering only gravity and air resistance.)

   a. Lax pair
   b. Structural stability
   c. Petrovsky lacuna
   d. Differential equation

5. In mathematics, in the field of differential equations, an _____ is an ordinary differential equation together with specified value, called the initial condition, of the unknown function at a given point in the domain of the solution. In physics or other sciences, modeling a system frequently amounts to solving an _____; in this context, the differential equation is an evolution equation specifying how, given initial conditions, the system will evolve with time.

Chapter 18. Second-Order Differential Equations

An _____ is a differential equation

$$y'(t) = f(t, y(t)) \quad \text{with} \quad f : \mathbb{R} \times \mathbb{R} \to \mathbb{R}$$

together with a point in the domain of f

$$(t_0, y_0) \in \mathbb{R} \times \mathbb{R},$$

called the initial condition.

- a. ALGOR
- b. ACTRAN
- c. Initial value problem
- d. AUSM

6. In mathematics, a _____ is a constant multiplicative factor of a certain object. For example, in the expression $9x^2$, the _____ of x^2 is 9.

The object can be such things as a variable, a vector, a function, etc.

- a. Leading coefficient
- b. Degree of the polynomial
- c. Coefficient
- d. Difference polynomial

7. In mathematics, _____ also known as variation of constants, is a general method to solve inhomogeneous linear ordinary differential equations. It was developed by the Italian-French mathematician Joseph Louis Lagrange with noteworthy help from the American mathematician and physicist Noah LaMoyne.

For first-order inhomogeneous linear differential equations it's usually possible to find solutions via integrating factors or undetermined coefficients with considerably less effort, although those methods are rather heuristics that involve guessing and don't work for all inhomogenous linear differential equations.

- a. Variation of parameters
- b. Sturm separation theorem
- c. Riccati equation
- d. Regular singular point

8. _____ is the motion of a simple harmonic oscillator, a motion that is neither driven nor damped. The motion is periodic - as it repeats itself at standard intervals in a specific manner - and sinusoidal, with constant amplitude; the acceleration of a body executing _____ is directly proportional to the displacement of the body from the equilibrium position and is always directed towards the equilibrium position.

The motion is characterized by its amplitude (which is always positive), its period, the time for a single oscillation, its frequency, the reciprocal of the period (i.e. the number of cycles per unit time), and its phase, which determines the starting point on the sine wave.

- a. Holonomic
- b. 15 theorem
- c. BDDC
- d. Simple harmonic motion

Chapter 18. Second-Order Differential Equations

9. The most commonly encountered form of Hooke's law is probably the spring equation, which relates the force exerted by a spring to the distance it is stretched by a _____, k, measured in force per length.

$$F = -kx$$

The negative sign indicates that the force exerted by the spring is in direct opposition to the direction of displacement. It is called a 'restoring force', as it tends to restore the system to equilibrium.

a. Spring constant
b. 15 theorem
c. Navier-Stokes equations
d. Polar moment of inertia

10. In acoustics and telecommunication, a _____ of a wave is a component frequency of the signal that is an integer multiple of the fundamental frequency. For example, if the fundamental frequency is f, the harmonics have frequencies f, 2f, 3f, 4f, etc. The harmonics have the property that they are all periodic at the fundamental frequency, therefore the sum of harmonics is also periodic at that frequency.

a. BDDC
b. BIBO stability
c. 15 theorem
d. Harmonic

11. _____ is any effect, either deliberately engendered or inherent to a system, that tends to reduce the amplitude of oscillations of an oscillatory system.

In physics and engineering, _____ may be mathematically modelled as a force synchronous with the velocity of the object but opposite in direction to it. If such force is also proportional to the velocity, as for a simple mechanical viscous damper (dashpot), the force F may be related to the velocity v by

$$\mathbf{F} = -c\mathbf{v}$$

where c is the viscous _____ coefficient, given in units of newton-seconds per meter.

a. BIBO stability
b. 15 theorem
c. BDDC
d. Damping

12. In mathematics and physics, a _____ associates a scalar value, which can be either mathematical in definition to every point in space. Scalar fields are often used in physics, for instance to indicate the temperature distribution throughout space or more specifically, differential geometry, the set of functions defined on a manifold define the commutative ring of functions.

a. Jacobian
b. Differential operator
c. Shift theorem
d. Scalar field

13. In mathematics, _____, first defined by the mathematician Daniel Bernoulli and generalized by Friedrich Bessel, are canonical solutions y(x) of Bessel's differential equation:

$$x^2 \frac{d^2y}{dx^2} + x\frac{dy}{dx} + (x^2 - \alpha^2)y = 0$$

for an arbitrary real or complex number α (the order of the Bessel function.) The most common and important special case is where α is an integer n.

Although α and −α produce the same differential equation, it is conventional to define different _____ for these two orders (e.g., so that the _____ are mostly smooth functions of α.)

- a. Bessel functions
- b. Logarithmic integral function
- c. Multiplication theorem
- d. 15 theorem

Chapter 1

1. d	2. a	3. d	4. d	5. c	6. d	7. d	8. d	9. c	10. d
11. b	12. a	13. d	14. c	15. d	16. b	17. d	18. b	19. b	20. a
21. d	22. b	23. b	24. a	25. d	26. a	27. d	28. d	29. d	30. d
31. d	32. d	33. b	34. a	35. d	36. b	37. a	38. d	39. b	40. c
41. d	42. d	43. d	44. a	45. d	46. d	47. d	48. a	49. d	50. d
51. d	52. d	53. a	54. a	55. c	56. d				

Chapter 2

1. c	2. a	3. a	4. d	5. c	6. d	7. b	8. c	9. d	10. b
11. d	12. b	13. d	14. d	15. c	16. a	17. d	18. a	19. c	20. c
21. c	22. d	23. d							

Chapter 3

1. d	2. d	3. b	4. d	5. d	6. d	7. c	8. a	9. d	10. c
11. d	12. c	13. c	14. d	15. d	16. d	17. d	18. d	19. c	20. c
21. b	22. a	23. d	24. a	25. c	26. d	27. d	28. d	29. d	30. b
31. c	32. a	33. d	34. d	35. c	36. a	37. b	38. a	39. b	40. a
41. a	42. c	43. a	44. a	45. b	46. a	47. d	48. d	49. a	50. d
51. c	52. d	53. b	54. c	55. c	56. d	57. d	58. d	59. a	60. a
61. d	62. d	63. d	64. c	65. d	66. a	67. a	68. d	69. d	70. a
71. b	72. d								

Chapter 4

1. d	2. a	3. d	4. b	5. d	6. a	7. a	8. a	9. b	10. d
11. a	12. d	13. d	14. d	15. d	16. d	17. d	18. b	19. c	20. c
21. d	22. a	23. d	24. d	25. a	26. d	27. c	28. d	29. d	30. d
31. d	32. a	33. b	34. a	35. d	36. d	37. b	38. d	39. c	40. d

Chapter 5

1. c	2. d	3. b	4. d	5. a	6. d	7. b	8. d	9. b	10. d
11. c	12. d	13. d	14. b	15. c	16. d	17. b	18. c	19. a	20. d
21. a	22. d	23. a	24. b	25. a					

Chapter 6

1. a	2. d	3. d	4. a	5. d	6. b	7. c	8. d	9. d	10. d
11. a	12. c	13. c	14. b	15. c	16. d	17. d	18. d	19. a	

Chapter 7

1. b	2. a	3. b	4. b	5. c	6. d	7. d	8. d	9. b	10. b
11. a	12. b	13. d	14. d	15. d	16. b	17. b	18. d	19. c	20. c
21. d	22. d	23. d	24. b	25. b	26. c	27. b	28. c	29. d	30. d
31. d	32. d	33. b	34. d	35. b	36. c	37. d	38. d	39. d	40. b
41. d	42. d	43. a	44. a	45. b	46. b	47. d			

ANSWER KEY

Chapter 8
1. d 2. a 3. a 4. d 5. b 6. d 7. d 8. c 9. a 10. d
11. d 12. d 13. c 14. d 15. a 16. d 17. a 18. a 19. b 20. a
21. a 22. a 23. a 24. d 25. a 26. d 27. b 28. d 29. d 30. b
31. d 32. d 33. a

Chapter 9
1. d 2. c 3. c 4. b 5. c 6. a 7. a 8. c 9. c 10. c
11. a 12. d 13. d 14. d 15. d 16. d 17. b 18. d 19. d 20. a
21. b 22. a 23. a 24. b 25. d 26. b 27. a

Chapter 10
1. d 2. d 3. d 4. c 5. d 6. a 7. b 8. c 9. d 10. a
11. d 12. d 13. b 14. d 15. d 16. b 17. d 18. d 19. c 20. d
21. d 22. d 23. a 24. d 25. a 26. d 27. d 28. d 29. c 30. d
31. b 32. a 33. a 34. b 35. d 36. a

Chapter 11
1. c 2. d 3. d 4. b 5. a 6. a 7. b 8. d 9. d 10. a
11. c 12. c 13. d 14. d 15. d 16. d 17. d 18. d 19. d 20. b
21. c 22. c 23. d 24. a 25. d 26. a 27. c 28. d 29. d 30. d
31. d 32. d 33. d 34. a 35. c 36. d 37. a 38. d 39. d 40. a
41. d 42. c 43. a 44. c 45. c 46. a 47. a 48. b 49. c 50. c

Chapter 12
1. c 2. c 3. a 4. d 5. a 6. a 7. d 8. a 9. d 10. a
11. b 12. d 13. a 14. c 15. d 16. b 17. b 18. d 19. c 20. d
21. a 22. b 23. d 24. d 25. b 26. c 27. d 28. d 29. d 30. a
31. d 32. d 33. d 34. b 35. a 36. d 37. c 38. b 39. d 40. d
41. d 42. a 43. c 44. a 45. b 46. d 47. c 48. d 49. c 50. d
51. d 52. d 53. b 54. d 55. a 56. a 57. d 58. a 59. d 60. d

Chapter 13
1. d 2. d 3. a 4. d 5. d 6. a 7. d 8. d 9. d 10. c
11. d 12. c 13. a 14. c 15. a 16. b 17. c 18. b 19. b 20. b
21. a 22. d 23. d 24. a 25. d 26. d 27. d 28. c 29. d 30. a
31. d 32. a 33. b 34. a 35. d 36. a 37. d 38. d 39. d 40. d

Chapter 14
1. d 2. b 3. d 4. d 5. a 6. d 7. d 8. c 9. d 10. a
11. c 12. b 13. a 14. b 15. a 16. a 17. d 18. a 19. d 20. b
21. c 22. d 23. c 24. d 25. d 26. d 27. c 28. d 29. d 30. b
31. d 32. d 33. a 34. d 35. b

Chapter 15

1. d	2. d	3. d	4. d	5. d	6. b	7. b	8. d	9. d	10. d
11. d	12. d	13. d	14. d	15. a	16. a	17. d	18. b	19. b	20. a
21. d	22. d	23. d	24. a	25. d	26. d	27. b	28. d	29. d	30. d
31. c	32. d	33. a	34. c	35. a	36. d	37. d	38. c	39. d	40. d
41. d	42. d	43. a	44. b	45. c	46. d	47. d	48. d	49. b	

Chapter 16

1. d	2. a	3. d	4. c	5. b	6. d	7. c	8. d	9. b	10. d
11. d	12. d	13. a	14. d	15. b	16. a	17. d	18. a	19. d	20. b
21. a	22. d	23. d	24. c	25. b	26. a	27. d	28. d	29. d	30. d
31. d	32. a	33. d	34. a	35. d	36. a				

Chapter 17

1. a	2. d	3. d	4. d	5. a	6. b	7. d	8. a	9. b	10. d
11. b	12. a	13. c	14. a	15. d	16. d	17. d	18. d	19. d	20. d
21. b	22. a	23. d	24. b	25. c	26. d	27. a	28. b	29. b	30. d
31. a	32. a	33. d	34. c	35. d	36. c	37. a	38. b	39. c	40. a
41. b	42. c								

Chapter 18

1. b	2. b	3. b	4. d	5. c	6. c	7. a	8. d	9. a	10. d
11. d	12. d	13. a							